T0344040

Bankers without Borders

Bankers without Borders

© 2018 International Bank for Reconstruction and Development / The World Bank
1818 H Street NW, Washington, DC 20433
Telephone: 202-473-1000; Internet: www.worldbank.org

Some rights reserved

1 2 3 4 21 20 19 18

This work is a product of the staff of The World Bank with external contributions. The findings, interpretations, and conclusions expressed in this work do not necessarily reflect the views of The World Bank, its Board of Executive Directors, or the governments they represent. The World Bank does not guarantee the accuracy of the data included in this work. The boundaries, colors, denominations, and other information shown on any map in this work do not imply any judgment on the part of The World Bank concerning the legal status of any territory or the endorsement or acceptance of such boundaries.

Nothing herein shall constitute or be considered to be a limitation upon or waiver of the privileges and immunities of The World Bank, all of which are specifically reserved.

Rights and Permissions

This work is available under the Creative Commons Attribution 3.0 IGO license (CC BY 3.0 IGO) http://creativecommons.org/licenses/by/3.0/igo. Under the Creative Commons Attribution license, you are free to copy, distribute, transmit, and adapt this work, including for commercial purposes, under the following conditions:

Attribution—Please cite the work as follows: World Bank. 2018. *Global Financial Development Report 2017/2018: Bankers without Borders.* Washington, DC: World Bank. doi:10.1596/978-1-4648-1148-7. License: Creative Commons Attribution CC BY 3.0 IGO

Translations—If you create a translation of this work, please add the following disclaimer along with the attribution: *This translation was not created by The World Bank and should not be considered an official World Bank translation. The World Bank shall not be liable for any content or error in this translation.*

Adaptations—If you create an adaptation of this work, please add the following disclaimer along with the attribution: *This is an adaptation of an original work by The World Bank. Views and opinions expressed in the adaptation are the sole responsibility of the author or authors of the adaptation and are not endorsed by The World Bank.*

Third-party content—The World Bank does not necessarily own each component of the content contained within the work. The World Bank therefore does not warrant that the use of any third-party-owned individual component or part contained in the work will not infringe on the rights of those third parties. The risk of claims resulting from such infringement rests solely with you. If you wish to re-use a component of the work, it is your responsibility to determine whether permission is needed for that re-use and to obtain permission from the copyright owner. Examples of components can include, but are not limited to, tables, figures, or images.

All queries on rights and licenses should be addressed to World Bank Publications, The World Bank Group, 1818 H Street NW, Washington, DC 20433, USA; e-mail: pubrights@worldbank.org.

ISBN (paper): 978-1-4648-1148-7
ISBN (electronic): 978-1-4648-1196-8
ISSN: 2304-957X
DOI: 10.1596/978-1-4648-1148-7

Cover image: © Shutterstock. Used with permission. Further permission required for reuse.
Cover design: Critical Stages, LLC.

The report reflects information available up to June 30, 2017.

Contents

BOXES

FIGURES

MAPS

TABLES

Foreword

This *Global Financial Development Report* is a key component in the ongoing debate over the role of international banking in supporting economic development and promoting shared prosperity.

This report, the fourth in its series, comes at a critical time when the global reform agenda is shaping financial globalization—in particular, banking. During the decade prior to the 2007–09 global financial crisis, banking activities across national borders increased dramatically. In many cases, the trend brought benefits, including additional capital, liquidity, and technological improvements, which resulted in greater efficiency and financial development. The global financial crisis, however, led to a reevaluation of the virtues of bank globalization, with global banks seen as culpable for transmitting the financial crisis across borders. In fact, the Financial Stability Board (FSB), the G20, and policy makers throughout the developing world voiced concerns about the effects of global banking.

The *Global Financial Development Report 2017/2018* offers new research and data that help fill gaps in the knowledge of international banking and contributes key insights to the policy discussion. The report provides stylized facts and examines existing and new evidence of the causes and effects of bank globalization—in particular, for economic growth, shared prosperity, and poverty reduction.

For many years, the World Bank Group has supported developing countries in reaping the benefits of international banking while also minimizing risks to financial stability. This work is even more critical as the world seeks to meet the rising aspirations of the poor. Crowding in private sector investment will transform the billions of dollars that are available in development assistance into trillions for investment in developing countries. International banks are one conduit for these private sector investments, and effective financial sector policies will be key to creating the stability that can attract private capital.

The report provides a careful review and synthesis of recent and new research; it also notes where more research is needed. It argues that international banking is no panacea for guaranteeing financial development and stability, and that the right policies are central to generating benefits, while avoiding negative repercussions associated with cross-border banking. Consequently, to secure contract enforcement, governments and international bodies must strengthen regulations, improve information availability, and enhance legal and judicial systems. In designing policies to overcome institutional weaknesses, it is also important to take into account the differences in bank characteristics and conditions in both home and host countries.

We hope that this year's *Global Financial Development Report* will prove useful to a wide range of stakeholders, including governments, international financial institutions, nongovernmental organizations, think tanks, academics, the private sector, donors, and the broader development community.

Jim Yong Kim
President
The World Bank Group

Acknowledgments

The *Global Financial Development Report 2017/2018* reflects the efforts of a broad and diverse group of experts, both inside and outside the World Bank Group. The report was produced by the World Bank Research Department in collaboration with the Finance and Markets Global Practice, the Chief Economist's Office at the International Finance Corporation (IFC), and the Multilateral Investment Guarantee Agency (MIGA). Moreover, it includes inputs from a wide range of units within the World Bank Group.

Asli Demirgüç-Kunt was the report's director. Ata Can Bertay was the task manager of the project. The main authors in charge of the chapters were: Ata Can Bertay and Miriam Bruhn (chapter 1), Robert Cull and Claudia Ruiz Ortega (chapter 2), Juan Jose Cortina Lorente, Ruth Llovet Montanes, and Sergio Schmukler (chapter 3). Nan Zhou was responsible for the statistical appendices and was part of the core team. Maria Soledad Martínez Pería and Jeanne Verrier contributed to the concept note. Other authors that provided key contributions to the chapters include Nan Zhou (chapters 1, 2, and 3), and Maria Soledad Martínez Pería and Katia D'Hulster (chapter 2). Leila Aghabarari, Serhat Guven, and Can Sever provided excellent research

assistance. Inputs were received from Saniya Ansar (chapter 1), Leila Aghabarari (chapter 2, box 2.3), David Gerbrands and Bjorn Schrijver (chapter 2, box 2.5), Javier Pablo Garcia Tolonen, and Santiago Fernandez de Lis Alonso (chapter 2, box 2.11), Nan Zhou (chapter 2, box 2.10, chapter 3, boxes 3.2, 3.5, and 3.6).

Shanta Devarajan (Senior Director of Development Economics), Mahmoud Mohieldin (Senior Vice President), and Joaquim Levy (Managing Director and World Bank Group Chief Financial Officer) provided overall guidance and valuable advice.

External advisors to the report included Viral Acharya (New York University, Stern School of Business, and Deputy Governor of Reserve Bank of India); Franklin Allen (Executive Director of the Brevan Howard Centre and Professor of Finance and Economics at Imperial College London); Thorsten Beck (Professor of Banking and Finance at Cass Business School in London); Allen Berger (Professor of Banking and Finance at University of South Carolina); Charles Calomiris (Henry Kaufman Professor of Financial Institutions at Columbia University); Stijn Claessens (Head of Financial Stability Policy, Bank of International Settlements); Patrick

Honohan (Senior Fellow at the Peterson Institute for International Economics and Former Governor of the Central Bank of Ireland); Harry Huizinga (Professor at Tilburg University); and Ross Levine (Willis H. Booth Chair in Banking and Finance at the University of California at Berkeley).

The team also received valuable peer reviews and guidance from other staff members at the World Bank Group, including Dan Biller, Marcos Brujis, Ted Haoquan Chu, Augusto de la Torre, Neil Gregory, Ceyla Pazarbasioglu, Gloria Grandolini, and Peer Stein. Aart Kraay reviewed the concept note and drafts of the report for consistency and quality multiple times.

Ted Haoquan Chu and Neil Gregory were the key contacts at IFC, Ceyla Pazarbasioglu at the Finance and Markets Global Practice, and Dan Biller at MIGA. The authors benefited from informal discussions, and received valuable suggestions and other contributions from Irina Astrakhan, Stefan Avdjiev, Ana Maria Aviles, Steen Byskov, Cesar Calderon, Pietro Calice, Katia D'Hulster, Shantayanan Devarajan, Michael Edwards, Aurora Ferrari, Neil Gregory, Mario Guadamillas, David Michael Gould, Erik Feyen, William Haworth, Frank Heemskerk, Leora Klapper, Emmanuel K. Lartey, William Maloney, Yira J. Mascaro, Martin Melecky, Yigal Menashe, Margaret J. Miller, Cedric Mousset, Thomas Rehermann, Matthew Saal, James Seward, Lin Shi, Susan K. Starnes, and Emile J. M. Van der Does de Willebois. Data contributions were received from Subika Farazi and Diego M. Sourrouille.

A background research conference was held jointly with the Federal Reserve Bank of Chicago, and an edited volume with all contributions was produced (Demirgüç-Kunt, Evanoff, and Kaufman 2016). The individual chapters of the report were presented at Global Financial Development seminars. The seminars were presented by members of the core team and benefited from thorough discussions from David Michael Gould and Erik Feyen (chapter 1), Ted Haoquan Chu and Steen Byskov (chapter 2), Mario Guadamillas and Alfonso Garcia Mora (chapter 3) and the participants of these seminars.

In the Bank-wide review of the concept note and of the report, substantial comments were received from Mahmoud Mohieldin (Senior Vice President); Yvonne M. Tsikata (Vice President and Corporate Secretary); Michael Edwards, Erik Feyen, Aurora Ferrari, and Pietro Calice (all Finance and Markets Global Practice); Keiko Honda, Merli Baroudi, Dan Biller, Persephone Economou, Paul Barbour, Gianfilippo Carboni, and Petal Jean Hackett (all Multilateral Investment Guarantee Agency); Nena Stoiljkovic Hans Peter Lankes, Bill Haworth, Facundo Martin, and Mahima Khanna (all International Finance Corporation); Xiaoqing Yu, Shabih Mohib, Tatiana Nenova, and Nikola Spatafora (all East Asia and Pacific Region); Mariam J. Sherman and David Gould (both Europe and Central Asia Region); Antonella Bassani, Samia Msadek, Jean Denis Pesme, Christina Wood, and Omer Karasapan (all Middle East and North Africa Region); Martin Rama and Martin Melecky (both South Asia Region); Makhtar Diop, Cesar Calderon, Souleymane Coulibaly, Vinaya Swaroop, and Luis Diego Barrot (all Sub-Saharan Africa Region); Caroline Heider, Anjali Kumar, Beata Lenard, and Stoyan Tenev (All Independent Evaluation Group); Axel van Trotsenburg, Lisa Finneran, Stuart James Stephens, and Anton Dobronogov (all Development Finance Vice Presidency); Manuela V. Ferro, Theo Thomas, Ashley Taylor, and Jane Hwang (all Operations Policy and Country Services Vice Presidency); Caren Grown and Tamova Christie (both Gender Cross-Cutting Solution Area); Alberto Ninio and Sandie Okoro (both Legal Vice Presidency); and Galina J. Mikhlin-Oliver (Integrity Vice Presidency).

The report would not be possible without the production team, including Patricia Katayama (acquisitions), Aziz Gokdemir (publishing officer), Susan Graham (project manager), Sabra Ledent (copy editor), and Deb Appel-Barker and Nora Leah Ridolfi (print coordinators). Bruno Bonansea was responsible for maps, and Sheela Na Cao designed the cover. Roula Yazigi assisted the team with the website. The communications team included Phil Hay and Ryan Douglas Hahn. Excellent administrative and budget assistance was provided by Tourya Tourougui. William Prince, Tariq Afzal Khokhar, Jomo Tariku, Ana Florina Pirlea, and Omar Hadi supported the publication of the *Global Financial Development Database* and the *Financial Development Data Tables*, associated with the report. Ana Florina Pirlea provided valuable feedback from the World Bank Data Help Desk for the team to enhance the statistics of the Database.

The authors would like to thank the many country officials and other experts who participated in the surveys underlying this report, including the Financial Development Barometer.

Financial support from the Knowledge for Change Program's research support budget is gratefully acknowledged.

Abbreviations and Glossary

AML/CFT	anti-money laundering and combating the financing of terrorism
BCBS	Basel Committee on Banking Supervision
BIS	Bank for International Settlements
CBS	Consolidated Banking Statistics, BIS
CGFS	Committee on the Global Financial Systems
EAP	East Asia and Pacific
EBRD	European Bank for Reconstruction and Development
ECA	Europe and Central Asia
EU	European Union
FDI	foreign direct investment
FSB	Financial Stability Board
G-20	Group of 20
G-SIB	global systematically important bank
IC	immediate counterparty
IFC	International Finance Corporation
IMF	International Monetary Fund
LAC	Latin America and the Caribbean
LBS	Locational Banking Statistics, BIS
M&A	mergers and acquisitions
MENA	Middle East and North Africa
NPL	nonperforming loan
OECD	Organisation for Economic Co-operation and Development
ROA	return on assets
SAR	South Asia
SME	small and medium enterprise
SRM	Single Resolution Mechanism
SSA	Sub-Saharan Africa
SSM	Single Supervisory Mechanism
TLAC	total loss absorbing capacity
UR	ultimate risk
WTO	World Trade Organization

Note: All dollar amounts are U.S. dollars ($) unless otherwise indicated.

GLOSSARY

Country	A territorial entity for which statistical data are maintained and provided internationally on a separate and independent basis (not necessarily a state as understood by international law and practice). The term, used interchangeably with *economy*, does not imply political independence or official recognition by the World Bank.
Domestic bank	A bank restricted to the home country operations, neither owning foreign subsidiaries nor being owned by any foreign banking entity.
Financial development	Conceptually, a process of reducing the costs of acquiring information, enforcing contracts, and making transactions.
Financial system	A country's financial institutions (banks, insurance companies, and other nonbank financial institutions) and financial markets (such as those in stocks, bonds, and financial derivatives). Also includes the financial infrastructure (for example, credit information–sharing systems and payments and settlement systems).
Global bank	Conceptually, a bank with significant asset size and an international reach of business. Although there is no single standard definition, in this report global bank refers to a large international bank with activities in multiple regions.
Institutional investors	Public and private pension funds, life insurance companies, non–life insurance companies, and mutual funds.
International bank	A bank with significant cross-border operations or international subsidiaries.
Nonbank financial institutions	Institutional investors and other nonbank financial intermediaries (such as leasing companies and investment banks).
Offshore financial center	A country or jurisdiction providing financial services to nonresidents beyond a scale commensurate with the size and financing of the domestic economy.
Regional bank	A bank owning foreign subsidiaries with a focus on a specific host region or set of countries.

Overview

Successful international integration, supported by sound national policy and effective international cooperation, has underpinned most experiences of rapid growth, shared prosperity, and reduced poverty. Perhaps no sector than banking better illustrates both the potential benefits and perils of deeper international integration. International banks—banks that do business outside the country where they are headquartered—are often considered important contributors to sustainable financial development, by promoting economic growth. The decade before the 2007–09 global financial crisis was characterized by a significant increase in financial globalization, particularly for banking institutions, which coincided with increases in bank size to unprecedented levels (Claessens 2016; Demirgüç-Kunt, Evanoff, and Kaufman 2016). These changes were manifested in both a rise in cross-border lending and a growing participation of foreign banks around the world as they became an integral part of financial systems, especially in developing countries.

International banking activities may contribute to faster growth, greater welfare, and enduring stability in two important ways: first, by bringing much-needed capital, expertise, and new technologies, thereby leading to more competitive banking systems; and second, by enabling risk sharing and diversification, thereby smoothing out the effects of domestic shocks (Claessens, Demirgüç-Kunt, and Huizinga 2001; Cull and Martínez Pería 2010; Goldberg, Dages, and Kinney 2000). Depending on the conditions, however, international banking may also lead to costs. Risk sharing will inevitably expose host countries to systemic risks from time to time; and more recently, international banks have been criticized for playing a role in the transmission of shocks across borders during the global financial crisis (De Haas and van Lelyveld 2014). Cross-border bank flows also play a crucial role in transmitting global liquidity to local financial systems, and international banking may promote destabilizing boom-bust cycles in poor institutional environments (Borio, McCauley, and McGuire 2011; Bruno and Shin 2015a).

In the wake of the global financial crisis, the globalization trend has been partially reversed, as multinational banks from developed countries—"the North"—have scaled back their international operations, coinciding with a general backlash against globalization. While banks based in high-income countries drove exits, developing country banks continued their international expansion, accounting for the bulk of new entry into foreign markets. Cross-border bank claims and syndicated loans also saw significant retrenchments, but "South–South" transactions—from developing countries to other developing countries—started growing, starting to replace the leading role of "North–South" transactions in the aftermath of the global financial crisis. This greater South–South activity has also coincided with regionalization, both in the roster of foreign banks in many host countries and in cross-border flows.

The full causes and implications of these changes are not yet completely understood. Postcrisis supervisory and regulatory reforms intended to enhance bank balance sheets and financial stability, such as more stringent capital requirements for banks and macroprudential regulations, have been at least partially responsible for these changes, affecting the supply of credit. During the crisis, banks also reduced lending as demand for external financing abroad declined, and sovereign and other risks increased. In addition, the crisis highlighted the need for greater cooperation in resolving troubled banks with multinational operations and a more explicit ex ante understanding of the associated burden sharing. More generally, the regionalization of international banking is prompting countries to contemplate regional regulatory and supervisory approaches.

Given these developments, international banking has attracted heightened interest from policy makers, researchers, and other financial sector stakeholders. The global financial crisis has certainly led to a reevaluation of the potential benefits and costs of bank globalization because many observers perceive global banks to have been mainly responsible for the transmission of shocks across borders during the recent financial crisis (Demirgüç-Kunt, Evanoff, and Kaufman 2016). Concerns about the effects of international banking—in particular, global systemically important banks (G-SIBs), which are deemed to be too big and interconnected to fail—have been voiced by the Financial Stability Board (FSB), the G-20, and policy makers around the world.

The *Global Financial Development Report 2017/2018: Bankers without Borders* seeks to contribute to this debate on the benefits and costs of international banks and provide evidence-based policy advice. The report examines both new and existing evidence on the activities of international banks, focusing on their international brick-and-mortar operations as well as their cross-border activities, and their drivers and economic effects. Overall, the report sifts through research evidence to shed light on the following long-standing policy concerns: To what extent should developing countries trust international banks with the local provision of their financial services, given that they may retrench and lead to a significant erosion of skills and services due to pressures from their home countries? Should developing country authorities be especially cautious in their approach to admitting South–South international banking activities? Is a lack of experience or insufficient home country prudential regulation and supervision a concern, or is it offset by the region-specific knowledge that gives these banks a better potential to provide banking services in developing countries? Does allowing foreign banks to have a larger market share risk reducing access to and increasing the price of banking services for small and medium-sized enterprises (SMEs) and lower-income households? Finally, how is technology—especially financial-technology (fintech) firms that work globally and across borders through digital products—likely to influence international banking? The report provides a synthesis of what we know, as well as areas where more evidence is still needed and recent developments that raise many new questions. Box O.1 provides the main messages.

Policy makers and other financial sector practitioners are divided on policies toward foreign bank entry. According to the fourth Financial Development Barometer—an informal poll of policymakers in developing countries undertaken for this *Global Financial Development Report*; see box O.2—respondents recognize both positive and negative effects of foreign banks. Although foreign banks are credited with providing financial services to firms and households and with introducing new ways of improving access to

BOX 0.1   Main Messages of This Report

Following a decade of increased globalization, international banking suffered a setback after the global financial crisis. There have been large reductions in cross-border flows, and less foreign bank entry. The trends in foreign bank entry differ across countries, however. While developed country banks retrenched, developing country banks continued to invest abroad, both through cross-border and brick-and-mortar operations, leading to a more regionalized banking system with greater South–South presence. Hence, international bank lending remains an important source of finance for developing countries, although its composition has changed since the crisis. And although regulatory barriers to foreign banking increased over this period, large international banks continued to become larger.

Remaining open despite rising protectionism is important for countries to continue to benefit from global flows of funds, knowledge, and opportunity. International banking activities have the potential to improve the degree of competition in the local banking sector, help upgrade skills, and improve the efficiency of resource allocation. Risks can be shared and diversified. Through the threat of exit, international banking can also discipline domestic financial policies, regulations, and supervisory practices and can weaken the political entrenchment between domestic financial institutions and governments. Overall, more capital and increased efficiency of allocation will promote faster economic development and greater financial stability.

However, international banking is no panacea for guaranteeing financial development and stability. Openness also introduces more volatility and exposes countries to foreign exchange risks, foreign monetary policy shocks, and other mismatches. In weak institutional environments with poor information, inadequate contract enforcement, and weak regulation and supervision, global finance may lead to destabilizing boom-bust cycles; and competition from foreign banks may drive out domestic banks and reduce access to finance and inclusion. Moreover, risk sharing also has a downside. International banks that export risks will also import them. And international banking can magnify distortions in domestic bank policy, regulation, and safety nets.

There is an important role for policy in maximizing international banking's benefits and minimizing its costs. International banking can have important benefits for development by improving efficiency and risk sharing, but benefits do not accrue unless the institutional environment is developed and the right policies are adopted. Research suggests that institutionally better developed countries tend to reap both more of the development and risk-sharing benefits of international banking. Specifically, good information sharing, property rights, contract enforcement, and strong regulation and supervision are key. Of particular importance, these improvements prevent foreign banks from just displacing domestic banks and exploiting regulatory weaknesses. And with strong institutions, both the foreign banks and domestic banks that are now exposed to greater competition can go downmarket and improve access and inclusion for small and medium-sized enterprises (SMEs) and households that were previously excluded.

Recent research suggests that for designing effective policies, it is important to keep in mind differences in bank characteristics and home and host country conditions. For development considerations, larger banks and those that are culturally closer, with a greater share of domestic financial intermediation including deposit taking, tend to provide better access to SMEs and households and are less likely to focus only on large corporate customers. As for stability, the risk-sharing benefits of globalization need to be considered over the long term. Cross-border flows tend to be more volatile and less resilient than a brick-and-mortar bank presence. Foreign banks with a greater commitment, as reflected in closeness both in distance to headquarters and in culture, that have larger local market shares, and rely more heavily on local funding, are more willing both to incur temporary costs when faced with external shocks and to support the local economy.

It is challenging to encourage the right type of foreign bank presence or forms of capital flows without causing distortions. Many supervisory agencies no longer rely on the home supervisor of their local affiliates for ensuring stability. Compared with branches, foreign subsidiaries can be self-sufficient—with high capitalization requirements and a high share

(box continued next page)

BOX 0.1 **Main Messages of This Report** *(continued)*

of funding through retail deposits—which therefore improves stability. Among subsidiaries, a mix of new, greenfield entrants and takeovers or mergers of existing domestic banks by foreign banks may also help diversify risks. Research has found that foreign bank entry has a stronger positive effect on competition with greenfield investments than with mergers and acquisitions, though greenfield investments are not necessarily associated with greater access to financial services. Better integrated with the parent bank, greenfields may also help more during local downturns; however, investment through acquisitions may yield greater benefits in response to home country or global shocks. In addition, to the extent possible, host economies can opt—for example, during privatization—to allow foreign banks from home countries with stricter bank regulations, or to diversify foreign banks by their home country to mitigate the impact of foreign shocks from a specific country. For many countries, however, options to shape foreign entry may be more circumscribed, depending on their obligations under multilateral and preferential services trade agreements.

The regulation and supervision of international banking are complex, and should involve extensive cross-border coordination. There is a need for more intensive cooperation between home and host countries, going beyond memorandums of understanding and information exchanges. This need reflects the limited ability of host country authorities to supervise appropriately larger international banks, along with the distorted incentives of both home and host country supervisors who do not consider the effects of their decisions beyond their borders. Ideally, coordination should include an international agreement on crisis management that explicitly outlines responsibilities and processes to follow in case of a resolution. With the changing composition of the industry and the increased role of technology, coordinating regulation and supervision remains a major challenge for policy makers. And because this is very much an ongoing agenda, a more in-depth analysis of regulatory reform will be included in a future *Global Financial Development Report.*

The rise of South–South banking and banking's greater regionalization come with benefits but also

possible risks. Greater South–South banking is likely to increase local competition and financial development, as any other entry would. But to the extent that banks from the South are more familiar with the institutions and the culture of other developing countries, they tend to be better at serving smaller and more informationally opaque segments, such as SMEs and households. They are also likely to be more committed to host countries and less likely to exit during downturns. However, to the extent that shocks are more correlated within regions than globally, greater regionalization will limit risk sharing and the diffusion of the best banking technology and skills. Greater South–South banking also entails additional risks from having foreign banks from less-regulated and institutionally weaker home countries. The net effect of regionalization is not clear a priori and is a topic for further research. Questions remain about whether there is an optimal mix of foreign entry through global and regional banks in order to maximize the benefits and minimize the costs of bank internationalization.

After the crisis, there was also a disintermediation trend, whereby cross-border bank credit was substituted with capital market funding. The importance of well-functioning domestic capital markets as a "spare tire" was confirmed during the global financial crisis, when in many countries they substituted at least partially for the decline in bank funding. The patterns illustrated here highlight not only the benefits of having alternative sources of finance but also the need to broaden the policy discussion to consider the financial system as a whole, and not focus just on one type of financial intermediary such as global banks. These shifts do not alleviate the funding constraints of smaller firms without access to markets, however. For smaller firms with limited or no access to capital markets, the important role of banks remains.

Fintech developments may have important implications for the global banking landscape. Fintech firms are rapidly expanding and speeding up transactions at a lower cost, and developing technologies for data security, risk management, mobile banking and alternative currencies. Large foreign banks that can devote more resources to research and development are likely to play an important role in this

(box continued next page)

BOX 0.1   **Main Messages of This Report** *(continued)*

---

area. So far, the relationship between global banks and fintech firms has been mostly complementary, with incumbent firms pouring investment into the fintech sector. The trend toward digitalization and technological innovation will likely increase the role of nonphysical distribution channels. Fintech also comes with risks; hence, regulators are paying close attention to it and to how it is revolutionizing the sector, bringing new challenges to the already-

complex supervision and regulation of foreign banks. Regulators need to keep pace with the rapid entry of new, nonbank providers into the market and of the rapid rolling out of digital services. And they need to pay attention to the potential risks that these changes may entail—such as the protection of vulnerable customers, discrimination, disclosure requirements for SMEs, and privacy concerns related to the sharing of consumer data.

---

finance, there are also concerns about stability and the "cherry picking" of best clients. Financial market practitioners and policy makers also note that international banks may have become too large and complex, with only half the respondents indicating confidence that their national policy frameworks are sufficient to address the potential stability risks posed by these institutions.

Given the trade-offs facing policy makers, it is crucial to thoroughly examine the costs and benefits of international banking and to devise effective policies based on the evidence. *Global Financial Development Report 2017/2018: Bankers without Borders* seeks to bring new data and research and to draw on available insights and experience to contribute to this discussion.

BOX 0.2   **Views on International Banking by Practitioners: Global Financial Development Barometer**

To examine views on international banking among the World Bank group's clients, the *Global Financial Development Report* team undertook new rounds of the Financial Development Barometer in 2015 and 2016. The barometer is an informal global poll of financial sector practitioners focusing on development issues. This poll examines trends and sentiments regarding financial sector issues that are under policy debate. The latest barometer explored the perceived drivers and effects of international banking as well as the efficacy of regulatory policies designed in the aftermath of the global financial crisis. It reveals interesting insights from central bankers, finance ministry officials, regulatory/supervisory authorities, market participants, and practitioners at various international financial institutions.

Of the 222 individuals polled, 112 (50 percent) from 9 developed and 42 developing countries responded to the survey.

More than 70 percent of the participants perceive international banking to play an important role in providing financial services to firms, and to a lesser extent in serving households (see figure BO.2.1). More than two-thirds of the respondents acknowledge the novel ways international banks introduce products to improve financial access. Nevertheless, more than 80 percent of respondents are concerned that foreign banks may be aggressive in cherry picking the most profitable and established borrowers. Also, more than 70 percent of respondents agree that international banks contribute to the transmission of international shocks. The perceptions of global and

(box continued next page)

BOX 0.2   Views on International Banking by Practitioners: Global Financial Development Barometer *(continued)*

FIGURE BO.2.1   **The Impact of Global and Regional Banking**

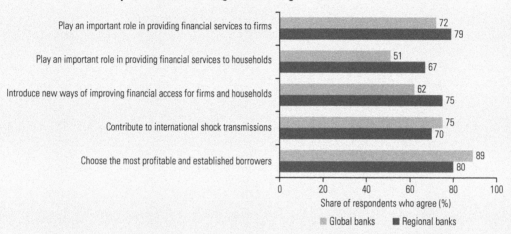

Source: Financial Development Barometer.

regional banks vary, because regional banks are seen as having stronger political and cultural links to the host country. Hence, positive effects are more commonly associated with regional banks and negative effects with global banks.

An overwhelming proportion of survey participants sees global banks as having become unwieldy and complex, potentially posing stability risks

to home and host country jurisdictions (see table BO.2.1). Views differ quite a bit on whether existing national policy frameworks will be sufficient to address such risks in light of the crisis experience, where respondents are roughly split in the middle. The widespread stability concerns are also reflected in strong support for regulatory interventions to address such risks.

TABLE BO.2.1   **Selected Results from the Financial Development Barometer**
Percentage of respondents agreeing with the statements

In your view...	
". . . global banks have become excessively complex."	93
". . . global banks have become too large from an operational efficiency viewpoint."	86
". . . global banks could pose excessive stability risks to their home (host) country."	89 (89)
". . . existing national policy frameworks would be sufficient to address such stability risks."	54
". . . the global reform agenda should be complemented by reforms of banking structures (separation of bank activities) to effectively address the risks posed by global, cross-border banks and reduce their complexity."	92
". . . in your country, macroprudential policies should be relied on to mitigate the risks of crises and their related cost associated with the activities of global banks."	85

Source: Financial Development Barometer.

INTERNATIONAL BANKING: MEASUREMENT AND RECENT TRENDS

International banks are involved in two main types of international activities: cross-border flows, and foreign participation in domestic banking systems through brick-and-mortar operations. Trade in financial services most commonly takes place through (1) cross-border operations of a bank, in lending, deposit taking, or insurance; and (2) provision of these services through a foreign bank's presence, which can take the form of a subsidiary or a branch in a foreign country. Here, an *international bank* is defined as a bank with cross-border activities or foreign subsidiaries or branches, or both. A *global bank* is defined as an international bank with operations in multiple regions. *Regional banks* are defined as banks that focus their operations in a specific region. And a *domestic bank* is defined as a bank that does not have international operations.

The decade before the financial crisis saw significant increases in international banking activities, a trend that coincided with general globalization during this period, including trade and foreign direct investment (FDI) in goods and services. Deregulation and liberalization across the world also promoted increases in cross-border activities, as well as local bank presence. Hence, both types of activities displayed an increasing trend just before the global financial crisis hit in 2008, yet declined afterward (figure O.1).[1] Developing countries experienced a shorter-lived decline than developed countries, particularly in foreign brick-and-mortar presence. It is particularly important that the volume of foreign bank claims via local lending now exceeds that of cross-border lending in developed countries and is comparable in developing countries, because lending by brick-and-mortar banks has proven to be more resilient in response to the financial crisis.

Local lending was more resilient than cross-border flows after the global financial crisis, but net foreign bank entry has become

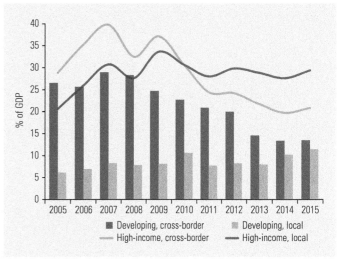

FIGURE O.1   **Cross-Border and Local Claims by Foreign Banks, 2005–15**

Source: Consolidated Banking Statistics (Ultimate Risk Basis), Bank for International Settlements. *Note:* Figures are country-level averages by income level of the borrowing countries over the period 2005–15. Borrowing countries are categorized as high-income and developing countries according to the World Bank's country classifications as of 2017. Cross-border claims refer to those extended by foreign bank offices outside the borrower's jurisdiction. Local claims refer to those extended by foreign bank offices within the borrower's jurisdiction. Total ratios of outstanding values to gross domestic product are provided in each case.

negative since 2010 (see figure O.2). Although the number of foreign banks exiting markets remained more or less the same, there was much less entry after the crisis. The number of foreign banks worldwide has declined, but not relative to the number of domestic banks, which saw an even greater decline. More important, banks based in high-income countries drove the exits, but developing countries continued their foreign bank expansion, accounting for close to 60 percent of new entries. Hence, two important trends have emerged: South–South banking, and regionalization. By 2013, banks based in high-income countries still represented 89 percent of foreign bank assets globally, but this share was 6 percentage points lower than before the crisis, representing a greater diversity of foreign bank ownership. Foreign bank presence also became more regionally concentrated, with the average intraregional share increasing by 4 percentage points. This largely reflected the expansion of developing country banks

FIGURE O.2 **Number of Entries and Exits of Foreign Banks, 1995–2013**

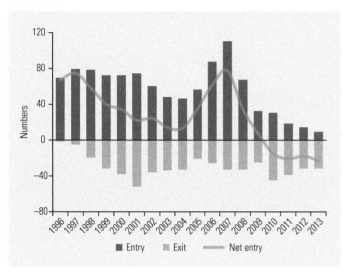

Source: Foreign Bank Ownership Database (Claessen and van Horen 2015).

into space opened up by the retrenchment of global banks.

These aggregate trends hide important differences across different regions. Since the crisis, while the share of foreign bank assets in total banking assets has declined in Europe and Central Asia (ECA), the Middle East and North Africa (MENA), and Sub-Saharan Africa (SSA), it has continued to increase in East Asia and the Pacific (EAP) and Latin America and the Caribbean (LAC) (see figure O.3). High-income countries also saw a decline. Nevertheless, despite these developments, foreign banks continue to constitute 40–60 percent of the banking industry in the ECA, LAC, and SSA regions. Hence, lending by international banks remains an important source of finance, particularly in these regions.

Despite the overall drop in cross-border flows since the global financial crisis, developing countries have increased their role as providers of cross-border funds to other developing countries. The share of Southern economies in cross-border bank credit channeled to the South has almost doubled since 2007, to 8.5 percent in 2014. The same pattern can be observed for syndicated loans, where South–South shares have grown from 3.5 percent before the crisis to 7.7 percent since it (figure O.4). Although most developing countries have expanded their bank credit toward Southern economies after the crisis, the EAP region accounts for the bulk

FIGURE O.3 **Share of Foreign Bank Assets, by Region, 2005–13**

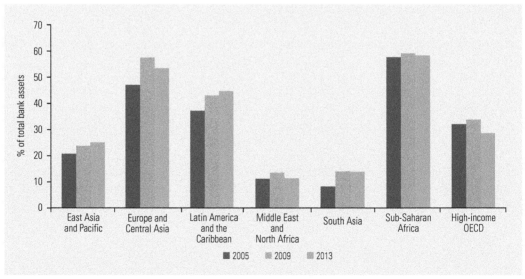

Source: Calculations based on Foreign Bank Ownership Database (Claessens and van Horen 2015).
Note: Regions exclude high-income countries that belong to the Organisation for Economic Co-operation and Development (OECD).

FIGURE O.4 **Direction of Cross-Border Bank Lending, before and after the Global Financial Crisis**

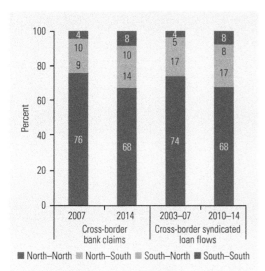

Source: Broner and others 2017.
Note: This figure shows the value of the stocks (flows) of cross-border bank claims (syndicated loans) scaled by worldwide bank claims (syndicated loans). Data are aggregated for all economies within a source region to all economies within a receiver region. For cross-border bank claims, the end-of-year statistics are shown. For syndicated loans, the statistics are calculated year by year and then averaged over time. The North includes the G-7 economies and 15 other Western European economies. The South includes the remaining economies not included in the North. Offshore financial centers are excluded from the sample.

of South–South transactions. Specifically, on average, EAP originated 25 percent of the total cross-border syndicated loans to developing countries during the postcrisis period, up from 12 percent during the precrisis average. An important part of the expansion in South–South bank credit since the crisis has been associated with a trend toward regionalization—with Brazil, China, India, and South Africa playing an increasingly important role in their regions. In particular, intraregional syndicated lending accounted on average for 75 percent of South–South syndicated lending during the 2010–14 period, up from 70 percent during the 2003–07 period. This pattern held across most regions, except for LAC and MENA (Broner and others 2017).

The rise of South–South brick-and-mortar banking since the crisis has also varied across regions. As in the case of cross-border activities, the increase in South–South brick-and-mortar banking operations and regionalization since the global financial crisis has been more prominent in some regions than others (figure O.5). Specifically, a greater share of foreign banks in the MENA and SSA regions are now regional banks compared with precrisis years.

FIGURE O.5   **Share of Regional Foreign Banks among Foreign Banks, Country-Level Averages, 1997–2013**

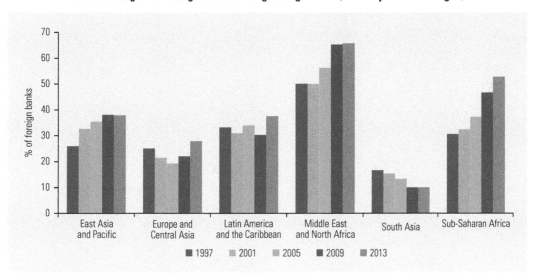

Source: Calculations based on Foreign Bank Ownership Database (Claessens and van Horen 2015).
Note: Regions exclude high-income countries that belong to the Organisation for Economic Co-operation and Development (OECD).

FIGURE O.6 **Trends in Bank Size**

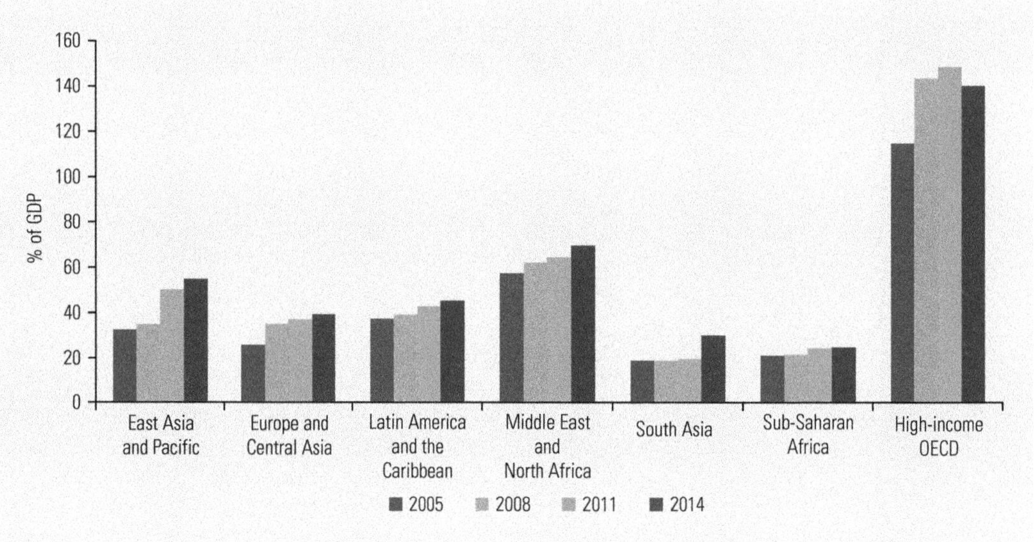

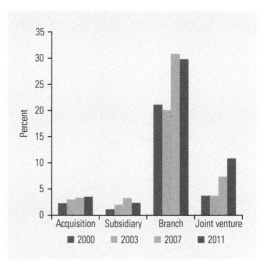

Source: Bureau van Dijk Bankscope (database).
Note: Values represent regional country-level averages of combined assets of the top five banks relative to GDP, for the period 2005–14.

Another trend in bank internationalization is a dramatic increase in bank size. From 2005 to 2014, the total asset size of the world's largest banks increased by more than 40 percent. Despite regulatory efforts after the crisis to address too-big-to-fail issues, bank size has not shrunk in either absolute terms or—as seen in figure O.6—relative to gross domestic product (GDP). The largest banks are also the ones that are active at the international level.

Finally, since 2007, with the backlash against globalization, many countries, including many developing countries, have adopted increasingly restrictive policies toward foreign banking. These policies take the form of direct restrictions (see figure O.7) or indirect policies affecting foreign bank presence—such as macroprudential policies affecting foreign bank operations (see figure O.8), countercyclical buffers, or even ring fencing—in an effort to regulate capital flows. All in all, restrictions on international banking activities increased after the global financial crisis, coinciding with the reduction in cross-border flows and net entries.

In summary, following a decade of increased globalization, international banking has suffered a setback since the global

FIGURE O.7 **Share of Developing Countries with Restrictions on Foreign Bank Entry through Alternative Modes**

Source: World Bank Regulation and Supervision (database).
Note: The analysis includes 78 developing countries providing complete responses to relevant questions in the 2003, 2007, and 2011 survey waves of the Banking Regulation and Supervision Surveys.

financial crisis. There have been large reductions in cross-border flows, and fewer foreign bank entries. The trends in foreign bank entry differ across countries, however.

FIGURE O.8   **Share of Home and Host Countries That Tightened Macroprudential Policies, 2005–13**

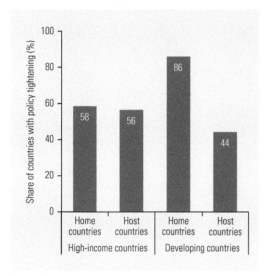

Sources: Claessens and van Horen 2015; Cerutti, Claessens, and Laeven 2015.
Note: Countries are defined as home countries when they own more banks in other countries than the number foreign subsidiaries they host and as host countries if they host more foreign subsidiaries than the banks they own abroad.

While developed country banks retrenched, developing country banks continued to invest abroad, through both cross-border and brick-and-mortar operations, leading to a more regionalized banking system with a greater South–South presence. Large international banks continued to become larger. During this period, regulatory barriers to foreign banking have also increased.

WHY DO WE CARE ABOUT INTERNATIONAL BANKING?: FINANCIAL DEVELOPMENT, STABILITY TRADE-OFFS, AND THE ROLE OF POLICY

Financial globalization comes with both opportunities and risks. Possible benefits include a globally more efficient allocation of capital and enhanced risk sharing. A liberalized capital account promotes external financing, and increased competition due to foreign entry is likely to improve efficiency and domestic resource allocation. Better know-how and financial skills are imported, as well as specialized

technologies. Pressures from foreign capital may discipline countries' macroeconomic and financial management, and the entry of foreign institutions may help improve regulation and supervision, as well as possibly breaking the political entrenchment between domestic financial institutions and governments. All in all, more capital and increased efficiency of allocation will promote faster economic development and greater financial stability, because risks can be exported and shared more efficiently (Cetorelli and Goldberg 2012b; Claessens, Demirgüç-Kunt, and Huizinga 2001; De Haas and van Lelyveld 2010; Goldberg 2009). However, openness also comes with its own risks, exposing the countries to foreign risks, foreign monetary policy shocks, and other types of mismatches (Morais and others, forthcoming). Rapid growth in international credit may more easily lead to boom-bust cycles in poor institutional environments (Borio, McCauley, and McGuire 2011). When international banks focus on prime customers and increase competition, poor information and contract enforcement may make it difficult for domestic banks to move to other segments and serve previously underserved clients. This can reduce the franchise values of domestic banks, and possibly have a negative impact on access and inclusion by driving them out altogether. Also, risk sharing inevitably implies that systemic risks in source countries may be imported from time to time (Peek and Rosengren 1997, 2000; Schnabl 2012). Moreover, existing policy distortions in domestic systems—such as poorly designed safety nets, and weak regulation and supervision that generate excessive risk-taking incentives—tend to be magnified through international banking that expands risk-taking opportunities (Demirgüç-Kunt, Kane, and Laeven 2014).

Bank internationalization, on its own, is no panacea for guaranteeing financial development and stability. International banking can have important benefits for development by improving efficiency and risk sharing, but these benefits will not accrue unless the institutional environment is developed and the right policies are adopted (Detragiache, Tressel, and

Gupta 2008; Gormley 2014; Mian 2006). Thus, the challenge for policy makers is to provide an environment that will maximize the benefits of internationalization while minimizing the costs. Research suggests that institutionally better developed countries tend to reap both more of the development and risk-sharing benefits of international banking.

Therefore, it is important for countries to ensure that they have the right regulations and infrastructure in place. Although foreign bank participation may help to break or mitigate the political entrenchment of incumbent banks, even in a bad institutional environment, those foreign banks may just replace incumbents and continue collecting profits and exploiting regulatory weaknesses without necessarily improving the competitiveness and efficiency of the banking sector (Detragiache, Tressel, and Gupta 2008; Ongena, Popov, and Udell 2013). Thus, financial liberalization should be accompanied by institutional reforms and may be introduced gradually, ensuring competitiveness in the banking industry to avoid foreign banks completely crowding out domestic banks. Having a host country with good institutions and a competitive banking industry will also help foreign banks become core operations for their parent banks—which could reduce their incentives to retrench during home country or global downturns. Other institutional factors—such as the information environment and the quality of contract enforcement—are also crucial for foreign banks to benefit host economies by expanding their services more widely beyond their niche customers, improving access and inclusion. Furthermore, when accompanied by improved information sharing—through credit registries, for example—foreign banks can help to lower average lending interest rates and increase average loan quality (Bruno and Hauswald 2013; Claessens, Hassib, and van Horen 2014).

The key to designing effective policies is to recognize that the benefits and costs of internationalization vary depending on bank characteristics and the conditions in the home and host countries. It is particularly important that differences in origins, types, and forms

of capital flows and foreign bank presence matter (Claessens 2016). Some flows, such as bank FDI in the form of brick-and-mortar operations, tend to be associated with the diffusion of technology and know-how compared with cross-border flows. Larger foreign banks and those that are culturally closer, with a greater share of domestic financial intermediation, including deposit taking, tend to provide better access to SMEs and households and are less likely to engage in cherry picking (Berger and Udell 2006).

For stability considerations, it is important to recognize that risk sharing also has a downside. International banks that export risks will also import them. Hence, the net risk-sharing benefits of globalization need to be considered over the long term. Again, the heterogeneity of flows and types of institutions and investors matter (Claessens 2016). Short-term, cross-border flows tend to be more volatile and less resilient than a brick-and-mortar bank presence. And some investors, such as international banks and mutual funds, are affected by global financial and monetary conditions to a greater extent, exposing countries to more volatility. Although these can be mitigated, they cannot be fully eliminated without giving up openness altogether. Nevertheless, research suggests that banks with a greater commitment, as reflected in closeness both in distance to headquarters and in culture, that have larger local market shares and a greater reliance on local funding, are more willing to incur temporary costs when faced with external shocks and to support the local economy (Claessens and van Horen 2014a).

Encouraging the right type of foreign bank presence or forms of capital flows without causing distortions is challenging. Many supervisory agencies no longer rely on the home supervisor of the local affiliates for ensuring stability. Compared with branches, foreign subsidiaries can be self-sufficient—with high capitalization requirements and a high share of funding through retail deposits—thereby improving stability. Among subsidiaries, a mix of new and greenfield units and takeovers or mergers may also help diversify risks. Research has found that foreign bank entry has stronger positive effects on the competition with greenfield investments than with mergers and acquisitions, though greenfield investments are not necessarily associated with greater access to financial services (Claeys and Hainz 2014; Delis, Kokas, and Ongena 2014; Jeon, Olivero, and Wu 2011). By being better integrated with the parent bank, greenfields may also help more during local downturns; however, investment through acquisitions may yield greater benefits in response to home country or global shocks (Jeon, Olivero, and Wu 2013). Finally, some diversification of foreign banks' business models may be desirable in shielding host economies from the negative outcomes associated with a specific type of activity (for example, in response to a negative shock to fee-based, non-interest-income-generating activities, or being overly reliant on wholesale funding, which could dry up during global downturns). When possible—as in a privatization—host country authorities could also try to diversify the roster of home countries and to make sure that the prospective parent banks are also diversified, so that they can provide liquidity and other support to their subsidiaries, even when they face shocks at home. Research shows that effective home country regulations, proximity to the home country—cultural or physical—and a core position in the banking group lower the probability of exit in response to shocks (Claessens and van Horen 2014b). For many countries, however, options to shape foreign entry may be more circumscribed, depending on their obligations under multilateral and preferential service trade agreements.

The regulatory and supervisory failures during the recent global financial crisis led to an intense effort to redesign the regulatory landscape, which is still ongoing. Two extreme approaches influencing the ongoing policy discussions entail *territoriality*—that is, the *ring fencing* of activities under a particular authority's domain, which inhibits an open financial system—and *universalism*, which entails an equitable distribution of bankruptcy costs involving cross-border burden sharing. The European Single Resolution Mechanism is a prospective example of the latter approach (Claessens 2016). Ring fencing is a local regulator's reaction to limit the potentially negative consequences of having foreign banks. Host authorities request local liquidity and capital to minimize the impact of external shocks. In terms of advantages, this approach provides better incentives for local supervision and no burden sharing requirements. Ring fencing, however, is also less efficient for financial institutions, because it lessens the benefits of cross-border banking in the first place, reducing the scope for risk sharing and potentially imposing costs in times of stress through possible runs and liquidity problems. This approach also undermines the incentives for cross-border regulation and supervision, thus impairing the general openness of financial systems. Although these two approaches may be too extreme for many countries, an intermediate model of cooperation that includes some elements of the universal approach may be feasible. Ideally, this intermediate model could adopt an international agreement on crisis management that explicitly outlines responsibilities and processes to follow in case of a resolution (Beck and Wagner 2016). Overall, despite progress since the financial crisis, the global regulatory reform agenda is at a crossroads; many aspects remain unfinished, and the finalization of the Basel III reform package appears to have been delayed. Hence, more comprehensive coverage of this topic will be included in a future issue of this report, when policy making is more advanced and additional data and research are available.

Within this broader context, this overview concludes with a discussion of three focus areas that are important in international banking and their policy implications: the rise of South–South banking, the shift toward alternative sources of funding, and the emergence of fintech. The focus on these areas reflects the importance of these new trends for policy, because they all present challenges and opportunities. These are also areas where research is new and limited, and recent developments raise many more questions for the future. For help in navigating the rest of the report, see box O.3.

BOX 0.3 **Navigating This Report**

The rest of the report consists of three chapters that cover the benefits and costs of international banking, key facts, and general guidelines for the role of policy. Within these broader topic areas, the report focuses on policy-relevant new developments where new evidence is emerging yet also raises many more questions for the future.

Chapter 1 defines international banking and presents a conceptual framework for evaluating the benefits and costs associated with globalization. It offers stylized facts about the importance of international banking across countries and over time, and highlights recent trends. The chapter also discusses the advantages and disadvantages of various data sources, which help differentiate between cross-border lending and the brick-and-mortar operations of international banks.

Chapter 2 examines the brick-and-mortar operations of international banks. It discusses and provides evidence on the determinants of foreign bank entry and its impact on bank competition, efficiency, access to finance, and financial stability. Implications for South–South banking and regionalization are discussed, as well as where fintech is influencing the financial sector. The current global regulatory reform agenda is discussed, with alternative approaches to regulation and supervision. The chapter provides policy guidance on maximizing the benefits of foreign entry and minimizing its costs.

Chapter 3 mirrors the preceding chapter but focuses on the cross-border activities of international banks. It discusses recent trends and presents evidence on the significance, drivers, and impact of cross-border bank flows. It focuses on three important developments that are shaping international banking: the role of the South, the substitution of financing across markets, and the rise of fintech. The chapter discusses these new trends and how they may shape the future global banking landscape, and it draws out policy implications.

There are two statistical appendixes. Appendix A presents basic country-by-country data on financial system characteristics around the world. It also presents averages of the same indicators for peer groups of countries, together with summary maps. It is an update of information from the *2015/2016 Global Financial Development Report*. Appendix B provides additional country-by-country information on key aspects of international banking around the world.

The accompanying website (http://www.worldbank .org/financialdevelopment) contains a wealth of underlying research; additional evidence, including country examples; and extensive databases on financial development—providing users with interactive access to information on financial systems. Users can provide feedback on the report, participate in an online version of the Financial Development Barometer, and submit their suggestions for future issues of the report. The website also presents an updated and expanded version of the Global Financial Development Database, a data set of more than 70 financial system characteristics for 203 economies since 1960.

FOCUS AREA 1: THE RISE OF SOUTH–SOUTH BANKING

One of the important recent trends in international banking has been the rise of South–South banking. As the stylized facts in the previous section illustrate, developing countries have become more prominent in international banking, and these activities have become more regionalized. Research in this area has been scarce, however, and its policy implications are not well understood.

South–South banking may be associated with better access. The increasing participation of developing countries in global financial transactions has allowed these economies to not only diversify their investments but also obtain financing from abroad, complementing domestic markets and widening their available funding choices. Greater South–South banking is likely to increase local competition and financial development, as with any foreign entry. But the recent trends in South–South banking are also likely to influence who gets credit and whether it helps improve access to financial services. Relative to a bank from the North, South–South banks invest in countries within their region and tend to be more familiar with the cultural, linguistic, legal, and institutional environment of the host country and may be better at collecting and processing soft information that allows them to overcome the common challenges that foreign banks face when lending downmarket to smaller and more informationally opaque segments, especially SMEs and households (Claessens and van Horen 2014b; Mian 2006). A recent study using firm-level data also finds that a foreign bank presence is more strongly linked to higher rates of business formation when those banks are headquartered in the South (Alfaro, Beck, and Calomiris 2015).

However, regionalization may also have costs. If foreign entry is more regionalized, this may constrain both the adoption of globally best banking technology and skills across countries and the most efficient allocation of capital. Increasing regionalization in the South also limits risk sharing and implies a larger exposure of an economy to shocks originating within the region.

Recent research has constructed an extensive, bank-level database that identifies international and domestic banks by developing indices of the internationalization of bank liabilities, and it investigates the performance of international banks vis-à-vis domestic banks in the 112 countries where they are headquartered (Bertay, Demirgüç-Kunt, and Huizinga 2017).

The results suggest that internationalization smooths banks' credit supply over the business cycle, particularly for developing country international banks. Figure O.9 shows the change in bank lending associated with a 1 percent increase in real GDP per capita growth, for domestic and international banks headquartered in high-income or developing countries. In general, bank lending is procyclical, increasing during booms and falling during downturns. Yet, particularly in developing countries, the lending pattern of domestic banks is significantly more procyclical in response to local business cycles compared with their international counterparts.

Furthermore, these data show that the funding of South–South subsidiaries has

FIGURE O.9   Change in Bank Lending Associated with a 1 Percent Increase in Growth in GDP per Capita

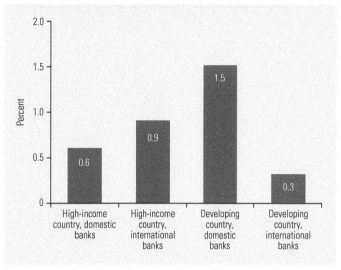

Source: Bertay, Demirgüç-Kunt, and Huizinga 2017.
Note: The figure shows marginal effects from a regression of bank lending on GDP per capita growth and a number of control variables and bank fixed effects, estimated using a sample of 2,750 banks based in 112 countries (47 high-income, and 65 developing) for the period 2000–15. International bank values are evaluated at the average level of internationalization; that is, the log of the number of countries in which the international bank is active. The coefficients are significant at the 10 percent level or better.

increasingly come from local customer deposits, which the global financial crisis proved to be a more stable source of funding, enabling these banks to better smooth their lending throughout the crisis (figure O.10).

Nevertheless, South–South banks may also bring increased risks, which stem from more lax regulation in their home countries. Indeed, Claessens and van Horen (2016) and Mehigan (2016) find that foreign banks based in countries with relatively laxer regulatory requirements could amplify credit booms in host countries. The extent to which foreign banks based in the South will be committed to the host countries and therefore limit shock transmission versus the extent to which their potentially weaker regulatory and supervisory frameworks will become a source of instability is not clear a priori, and thus needs future research. Also, because regionalization by definition means less risk sharing, questions remain whether there is an optimal mix of foreign bank entries from global as well as regional banks, so as to maximize the potential benefits.

FIGURE O.10 **Contribution of Local Deposits to Banks' Total Funding**

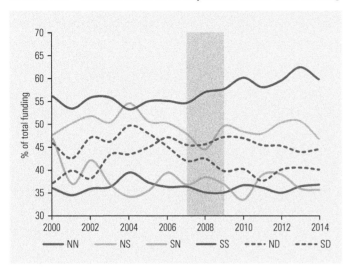

Source: Calculations based on Bertay, Demirgüç-Kunt, and Huizinga 2017.
Notes: NN corresponds to bank subsidiaries from developed countries operating in developed countries. NS corresponds to bank subsidiaries from developed countries operating in developing countries. SN corresponds to bank subsidiaries from developing countries operating in developed countries. SS corresponds to subsidiaries from developing countries operating in developing countries. ND corresponds to domestic banks in developed countries. SD corresponds to domestic banks in developing countries.

FOCUS AREA 2: THE SHIFT TOWARD ALTERNATIVE SOURCES OF FUNDING

When the global financial crisis suddenly hit the banking sectors of major high-income countries, firms around the world compensated for this contraction by substituting across funding sources. Cortina, Didier, and Schmukler (2016) use issuance data for large corporates in domestic and international bond markets and syndicated loan markets to show that in high-income and developing countries, firms with access to capital markets moved to bond markets (figure O.11). In developing countries, these firms also switched to domestic banks and away from international banks. Due to these switches, global financial activity during the crisis declined less than the collapse in cross-border loans. These changes in debt composition continued during the postcrisis period.

The importance of well-functioning domestic capital markets as a "spare tire" was confirmed during the global financial crisis period in many countries, as they substituted

at least partially for the decline in bank funding. Demirgüç-Kunt, Martínez Pería, and Tressel (2017) analyze the capital structures of firms during the crisis by investigating a large panel of listed and nonlisted firms over the 2004–11 period, with good coverage of SMEs. They show that firms listed on a stock market have, on average, experienced a much more moderate decline in leverage and in the use of long-term debt (figure O.12). These findings are consistent with the view that capital markets may have played the role of a spare tire for publicly listed firms, by providing an alternative source of external finance and better information when the functioning of the banking system was impaired during the crisis (Levine, Lin, and Xie 2016).

These patterns highlight not only the benefits of having alternative sources of finance but also the need to broaden the policy discussion to consider the financial system as a whole. When firms obtain financing from different sources, it is important to jointly analyze the different types of financing. Having access to different markets might allow firms to compensate for fluctuations in particular markets by raising funds elsewhere. As such, countries might reduce contagion risks by diversifying the sources of finance and, to the extent possible, having more complete markets, including equity markets. Policy initiatives, such as the Capital Markets Union in Europe, aimed to increase the substitutability between bank loans and other sources of external finance (European Commission 2015), as well as those that aimed to develop innovative instruments, such as minibonds, and securitization may be important (Borensztein and others 2008; Giovannini and others 2015).

However, these shifts do not alleviate the funding constraints of smaller firms without access to markets. Cortina, Didier, and Schmukler (2016) discuss the importance of considering the compositional change in the types of issuers that are tapping each market over time. For instance, during domestic crises, only the relatively larger firms have access to alternative markets such as bonds and international loans. The work of these researchers shows that during foreign shocks,

FIGURE O.11   **Volume of Debt Issuance over Time for Real Purposes**

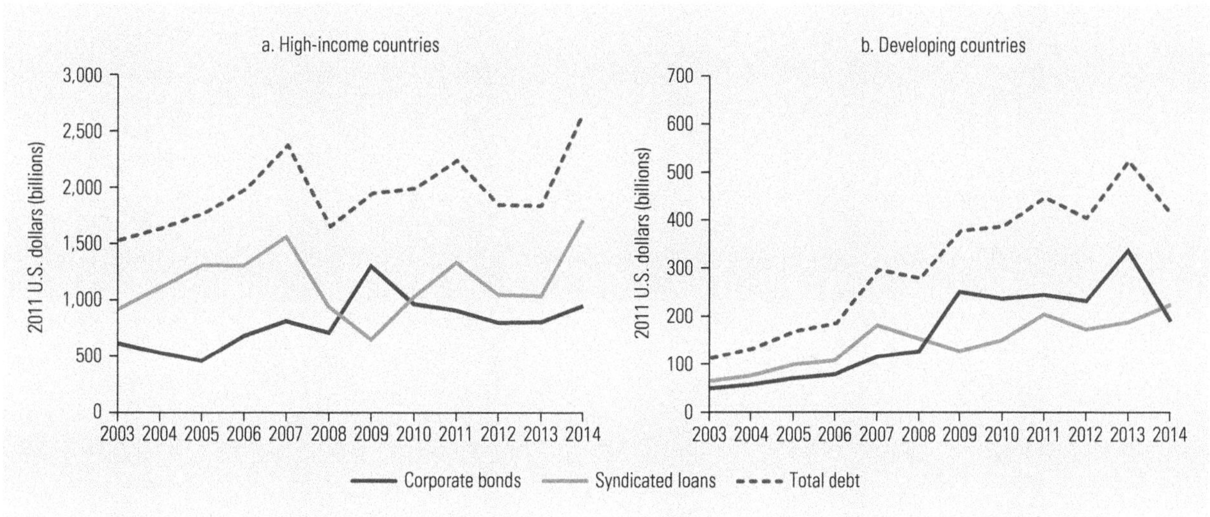

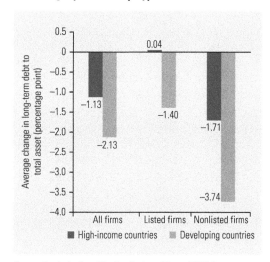

a. High-income countries

b. Developing countries

— Corporate bonds   — Syndicated loans   ---- Total debt

Source: Thomson Reuters SDC Platinum (database).
Note: This figure displays the aggregate amount raised per year for real purposes in corporate bond and syndicated loan markets by high-income (panel a) and developing countries (panel b). Real purposes refer to the exclusion of bonds and loans used for acquisition financing and leveraged buyout operations, refinancing, and capital structure management, as well as other issuances whose purposes cannot be categorized as real investments (such as those with unspecified purposes or with missing information).

FIGURE O.12   **Average Change in Long-Term Debt Financing, by Ownership Type**

■ High-income countries   ■ Developing countries

Sources: Demirgüç-Kunt, Martínez Pería, and Tressel 2017; Bureau van Dijk ORBIS (database); and staff calculations.
Note: The data set covers 277,000 firms across 79 countries over the period 2004–11 and is composed mostly of SMEs; 98.7 percent of firms are not listed on a stock exchange.

large international firms switching to domestic markets can potentially crowd out smaller domestic issuers from the market. In the work of Demirgüç-Kunt, Martínez Pería, and

Tressel (2017) as well, the decline in leverage and in long-term debt financing after the crisis was particularly pronounced among all non-listed firms, a large proportion of which are SMEs (figure O.12). Hence, for smaller firms with limited or no access to capital markets, the important role of banks remains.

FOCUS AREA 3: THE RISE OF FINTECH—OPPORTUNITIES AND CHALLENGES

Technology is also changing the banking sector and could have major implications for access, efficiency, and financial sector stability. Fintech—technology-driven new companies providing financial services outside the traditional financial sector—can reshape competition among financial providers and thus improve the delivery of financial services and increase access. Global investment in fintech companies has expanded very rapidly worldwide. Although data on fintech are as yet very scant, there were at least 4,000 active fintech firms in 2015; and more than a dozen of them were valued at over $1 billion (*The Economist* 2015).

Large foreign banks that can devote more resources to research and development are likely to play an important role in this process. Although, at first, fintech helped financial institutions speed up transactions at a lower cost, the most recent technologies encompass a variety of services, such as data security, risk management, mobile banking and alternative currencies. For example, Blockchain, which is an immutable shared electronic record, makes lightning-fast transactions possible compared with traditional bank transfers or settlements of securities trades. In principle, digital financial services, and in particular those provided via mobile telephony, hold the promise of deepening financial inclusion to market segments that have been underserved (Ahmed and others 2015). Hence, fintech is likely to facilitate the provision of financial services and affect how banks compete with each other (and with other, nonbank providers of financial services) for all market segments and across geographical boundaries, which could have broader implications for access, efficiency, and financial sector stability.

Despite its potential, fintech can also pose new challenges for both the financial system and policy makers. The main vulnerabilities that the new digital financial practices are bringing to the financial sector include the lack of safety nets in their business models, the misuse of personal data, difficulties in identifying customers, and electronic fraud. Most peer-to-peer lending platforms act as brokers between borrowers and investors, and thus they do not bear the risk of those loans on their balance sheets. Because they rely on new transactions to make profits, their main source of funding might evaporate during a downturn. Moreover, the algorithms used to evaluate credit profiles might involve discriminatory systems—by, for example, discriminating against borrowers in poorer areas and other vulnerable segments (U.S. Department of the Treasury 2016). With respect to payments, the anonymity, speed, and global reach of the cryptocurrency payment system makes illicit transfers easier. An example of this was "Silkroad," an anonymous e-commerce platform that allowed customers to buy and sell any products—including illegal ones, such as drugs and guns—by using Tor, an anonymous browser, and bitcoin, an anonymous form of payment.

Because certain aspects of fintech's development remain lightly regulated, how this new area of finance should be regulated and supervised is generating an active debate. The new lending practices used by the online platforms seem to be one of the main hot spots for regulators to date. For instance, lending discrimination against consumers, disclosure requirements for SMEs, and the sharing of consumer data are some of the most relevant areas of concern currently being dealt with by regulators in the United States (*Politico* 2016). Moreover, because fintech companies usually have a base of more vulnerable customers— they are bringing some customers into the financial system for the first time—consumer education and protection measures are much needed. Another source of concern is that financial regulation remains region-specific and fragmented, but many fintech firms work globally or offer digital products that are difficult to contain within the borders of a particular economy. Thus, it is not clear which economy's laws would be applied to a company. Some regulators seem to understand that excessive regulation might be deadly for the fintech start-ups and are developing regulatory sandboxes to manage the transition to a new landscape. This approach allows for the live testing of fintech services with a low level of regulation for a defined period, helping to understand the risks that the new products might entail in a controlled environment. This way, the sandbox enables regulators to work with fintech companies to ensure that appropriate consumer protection safeguards are built into their new products and services before these reach a mass market (Financial Conduct Authority 2015). The United Kingdom has launched its sandbox, and other jurisdictions are following similar initiatives—such as Australia, Singapore, and, more recently, Hong Kong SAR, China (*Financial Times* 2016a). Regulators in the United States are also contemplating a sandbox approach (*Wall Street Journal* 2016). New, digitally enabled methods can also potentially be used to address compliance requirements and the monitoring of digital financial services, such as "regtech" (Arner, Barberis, and Buckley 2016; *Financial Times* 2016b).

Regulating and monitoring the development of an industry that is rapidly growing will remain a key challenge in the future. On one hand, redundant and inefficient regulations may hinder fintech's potential for promoting overall financial development. On the other hand, policy makers need to constantly monitor and adapt proper regulatory frameworks that keep pace with the speed at which financial innovations occur. Although the new players are increasing competition and pushing digital transformation in the global financial sector, to date the level of disruption seems low and their services appear highly complementary to the ones provided by the more established banking sector. Banks enjoy

the advantage of scale and incumbency in a heavily regulated industry. This fosters cooperation between banks and fintech companies. Fintechs gain access to banks' scale and customers, and banks can exploit fintechs' expertise in programming and in analyzing large databases. Nevertheless, the impact of fintech and newly developed digital technologies on the global financial sector is expected to keep rising in the years to come.

NOTE

1. Cross-border bank lending activity is comparable to bond issuances and equity market activity. The annual total value of foreign syndicated loans issued globally, which represents only a subset of new foreign bank lending, was $2.5 trillion in 2006 and $3.0 trillion in 2015. For comparison, the total value of global cross-border bond issuances was $3.2 trillion in 2006 and $3.8 trillion in 2015.

CHAPTER 1: KEY MESSAGES

- International banks operate in foreign countries through local affiliates and cross-border lending. They offer opportunities to promote economic development because they bring with them capital, liquidity, expertise, and new technologies, which can lead to more investment, greater competition, and better resource allocation. International banks also play a risk-sharing role—that is, they can help host countries stabilize their credit supply during a local downturn, and they can shift resources back to the home country when conditions at home worsen. However, there are also reasons for caution. Borrowing from abroad involves risks such as foreign exchange exposures and other mismatches. Risk sharing can also expose host countries to systemic risks from time to time. And because global finance tends to be more procyclical than domestic finance, this factor could more easily lead to boom-bust cycles in poor institutional environments.

- The presence of international banks, as measured by their foreign claims, quadrupled in the decade leading up to the global financial crisis in 2007–09, but it has since dropped and stagnated. In fact, although the number of foreign banks exiting markets remained more or less the same, there was much less entry after the crisis, and net entry became negative for the first time since 1995. Despite this decline, lending by international banks remains an important source of finance for private and public sectors across the world. Notably, the volume of foreign bank claims via local lending now exceeds that of cross-border lending because lending by brick-and-mortar banks has proven to be more resilient in response to financial distress.

- Indeed, the participation of foreign banks through branches and subsidiaries was rising in all regions until recent years when the major global banks began to retrench their international operations. Although banks from high-income countries drove exits, developing countries continued their foreign bank expansion, accounting for close to 60 percent of new entries. Thus, two important trends have emerged: South–South banking and regionalization. By 2013, banks from high-income countries still represented 89 percent of foreign bank assets globally, but this share was 6 percentage points lower than before the crisis, representing a greater diversity of foreign bank ownership. Foreign bank presence also became more regionally concentrated, with the average intraregional share increasing by 4 percentage points, largely reflecting developing country banks expanding into space opened up by the retrenchment of global banks.

- Another trend in bank internationalization is the dramatic increase in bank size, with the assets of the largest banks worldwide increasing by more than 40 percent from 2005 to 2014. Despite regulatory efforts after the global financial crisis to address too-big-to-fail issues, bank size has not shrunk in either absolute terms or relative to gross domestic product (GDP). The largest banks are also the ones that are active at the international level.

- Since 2007, with the backlash against globalization, many countries, including many developing ones, have been adopting increasingly restrictive policies that directly and indirectly affect the presence of foreign banks. All in all, restrictions on international banking activities increased after the global financial crisis.

- Overall, international banking can have important benefits for development by improving efficiency and risk sharing, but benefits do not accrue unless the institutional environment is developed and the right policies are adopted. Thus, the challenge for policy makers is to provide an environment that will maximize the benefits from internationalization while minimizing the costs. The key to addressing this challenge is to devise policies acknowledging that benefits and costs vary, depending on bank characteristics and home and host country conditions. The rise of South–South banking ties as well as the emergence of new financial technologies will also present new challenges for policy makers.

1

Conceptual Framework, Stylized Facts, and the Role of Policy

INTRODUCTION

International banks can play an important role in shaping financial and economic development. They may bring much-needed capital, liquidity, and technological expertise to host countries. In return, however, they will expect high returns, diversification benefits, and growth opportunities. In fact, historically such international activities have been essential to banking (see box 1.1).

This chapter provides a conceptual framework for understanding the dynamics of international banking, its effects on economic development, and the scope for public policy. The chapter then introduces relevant definitions and stylized facts that shed light on recent trends and pave the way for the analyses in the rest of the report. The chapter concludes with a discussion of the policy implications and the prospective role of government in international banking.

A CONCEPTUAL FRAMEWORK FOR UNDERSTANDING INTERNATIONAL BANKING

Banks provide many important functions that facilitate economic activity. These functions include allocating scarce resources to their best uses, enabling diversification of risk, mobilizing and pooling savings (thereby enabling large, indivisible, and long-term investments through maturity transformation), facilitating the exchange of goods and services (such as via payment services), and monitoring firms and managers (Levine 1997). The ability of a bank to perform these functions changes when it operates in an international setting as opposed to autarky, and this change has implications for the owners of the bank and its home country (the country in which the bank is headquartered) and for the clients of the bank in both home countries and host countries (the foreign countries in which banks operate). Box 1.2 provides the definitions needed to understand international banking and illustrates how stakeholders in different countries interact through international banks.

Banks expand their activities to other countries to further diversify risk, to realize higher profits, and to achieve economies of scale. Banks also have a long tradition of financing trade across borders—and sometimes even following their client firms involved in international trade (Cull and Martínez Pería 2010). Risk diversification is particularly successful if the home country faces shocks that are not highly correlated with shocks in the

---

BOX 1.1   A Brief Historical Perspective on International Banking

The internationalization of money and finance can be traced back to the fourth century A.D., when the bezant was introduced by Emperor Constantine of Byzantium and effectively used as an international currency in the Mediterranean region (Lothian 2002). Although not on a scale comparable with globalization in modern times, banks were involved in cross-jurisdictional activities for centuries. What follows, based largely on Roussakis (1997), is an account of the historical international banking strongholds that dominated global finance.

Early banks from 15th-century Italy. Even in the Middle Ages, banks that were succeeding in local city-states sought to increase the geographical reach and scope of their operations. Their efforts contributed to international trade and sovereign debt funding. For example, in the mid-15th century Medici Bank in Florence had branches in Rome, Venice, Avignon, London, Bruges, and Geneva; it distributed liquidity from the papal deposits through its branch network (Roussakis 1997). Eventually, the bankruptcy of the bank resulted at least in part from the losses in its "foreign" branches stemming from sovereign delinquencies (De Roover 1963).

Emergence of German merchant banks. In the 16th century, German banks emerged, sometimes replacing the services provided by Italian banks. They became widely involved in financing trade, providing credit to industry, and financing sovereigns such as the Tudors of England and the Hapsburgs of Europe. The German banks, notably the Fugger, financed assets in part through the money markets in Antwerp (Roussakis 1997).

Dutch banks and syndications. In addition to financing trade, Dutch banks funded foreign governments throughout the 17th and 18th centuries. In the latter period, they began to share the financing of these loans with other merchants and wealthy individuals and to sell these bonds to the rest of Europe through the Amsterdam stock exchange—early examples of syndicated loans and securities underwriting.

Industrialization and the rise of modern global banks. At the dawn of 19th century, the long-term financing needs for industrial investments were met through bond and equity issuance, largely in London. Merchant banks such as Baring Brothers[a] were among the most important players, channeling capital across the Atlantic. It was also common practice for foreign governments to raise funds in London (see, for example, Reinhart and Rogoff 2008) and for foreign banks to be established with foreign capital.[b] Indeed, it has been widely acknowledged that the second half of the 19th century saw the first wave of globalization, in which multinational banking activity increased dramatically. For example, Battilossi (2006) reveals that the number of foreign branches of British, French, and German banks increased from 525 in 1880 to 1,610 in 1913. Accompanied by the gold standard in many countries, which provided monetary stability and reduced exchange rate risk, capital moved almost freely around the world, mostly from Europe to North America and Latin America. Finally, the 20th century saw U.S. and Japanese banks emerging as global banks, which led to the globalization trend in recent decades, strengthened by technological advances and financial deregulation.

a. In 1890 Baring Brothers suffered a liquidity crisis because of its deteriorating loan portfolio concentrated in Latin America. Eventually, leading financial institutions in London had to guarantee Baring's liabilities in an effort orchestrated by the Bank of England—an early example of a bank bailout/rescue (Baker and Collins 1999; Cassis 2013).
b. For example, the Ottoman Bank, established in the mid-19th century in Istanbul, was founded mostly by British and French capital. See http://www.obarsiv.com/english/history.html.

---

host country (García-Herrero and Vázquez 2013). This situation often arises when the host country is in a different geographic region. More broadly, banking activity is one way in which capital flows from low- to high-return countries, and in many cases international banking activities interact with

other types of flows—such as when foreign banks help deepen local capital markets in host countries or increase the flows of foreign direct investment (FDI) to nonfinancial sectors (Ongena, Qi, and Qin 2014; Poelhekke 2015). From the perspective of borrowers in host countries, the diversity of funding sources

BOX 1.2   Useful Definitions for Understanding International Banking in the Financial System

After decades of internationalization, international banks remain quite heterogeneous, and further categorization is helpful in distinguishing their differences from each other and from other banks in their home countries. In this report, an *international bank* is defined as one with cross-border lending facilities or foreign bank subsidiaries or both. Some international banks have emerged as global giants in both size and international reach. A standard definition of a global bank does not exist.[a] Thus here a *global bank* is defined as a large international bank with activities in multiple regions. The banking landscape is also populated with *regional banks*—those that focus on a specific region (or set of countries)[b]—and *domestic banks*—those that have only home country operations. *Global* and *regional banks*—located in *home countries*—are interna-

tional banks that own foreign bank subsidiaries in *host countries*.[c] Domestic banks, by contrast, are banks that do not own foreign bank subsidiaries; nor are they owned by foreign (banking) entities. In short, *foreign banks* are defined by the nationality of their ownership, whereas *international banks* are defined by the geographical scope of their business and operations.

As shown in figure B1.2.1, all agents in both countries may directly interact with the financial markets through different operations. Bidirectional flows, including round-tripping transactions, are also identified in the figure. In addition to the net flows, these interactions are crucial, as noted by Avdjiev, McCauley, and Shin (2015)—that is, gross flows matter in assessing the amount of the risk in the banking system.[d]

FIGURE B1.2.1   How the International Banking System Works

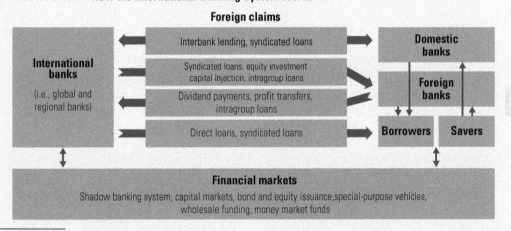

a. The most relevant official definition is that used for a global systemically important bank (G-SIB) by the Bank for International Settlements (BIS) in which factors such as bank size and cross-jurisdictional activities, among others, are considered (details are discussed in box 1.4).
b. For example, the Austrian Erste Group, which has assets totaling some €200 billion, is active in seven countries in the Europe and Central Asia (ECA) region. By contrast, as of the end of 2014, State Street Bank, a U.S. bank of similar size, was active in 29 jurisdictions—Canada, Germany, India, Ireland, Italy, and the United Kingdom, among others. The Austrian Erste Group is not in the global bank sample of BIS, whereas State Street Bank is a G-SIB.
c. International banks may also own foreign branches in host countries. The main difference between a foreign branch and a foreign bank subsidiary is that the branch is regulated by the home country and the subsidiary is regulated by the host country. Moreover, unlike foreign branches, foreign bank subsidiaries are locally chartered, self-standing banks with their own capital—see Cerutti, Dell'Ariccia, and Martínez Pería (2007) for details.
d. The aspect of currency denominations described by Avdjiev, McCauley, and Shin (2015) is not included in this framework. According to these authors, international currencies serve as "funding currency." For example, the U.S. dollar plays the preeminent role in international banking because non-U.S. banks also use the dollar in their transactions. In line with this, the currency mismatch in the real sector debt creates a "risk-taking channel," as noted by Bruno and Shin (2015b), and yields the relationship between the exchange rate and financial stability.

from foreign as well as domestic banks lowers the risk of losing credit during crises or domestic downturns (Goldberg, Dages, and Kinney 2000).

International bank flows are characterized by important differences when compared with other types of capital flows, such as debt and equity investments. These differences can be traced back to the uniqueness of the bank business model. First, banks have the ability to reduce information asymmetries between savers and users of funds through screening and monitoring (Diamond 1984; Fama 1985). Second, banks are vulnerable to bank runs because of their obligation to provide immediate access to depositors' funds on demand (Diamond and Dybvig 1983; Diamond and Rajan 2001). Third, because of this vulnerability, banks tend to be supported by a financial safety net (such as deposit insurance or bank access to the short-term discount windows provided by central banks), possibly inducing moral hazard and greater risk-taking incentives (Demirgüç-Kunt and Detragiache 2002). Finally, because of this tendency to take excessive risks, banks often face tight regulatory measures—mostly on a national level with limited cross-border coordination. These differences are conceptually important because they can determine the international banking landscape and the economic outcomes of international banking activities in both home and host countries. Depending on the institutional environment, quality of regulation and supervision, macroeconomic stability in home and host countries, and the different characteristics of international banks, cross-border banking activities that bring benefits may also lead to certain costs for stakeholders, suggesting an important role for government.

INTERNATIONAL BANKING AND ECONOMIC DEVELOPMENT

Foreign banks can increase competition in the banking industry, leading to more efficient resource mobilization and allocation and greater access to finance for both firms and households. International debt and equity investments should also create such competitive

pressures, but they apply mostly to large firms and not small and medium-sized enterprises (SMEs) and households because of fixed costs and information problems.[1] Those problems are directly addressed by bank business models through economies of scale and monitoring and screening activities (such as collecting valuable information from deposit services). Benefits for the underserved segments unable to tap into capital markets for funding could occur in two ways: (1) foreign banks could directly penetrate those segments through transactional lending approaches (Beck, Ioannidou, and Schäfer 2012) or relationship banking (Beck, Degryse, and others 2014); or (2) foreign banks could force domestic banks, in search of profit margins dimmed by foreign competition, to serve those previously neglected segments. In fact, foreign banks do not need to enter a contestable banking industry to create competitive pressures—the sheer threat of entry by foreign banks may lead to more efficient financial intermediation (Claessens, Demirgüç-Kunt, and Huizinga 2001; Claessens and Laeven 2004). And yet, the contribution of international banking to financial development depends on the characteristics of parent banks (such as the health of their balance sheets) and foreign subsidiaries (such as the use of relationship banking techniques), as well as the market conditions in the host country (such as the existence of credit information and contract enforcement).

By contrast, in weak institutional environments with poor information and contract enforcement, international banks may focus only on large corporations or governments (so-called cherry picking or cream skimming). Such a focus on large borrowers may result in the exclusion of poor households or SMEs from the financial system, thereby reducing access to finance (Detragiache, Tressel, and Gupta 2008).[2] Furthermore, intensified competition and reduced profitability may lead to higher risk taking by domestic banks (particularly in the presence of financial safety nets), which can lead to moral hazard.[3] For example, a domestic bank in a developing country may extend foreign currency–denominated credit to households that do not have any capacity to hedge, implying high credit risk and vulnerability to exchange rate fluctuations. High risk taking may also be associated with foreign banks if their parent banks try to use them to avoid relatively more stringent regulation and supervision in their home countries—that is, engage in regulatory arbitrage (Ongena, Popov, and Udell 2013). Indeed, international banks, and especially global systemically important banks (G-SIBs), are very complicated to supervise and to unwind, and thus they pose serious challenges in cross-border bank regulation, supervision, and resolution in both home and host countries and require cross-border cooperation.

Another channel through which international banking can promote financial and economic development in host countries is by providing additional human capital and knowledge. Foreign bank entry can lead to improvements in the technology of the host country's financial systems and business models of domestic banks, allowing firms and households to access more sophisticated financial services (de la Torre, Martínez Pería, and Schmukler 2010). Foreign banks could also impose discipline on policy makers and regulators by breaking the political entrenchment of certain connected firms in the financial system that often leads to highly inefficient resource allocation and bad development outcomes.[4]

Empirical evidence suggests that a foreign bank presence fosters a country's economic growth and entrepreneurship and, under some conditions, reduces inequality. For example, Bruno and Hauswald (2013) analyze data for 36 manufacturing industries across 81 countries and find that a foreign bank presence displays a strong positive correlation with economic growth in industries with greater dependence on external finance. This finding is particularly strong for developing economies, where informational and legal frictions often hinder access to credit. Similarly, according to Alfaro, Beck, and Calomiris (2015), in developing countries a greater foreign bank presence is associated with a higher share of business formation in industries with a greater need for external finance.

And yet in another study, for a large panel of countries a foreign bank presence is also positively related to inequality (Delis, Hasan, and Mylonidis 2016). This relationship, however, tends to turn negative when institutional and regulatory differences between home and host countries are sufficiently large or when foreign banks maintain a large presence in host countries for extended periods of time, suggesting gradual improvement. All in all, even though international banks can potentially increase efficiency and access, the informational, institutional, and regulatory environments in both home and host countries play a crucial role in determining the effect of international banking on economic development.

INTERNATIONAL BANKING AND FINANCIAL STABILITY

The presence of international banks is likely to be accompanied by greater financial inflows and outflows for host markets as part of risk sharing, which could be stabilizing for the local credit supply overall. For example, international banks are more likely than domestic banks to maintain their lending in host countries during local economic downturns, thanks to their deep pockets and possibly long-term investment horizons (De Haas and van Lelyveld 2010). On the other hand, international banks appear to curtail credit in host countries more aggressively than domestic banks when a crisis hits the international banks' home country. This then allows these international banks to perform better in their home country when compared with domestic competitors without foreign subsidiaries (De Haas and van Lelyveld 2014; Peek and Rosengren 1997, 2000). International banks thus share risk between host and home countries, transferring funds from home to host countries when a host country crisis hits, and transferring funds from host to home countries when a home country crisis hits. Although this risk-sharing arrangement implies greater financial flows, it allows both host and home countries to buffer the greatest shocks to their credit supply, thereby stabilizing credit overall.

Nevertheless, international banks may also fuel credit booms in host countries that end up in busts if domestic financial systems are not capable of handling such flows.[5] Credit booms may occur, for example, if international banks lower lending standards (Dell'Ariccia and Marquez 2006a). These booms may end up in busts that are exacerbated if international banks choose to exit. Such behavior—amplified by global risk and liquidity conditions—could be harmful to the financial stability of the home or host countries, ending in costly boom and bust cycles and cross-border contagion risks (Forbes and Warnock 2012).[6] Moreover, developing countries or small economies could also be negatively affected because their monetary policy cannot influence the decisions of large international banks, making monetary policy less effective.[7]

The global financial crisis revealed that the extent to which international banks shift funds from host to home countries during a home country crisis is related to a number of country and bank characteristics. These characteristics include the cultural and institutional distance between the home and host countries and their relative legal and regulatory frameworks, the structure of their respective banking industries, the existing financial and information infrastructure, the mode of entry of the international banks (cross-border lending versus brick-and-mortar operations via subsidiaries or branches, or greenfield versus mergers and acquisitions), and the financial characteristics (such as funding structure) of the parent bank or foreign affiliate (Bertay 2014; De Haas and van Horen 2013; Schnabl 2012). Policy making that affects or stipulates these characteristics may thus have an important influence on host country experiences with international banks, which is discussed in the coming chapters.

International bank lending is an important source of funds for developing countries compared with international financial market activity and FDI. International banks are involved in two main types of international activities: (1) cross-border lending and (2) foreign participation in domestic banking systems through brick-and-mortar operations—that is, where the bank is physically present in a country through an office, which can be a branch or part of a foreign bank subsidiary owned by the bank. These two activities are the main focus of this *Global Financial Development Report 2017/2018* (GFDR), and they are discussed in the next two chapters.[8] Figure 1.1 illustrates the importance of international banking activity in developing countries compared with foreign bond issuances and FDI. These comparisons are not straightforward because data on international bank activities include bond issuances and equity holdings (see box 1.4 later in this chapter), data on bond issuances include bonds held by banks, and FDI includes equity investments by banks. For a cleaner comparison, figure 1.1 focuses on issuances of syndicated loans led by foreign banking entities, which is only a fraction of all cross-border bank loans, but has the advantage of excluding bond and equity activity. These numbers thus provide a lower bound on the value of international bank lending. Despite being a lower bound, foreign syndicated loan issuances were much larger than foreign bond issuances before the global financial crisis (in 2006, $239 billion for syndicated loans versus $117 billion for

FIGURE 1.1 Foreign Financial Inflows to Developing Countries: Syndicated Loans, Bonds, and Foreign Direct Investment, 2000–15

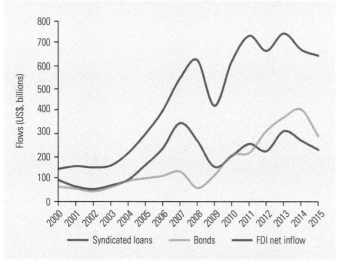

Source: World Bank, World Development Indicators (database) and FinDebt (database).

bonds). In the years following the global financial crisis, cross-border bond issuances overtook the foreign syndicated loans, but their sizes were still comparable (in 2015, $233 billion for syndicated loans versus $292 billion for bonds).[9] The issuance of syndicated loans led by foreign banks represented about one-third of the volume of FDI net inflows in the postcrisis years.

International banking activity increased dramatically from 2001 until the global financial crisis in 2007–09, but it did not recover from the retrenchment in high-income countries during the crisis. Figure 1.2 reveals that all foreign exposures of international banks from Bank for International Settlements (BIS) reporting countries increased from $8.6 trillion in 2000 to $31 trillion in 2008. After the crisis, the international banks reduced their exposures, leading to a significant retrenchment (by the end of 2015 total foreign claims were $24 trillion, or 22.5 percent lower than in 2008). This retrenchment came from a reduction of foreign claims in high-income countries rather than developing countries, where foreign exposures remain resilient in absolute terms. Another recent development in the global financial arena is the rise of international microfinance institutions (MFI) (see box 1.3).

Despite the significant decline after the global financial crisis, lending by international banks continues to represent an important share of total bank credit in many countries. Data on lending by international banks are provided primarily by BIS. BIS data on foreign claims cover both cross-border lending and loans made by foreign-owned banks within a country (see box 1.4 for a more detailed description of foreign claims and box 1.5 for alternative sources of data).[10] Despite the postcrisis decline, lending by foreign banks accounted for 27.6 percent of credit to the private sector in developing countries in 2014 (in high-income countries, 40.6 percent). As panel a of figure 1.3 shows, both the extent of the foreign bank presence and the impact of the crisis varied by region from 2005 to 2014. After the 2007–09 crisis, the Middle East and North Africa (MENA) and

FIGURE 1.2   **Foreign Claims Reported to BIS by Counterparty Income Level, 2000–15**

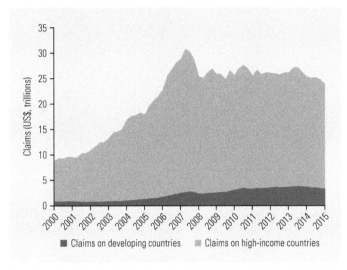

Source: Consolidated Banking Statistics (Immediate Risk Basis), Bank for International Settlements.

the Sub-Saharan Africa (SSA) regions witnessed the greatest declines in foreign lending; in both regions, foreign claims on the nonbank private sector, with respect to domestic credit to the private sector by banks, were half of their respective peak values in 2005 (SSA) and 2008 (MENA).

Foreign claims mostly fund the nonbank private sector, particularly in developing countries. At their highest level (in 2008), foreign claims going to the nonbank private sector reached almost 43 percent of gross domestic product (GDP) in high-income countries and 32 percent of GDP in developing countries. By contrast, foreign claims going to the official sector have typically remained below 10 percent of GDP in high-income countries and below 4 percent of GDP in developing countries. Panel b in figure 1.3 shows large reductions in foreign lending to banks and the nonbank private sector, as a percentage of GDP, after 2008 in both high-income and developing countries, whereas lending to governments by international banks increased. Given the relative resilience of total foreign claims in developing countries (see figure 1.2), these reductions in relative values to GDP indicate that international banking

BOX 1.3   The Rise of International Microfinance Institutions

Over the last two decades, international microfinance institutions (MFIs)—institutions affiliated with a common owner that have operations in different countries—have emerged and have focused on expanding access to financial services around the world. Many of these institutions follow the greenfield business model, which has two main elements: (1) creation of a group of "greenfield MFIs," defined as institutions that are newly created without preexisting infrastructure, staff, clients, or portfolios; and (2) use of central organizing bodies—often holding companies—that create these MFIs through common ownership and management. The holding company usually also plays a large role in backstopping operations, formulating standard policies and procedures, providing staff development and training, and cobranding the subsidiaries in the network (Earne and others 2014). Examples of these greenfield MFIs are Access, Advans, BRAC, FINCA, and ProCredit.

Some holding companies such as Access, Advans, and ProCredit were founded by specialized microfinance consulting firms with the purpose of investing in and building a global network of subsidiaries. Others, such as BRAC and FINCA, were established to consolidate the affiliates of existing microfinance networks and expand them by creating new greenfields.

Greenfield MFIs are typically driven by a mission to expand access to financial services and to promote economic development while offering commercial success for their shareholders. Shareholders and investors in these MFIs are primarily development finance institutions, including the African Development Bank (AfDB), European Investment Bank (EIB), International Finance Corporation (IFC), and KfW Development Bank. The holding company model has provided depository financial institutions with a single vehicle for making larger investments in microfinance and leveraging their participation with other investors (Earne and others 2014).

Cull and others (2015) have studied the role of greenfield MFIs in promoting the quality, breadth, and depth of usage of financial services in Sub-Saharan Africa (SSA). According to their analysis, relative to other African microfinance providers, greenfield MFIs grew faster, improved profitability to levels comparable to those of the top MFIs, and substantially increased their lending to women. Table B1.3.1 illustrates some of these findings. Greenfield MFIs in Africa started out with a smaller number of loans and deposits than other MFIs and with a worse financial performance, but they saw a rapid increase in both loans and deposits during their first few years of operation. The numbers also show that, after five years in operation, greenfield MFIs had a positive net income, whereas other MFIs had a negative net income. Overall, Cull and others (2015) conclude that, although the loan sizes of greenfield MFIs are larger than those of most African MFIs, indicating less outreach to the poorest market segments, greenfield MFIs have achieved rapid gains in financial inclusion for somewhat more affluent clients.

TABLE B1.3.1   **Evolution of Greenfield MFIs in Sub-Saharan Africa during Initial Years of Operation**

Measure	Greenfields			MIX young Africa
	Month 12	Month 36	Month 60	
No. of staff	131	318	524	69
No. of branches	9	22	31	10
No. of loans outstanding	9,495	25,009	36,714	11,255
Gross portfolio (US$, millions)	$2.3	$9.2	$20.0	$2.7
No. of deposit accounts	7,123	37,460	81,682	18,127
Deposits (US$, millions)	$0.8	$8.7	$23.1	$2.0
Share of portfolios at risk >30 days	3.9%	4.0%	3.4%	9.5%
Operating expenses/portfolio	200%	53%	36%	113%
Equity (US$, millions)	$3.6	$4.3	$6.6	$1.2
Net income/assets	−12.4%	−0.1%	3.1%	−2.4%
Net income/equity	−44.6%	−0.3%	18.9%	−3.4%

Source: Cull and others 2015.
Note: MIX young Africa refers to MFIs four to seven years old that report to the Microfinance Information eXchange (MIX). The original underlying data were provided by MIX and the International Finance Corporation. BRAC = Building Resources Across Communities; FINCA = Foundation for International Community Assistance; and MFI = microfinance institution.

BOX 1.4   **What Constitutes a Foreign Bank Claim? An Overview of the Banking Statistics of the Bank for International Settlements (BIS)**

A foreign bank claim is a financial claim extended by an international bank (as defined in box 1.2) to a nonresident of the bank's headquarters country (García-Herrero and Martínez Pería 2007). It typically includes financial assets such as loans, debt securities, equity holdings, and derivatives with positive market values (BIS 2015). At the banking system level, claim information is available from BIS International Banking Statistics through two parallel data sets.

Consolidated Banking Statistics (CBS). This data set measures the consolidated assets and liabilities of banks headquartered in 31 reporting countries. Intragroup transactions are netted out using an approach similar to that adopted by banking supervision. The CBS disaggregates along two important dimensions. First, it distinguishes between foreign claims booked by bank offices within counterparty jurisdictions as local claims and those booked outside from global or regional headquarters as cross-border claims (see figure B1.4.1). This approach provides a channel for understanding the sources of foreign credit for individual countries and sectors. Second, the CBS reports on an immediate counterparty (IC) basis according to the residences of the contracted parties, and it reports on an ultimate risk (UR) basis, accounting for risk transferals[a] to parent entities or third-party guarantors. This kind of reporting reveals the country risk exposures of international banks. And these two features make the CBS a valuable source of information for tracing shock transmissions across banking systems and economies. In addition, the CBS/IC contains maturity disaggregation for international claims (defined as the combination of cross-border

FIGURE B1.4.1   A Taxonomy of Foreign Claims

A + B = International claims

A	B	C
Cross-border claims	Local claims of foreign affiliates in foreign currency	Local claims of foreign affiliates in local currency

A + B + C = Foreign claims

Source: Adapted from Cerutti, Claessens, and McGuire 2012.
Note: The blocks indicate data availability: block A = CBS/UR only; blocks A + B and block C = CBS/IC only; block B = unavailable in CBS; and blocks A + B + C = CBS/UR and CBS/IC. CBS = Consolidated Banking Statistics; IC = immediate counterparty; and UR = ultimate risk.

claims and nonlocal currency claims by local bank affiliates). Quarterly stock value series are available from 2000 onward, and semiannual data for a smaller number of countries begin as early as 1983.

Locational Banking Statistics (LBS). The LBS provides the gross assets and liabilities of banks headquartered in 44 countries. However, unlike the CBS, under principles consistent with balance of payments accounting, it notably does not adjust for intragroup positions. Details in the LBS reveal the location and nationality of reporting banks, the residence and sector of counterparties,[b] as well as the currencies and instruments used by banks in transactions. The LBS is especially useful in understanding the capital flows, monetary spillovers, and funding risks of banking systems. Quarterly series of amounts outstanding and adjusted flows are available from as early as 1977.

a. Through credit commitments, guarantees, and derivative contracts.
b. As of December 2016, LBS information by reporting, parent, and counterparty country was unilateral.

---

has not kept up with the economic growth in developing countries.

Cross-Border Lending versus Local Lending by Foreign Banks

Almost all regions witnessed enormous increases in cross-border claims before the global financial crisis, followed by a postcrisis drop in cross-border claims. Although all regions saw such a drop immediately after the crisis, cross-border claims going to the Latin America and the Caribbean (LAC) and East Asia and Pacific (EAP) regions showed a significant recovery after this period (panel a, figure 1.4).[11] By contrast, the exceptional precrisis increase in

BOX 1.5   What Data Can Be Used to Understand the Activities of International Banks?

Data at different levels of granularity offer nuanced details on the evolution of global banking and shed light on bank activities from various perspectives.

Transaction-Level Data: Syndicated Bank Lending

Syndicated lending is one type of bank credit more systematically documented in commercially available data sets. Sources such as Dealogic, Thompson Reuters, and Bloomberg provide the number, volume, and currency denomination of syndicated loans, the country and sector of borrowers, and the identity and funding shares of syndicate members.

World Bank FinDebt Database. The World Bank's Finance and Markets Global Practice constructs the Global Bond and Syndicated Loan Database (FinDebt) quarterly using Dealogic information. The database reports at the borrower sector level syndicated lending volumes, maturities, pricing margins, currency decompositions, and fund uses. A timely source for identifying trends in domestic and cross-border bank lending activities, FinDebt provides data on 182 borrower countries as of early 2000.[a]

Bank-Level Data: Financials and Ownership Structures

As international bank lending via local affiliates expands, the equity structures of global banks and balance sheets of affiliates become essential elements in understanding risk propagation in banking systems. Although bank-level data are released by regulators in specific countries, comparable information at the international level is limited, except for systemically important banks.

BIS G-SIB Assessment. Following the methodology identified by the Basel Committee on Banking Supervision (BCBS), the Bank for International Settlements (BIS) publishes 12 indicators in five categories that capture the size, interconnectedness, substitutability, complexity, and cross-jurisdictional activity of an annually updated list of global systemically important banks, or G-SIBs (BIS 2013).[b] This list consists of 75 of the largest global banks (BIS 2013), including those from emerging markets in Brazil, China, India, and the Russian Federation. Notably, bank-level foreign positions not available in the BIS International Banking Statistics are disclosed annually by most of the G-SIBs in this sample. These data enable users to identify the most recent trends in the size and cross-border activities of global banks and compare global banks from developed and developing countries.

Other than regulatory disclosures, financials and ownership information are typically provided in packages, along with rating information, by private companies through data services such as Bureau van Dijk Orbis Bank Focus (formerly Bankscope), Fitch EM Banking Datawatch, and S&P Global Market Intelligence (formerly SNL Financials). Such commercial data sets may cover large samples with various degrees of comprehensiveness. Building on Bureau van Dijk Bankscope, two recent statistical efforts identify the nationality of majority owners and provide insights into the evolution of bank participation through foreign subsidiaries:[c]

Foreign Bank Ownership Database. Initially published as an annex by Claessens and van Horen (2014b), the updated database reveals the nationality of direct majority ownership for more than 5,000 banking entities[d] in 138 economies for each year an entity was active during 1995–2013. Having also absorbed information from bank reports, regulatory agencies, monetary authorities, and stock exchanges, this comprehensive data set covers more than 90 percent of banking assets in each country's banking system. It has been applied by researchers seeking to understand the relationship between foreign bank presence and private credit provision (Claessens and van Horen 2014b), business regulations (Kouretas and Tsoumas 2016), and the impact of the global financial crisis on banking globalization (Claessens and van Horen 2015). The Foreign Bank Ownership Database is available publicly.

Bertay, Demirgüç-Kunt, and Huizinga (2017). This recent study captures ownership structures from the viewpoint of ultimate shareholders for the period 2000–15. It maps direct owner and subsidiary links onto banking group-level equity networks. The data set identifies more than 2,750 banking groups with majority-owned affiliates, 325 of which control at least one foreign bank subsidiary. The data set also demonstrates evolutionary trends of bank foreign exposure and organizational complexity by linking subsidiary asset and liability information with that of controlling banks. It provides an alternative perspective of country exposures in contrast to those based

(box continued next page)

BOX 1.5   **What Data Can Be Used to Understand the Activities of International Banks?**
(continued)

on banking claims, and it reveals intragroup and intergroup differences in asset composition, funding strategy, operational efficiency, and risk transmission channels among global bank offices.

System-Level Data: Claims and Liabilities

The gross and net asset and liability positions of banking systems are useful from a financial development perspective for cross-country analysis.

BIS International Banking Statistics. As discussed in detail in box 1.4, such information is typically collected and reported by national monetary authorities and reported through the BIS International Banking Statistics. Recent studies such as Broner and others (2017) have applied bilateral locational banking

information derived from more nuanced, confidential bank-level reports of counterparty exposures. Covering banks from 44 reporting countries (mostly advanced economies, offshore centers, and emerging markets[e]), this type of information provides broad coverage because the global banking industry remains geographically concentrated. The information revealed on cross-border bank assets and liabilities is particularly useful for capturing bank flows to and from high-income economies.

Data challenges remain in addressing global banking systemic risk assessments and accounting for cross-border financial linkages. The IMF-FSB G-20 Data Gaps Initiative recommends the collection of consistent bank-level data for joint analyses and continued enhancement of existing aggregate statistics.

a. FinDebt was accessible only within the World Bank as of December 2016.
b. The list of G-SIBs/G-SIFIs (global systemically important financial institutions) was initially published by the Financial Stability Board (FSB) in November 2011 using end-2009 data. Since July 2013, it has been adjusted annually. In the end-2014 exercise, 30 banks were identified as G-SIBs that are required to meet higher loss absorbency as well as regulatory capital requirements under the Basel III framework (see http://www.bis.org/bcbs/gsib/gsib_assessment_samples.htm).
c. Bankscope does not contain information systematically covering foreign branches. Thus bank-level databases exclusively relying on it include foreign bank participation through subsidiaries only. The difference may have important implications, as discussed in chapter 2.
d. Including commercial banks, saving banks, cooperative banks, and bank holding companies.
e. With the exception of China and Russia.

FIGURE 1.3   **Lending by International Banks: Foreign Claims on Counterparty Nonbank Private Sector (Country-Level Average by Region) and on Counterparty Sectors (Country-Level Average by Income Level), 2005–14**

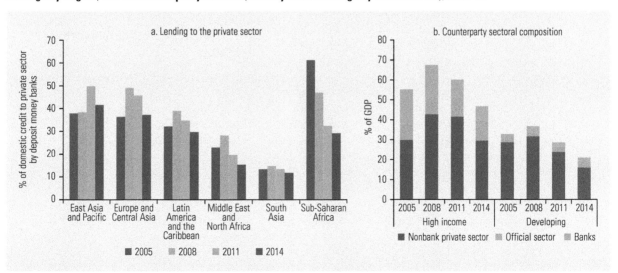

Sources: Consolidated Banking Statistics (Ultimate Risk Basis); Bank for International Settlements, and International Financial Statistics (database); and International Monetary Fund.
Note: Regions exclude high-income countries that belong to the Organisation for Economic Co-operation and Development (OECD).

FIGURE 1.4   Cross-Border Bank Flows: Cross-Border Claims on Counterparty Regions and Foreign Claims on Counterparty Economies by Position Type and Income Level, 2005–15

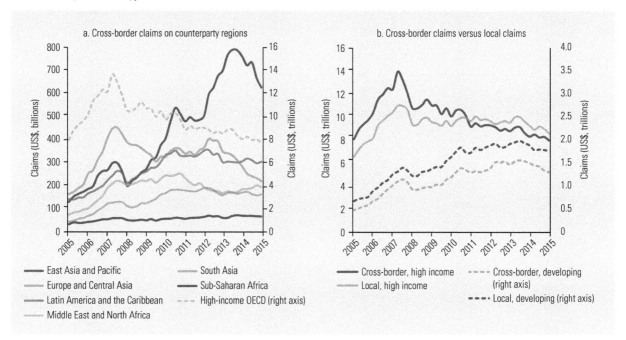

Source: Consolidated Bank Statistics (Ultimate Risk Basis), Bank for International Settlements.
Note: According to the World Bank's classification, developed countries are defined as high-income countries; the rest of the countries are defined as developing countries. Regions exclude high-income countries that belong to the Organisation for Economic Co-operation and Development (OECD).

cross-border claims in the Europe and Central Asia (ECA) region did not continue after the crisis, and claims on this region remained more or less fixed until 2013, when they began to fall significantly.[12] As of 2014:Q4, total cross-border claims by all bank nationalities reporting to the BIS Consolidated Banking Statistics (CBS) reached $12 trillion on an UR basis, accounting for about one-sixth of global banking assets.[13] High-income countries received about three-quarters of all cross-border claims in 2014.

Proving more resilient to the financial crisis, lending by local foreign banks is now a more important source of credit than cross-border lending in both high-income and developing countries. In high-income countries, cross-border claims, which used to be higher than local claims before the global financial crisis, fell significantly after the crisis, whereas local claims by foreign affiliates suffered much less from the financial crisis, making them more important than cross-border

claims over the last few years (panel b, figure 1.4). This difference is also pronounced for developing countries, where local claims were higher than cross-border claims before the global financial crisis and where local claims have increased even more than cross-border claims since the crisis.

New Developments in International Banking

Foreign bank participation in local markets was on the rise in all regions until recently, when some major banks began to retrench their international operations. In all regions, the shares of foreign banks of the total number of banks increased slightly from 2009 to 2013 and remained higher than during the precrisis period (see panel a, figure 1.5). From 1995 to 2013, the share of foreign banks increased about twofold in the EAP, LAC, and MENA regions and threefold in the ECA region. The asset shares of foreign banks also increased

FIGURE 1.5   **Foreign Bank Presence through Subsidiaries: Share of Foreign Banks of Total Banks (Country-Level Average by Region, 1997–2013) and Share of Foreign Bank Assets of Total Bank Assets (Country-Level Average by Region, 2005–13)**

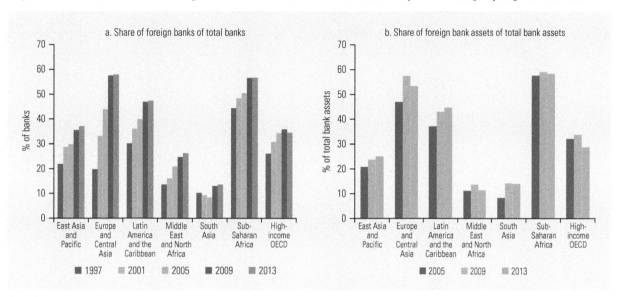

Source: Claessens and van Horen 2015.
Note: Regions exclude high-income countries that belong to the Organisation for Economic Co-operation and Development (OECD).

in all regions before the crisis (panel b, figure 1.5); but since the crisis the share of foreign bank assets has declined across the board, except in East Asia and Latin America.[14] In fact, several major international banks (such as Deutsche Bank) recently announced plans to drastically reduce the number of countries in which they operate. Overall, despite this retrenchment in the ECA and SSA regions, foreign banks continue to constitute over 40–50 percent of the banking industry in both numbers of banks and their asset shares—similar to the more resilient LAC region's foreign banking landscape.

In some regions, the retrenchment of global banks has been accompanied by an expansion of regional players, involving a greater variety of players. Indeed, the prospects for international banking might inspire developing countries to have their own international banks investing regionally or globally. On the one hand, such South–South international banking might offer greater potential to provide banking services. Developing country banks may be more successful in navigating weaker legal frameworks and solving asymmetric

information problems because of their short cultural and institutional distances and region-specific knowledge. On the other hand, the lack of experience and technical know-how, as well as the probable insufficient prudential and AML/CFT (anti–money laundering and combating the financing of terrorism) regulation and supervision in the home country, may be harmful to economic development and financial stability. Although internationally comparable data on developing country international banks are relatively limited, the available evidence suggests the rising importance of developing country banks as foreign participants. Panel a of figure 1.6 shows the large increases in absolute amounts of foreign claims originating from Brazil, India, Mexico, and Turkey. The increase mostly stems from the increases in the foreign claims of banks from Brazil and India, with Turkish and Mexican banks playing a small role. The increases in foreign claims of these countries suggest the greater international involvement of developing country banks. Indeed, in developing country banking systems, the share of foreign banks owned by other developing countries (in terms of

FIGURE 1.6 **Rise of South–South Banking: Foreign Claims by Banks in BIS-Reporting Countries (2003–15) and Nationality of Majority Ownership of Banks in Developing Countries (1995–2013)**

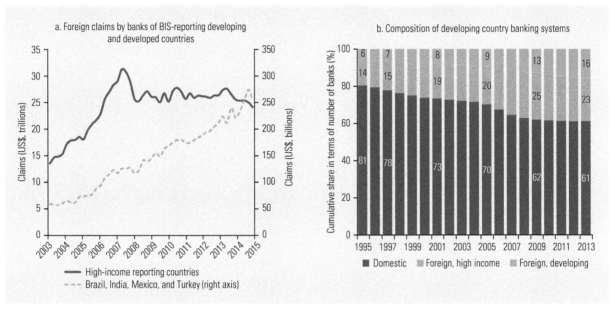

Sources: Panel a: Consolidated Bank Statistics (Immediate Risk Basis), Bank for International Settlements; and panel b: Claessens and van Horen 2015.

number of banks) has increased dramatically, from 8 percent in 2001 to 16 percent in 2013, whereas foreign banks owned by high-income countries have fallen to 23 percent from their peak of 25 percent during the global financial crisis (panel b, figure 1.6).

Banks have also become very large over the last decade, and most of the largest ones are international. During the last decade, but especially leading up to the global financial crisis of 2007–09, the size of the world's largest banks increased dramatically (panel a, figure 1.7). From 2005 to 2014, the total size (measured by real total assets from unconsolidated balance sheets) of the world's largest 10, 50, and 100 banks increased by more than 40 percent (from $14.2 trillion to $20 trillion in the case of the top 10). Interestingly, despite all the regulatory efforts to curb bank size and address too-big-to-fail problems, banks did not on average contract in size after the crisis.[15] In most regions, the largest banks increased their size not only in absolute terms but also relative to their national economies when compared with the precrisis period

(panel b, figure 1.7).[16] This trend suggests that a handful of banks have become very large compared with GDP, possibly leading to systemic problems in the banking system if one of them fails.[17] The share of foreign banks among the largest banks in developing countries is rather low (as suggested by panel b, figure 1.7). Nevertheless, in some regions such as ECA and SSA, the assets of the largest foreign banks correspond to a sizable 10–20 percent of GDP on average. These banks may be systemically important in the host countries but not necessarily in the home country or for the parent bank, which can have important implications for financial stability and cross-border policy coordination. Almost all banks tend to hold some foreign assets, but the largest banks dominate cross-border activities through subsidiaries and branches (Buch, Koch, and Koetter 2011). Data from the assessment of G-SIBs by BIS confirm that virtually all the banks in their sample of large banks have significant foreign claims,[18] making up on average 23 percent of their total on- and off-balance-sheet exposure. These figures suggest that bank size

FIGURE 1.7   Total Assets of Largest Banks (Absolute Amounts, on a Rolling Basis) and Size of Assets in Relation to National Economies (Combined Assets of Top Five Banks, Country-Level Average by Region), 2005–14

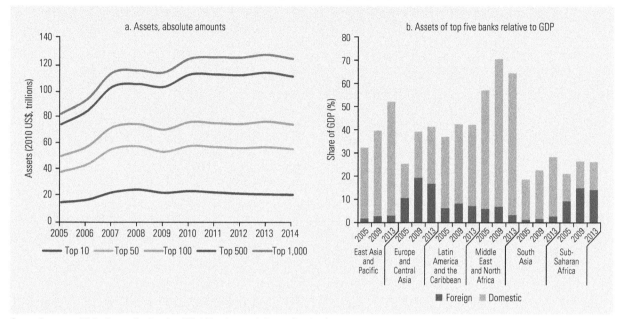

Sources: Bureau van Dijk Bankscope (database); and World Development Indicators (database).
Note: Panel b indicates asset decomposition on an unconsolidated basis. Regions exclude high-income countries that belong to the Organisation for Economic Co-operation and Development (OECD).

should be a central issue in any discussion of international banking.

Many countries, including many developing countries, have increased their restrictive policies on international banking. Regulatory and supervisory restrictions on foreign bank entry may reduce bank competition, leading to inefficiencies, inferior capital allocation, and a slower pace of economic development. Figure 1.8 presents an index proxying restrictions on foreign bank entry and rates of license application denials over the period 2000–11. In both developed and developing countries, foreign bank entry was easier during the first half of the 2000s than during the second half, which includes the global financial crisis. A recent survey by Ichiue and Lambert (2016) on postcrisis international banking regulation also reveals tighter regulation of international bank activities in both home and host countries (and especially in developed economies) from 2006 to 2014. Other recent policy changes, including macroprudential policies (such as increased

FIGURE 1.8   Regulatory Restrictions on Foreign Bank Entry and Ownership (Country-Level Average), 2000–11

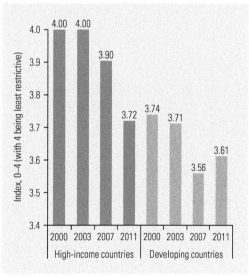

Source: Barth, Caprio, and Levine 2013.
Note: The index of foreign bank entry and ownership captures restrictions on foreign bank entry to a market through four channels: acquisitions, subsidiaries, branches, and joint ventures. At the country level, the index is equal to four minus the number of restricted channels.

capital requirements or discriminatory reserve requirement ratios) and ring-fencing of foreign bank subsidiaries, may also restrict international banking activities (Claessens 2016). All in all, various regulatory actions after the global financial crisis have led to de jure and de facto restrictions on international banking activities. This is also reflected in the reduction of entry after the crisis. Indeed, although the number of foreign banks exiting markets has remained more or less the same, there was much less entry after the crisis, and net entry became negative for the first time since 1995.

A recent factor in the global banking landscape is the new financial technology (fintech) firms. Fintech refers to technology-enabled financial innovation facilitating new products, services, and business models. After the global financial crisis, low interest rates and the departure of traditional banks from some specific segments created opportunities for fintech firms to disrupt the traditional financial intermediation process. Although the size of these firms is currently negligible compared with that of traditional banks, the services they provide can result in competition in many lines of bank business. Indeed, digital financial services lead to cost reductions and to better capture of new market segments, and therefore greater financial inclusion. Many traditional banks have already acknowledged these prospects and have begun to work with fintech firms, focusing on complementarities or pursuing new digital technologies in house (see chapter 3). From peer-to-peer (P2P) lending practices to payment services, many of the areas in which fintech firms operate have natural international extensions. For example, crowdfunding microloans to households or groups in developing countries saves the valuable capital of MFIs such as Kiva.org, and cross-border, P2P money transfer services (such as TransferWise) reduce the cost of sending remittances to developing countries. If successful, fintech firms will pose various challenges for regulators worldwide. There will be cross-jurisdictional concerns because fintech firms largely work globally, and it is not clear which country's laws would be applied to them. To achieve coordination among these companies, information sharing, supervision, and joint assessment of "systemically important" fintech firms will be important tasks for regulators.

POLICY IMPLICATIONS

Overall, efficient allocation of resources is key to economic development, and international banks can play an important role in introducing competition and improving the efficiency of the financial system. In addition, international banking can act as a risk-sharing scheme, smoothing downturns by sharing them among home and host countries. Risk sharing implies greater financial inflows and outflows for host markets, but it should stabilize the local credit supply overall. Nevertheless, a country's experience with international banks tends to depend on the characteristics of those banks as well as the country's institutional and regulatory environment, implying that policy can play a crucial role in shaping this experience. The global financial crisis provided crucial insights into the importance of international banking for economic development and financial stability, confirming the importance of heterogeneity of impact based on differences in home and host country policies.

The benefits and costs of international banking are two sides of the same coin, implying that good policy making is very important in ensuring that developing countries benefit from international banking. The challenge of policy is to maximize the benefits of bank internationalization while minimizing the costs and making international banking a reliable component of the global financial system for developing countries. Cross-border regulation, supervision, and resolution mechanisms; legal, information, and other institutional frameworks; and competition policy in the financial sector, including entry regulations—all can be designed with an eye toward minimizing the costs and maximizing the benefits of bank globalization. Finally, two new trends—the increasing South–South activity by internationalizing developing country banks and the potential of technological advances and fintech to modify global banking—present new challenges. We turn to these in the next chapters.

NOTES

1. Large domestic banks may receive funding from international capital markets to supply credit to firms and households. Yet they may still lack the necessary risk management tools or corporate governance practices, or they may behave politically if they are state-owned (Dinc 2005), channeling funds to less efficient firms and ending up with lower profits and higher costs than foreign banks (Micco, Panizza, and Yañez 2007). They may also not be able to roll over debt in the case of domestic turmoil (see Schnabl 2012), such as when internationally funded domestic banks cut credit more than foreign banks.

2. This may especially be severe when a lack of an information infrastructure prohibits domestic banks from reaching SMEs and the poorest households. In such an environment, even if domestic banks move down the market, that may be another example of excessive risk taking causing problems in the future.

3. Jeon and others (2016) show that domestic bank risk taking increases as the foreign bank presence increases in a developing country setting.

4. See Goldberg (2009) for an overview.

5. For example, in the early 2000s (2001–04) international banks played an important role in expanding credit in economies in Central and Eastern Europe (Enoch 2007), leading in some cases to excessive credit booms (Duenwald, Gueorguiev, and Schaechter 2005).

6. Boom/bust cycles similar to those in the traditional banking sectors may also apply to microfinance institutions in developing countries (Wagner 2012).

7. According to Wu, Luca, and Jeon (2011), compared with domestic banks, foreign banks are less responsive to host monetary policy shocks, weakening lending channels in emerging economies. Wu, Lim, and Jeon (2016) provide similar evidence for the Republic of Korea, emphasizing that foreign bank branches rather than subsidiaries drove the results during the global financial crisis.

8. See Smith, Walter, and DeLong (2012) for a general outlook on the activities of global banks, which include bond and equity issuance, wealth management, advisory or payment services, and trading.

9. The pattern looks similar when examining data for all countries, not just developing ones. Here, the value of foreign syndicated loan issuances was $2.5 trillion in 2006 and $3.0 trillion in 2015. The total value of global cross-border bond issuances was $3.2 trillion in 2006 and $3.8 trillion in 2015. The proceeds from initial public offerings (IPOs) globally were about $0.8 trillion in both 2006 and 2013, according to the "Global Equity Capital Markets Review" by Reuters (2014).

10. The BIS data contain information on the positions of banks, which include other financial assets such as debt securities and equity holding on top of loans. The series can be used as a proxy for international bank lending (see, for example, Cetorelli and Goldberg 2011).

11. These series look quite similar (except their magnitudes are smaller) when the BRICS countries (Brazil, Russia, India, China, and South Africa) are excluded—they are the largest receivers of cross-border funds. The only exception here is the South Asia (SAR) region, in which almost all cross-border claims go to India.

12. During the global financial crisis, the ECA region acted as a laboratory for international banking activities because of high foreign bank involvement. This experiment provided lessons for other countries, which are detailed in chapter 2.

13. Here, global assets include those of deposit money banks, which are restricted to depository institutions such as commercial banks, credit unions, savings institutions, and money market mutual funds, according to definitions in the International Financial Statistics of the International Monetary Fund. The World Bank's Global Financial Development Database indicates that by 2013:Q4, total assets owned by deposit money banks stood at $72.3 trillion.

14. The difference between increases in the share of number of foreign banks and in the share of foreign bank assets indicates domestic banking consolidation in some regions.

15. The total asset size of the 10 largest banks in 2013 was virtually the same as in 2007, although the list consists in part of different banks.

16. Percentage increases in the assets of the largest five banks with respect to national economies are higher in many regions (specifically,

the ECA, LAC, MENA, and SSA, and high-income OECD countries) than the asset growth of the remaining banking systems, relative to GDP.

17. Furthermore, the absolute and systemic size of banks could have consequences for their business models and funding structures. Bertay, Demirgüç-Kunt, and Huizinga (2013) analyze how absolute size—measured by real total assets—and systemic size—measured by total assets over the GDP of the home country—are associated with various bank characteristics such as risk and return, activity mix, and funding strategy. They show, for example, that banks with a larger systemic size have lower returns on assets without necessarily having lower risk as measured by the z-score, whereas those with a larger absolute size have higher returns on assets without necessarily having high risk as measured by the z-score.

18. The term used in the assessment templates is *cross-jurisdictional claims*.

CHAPTER 2: KEY MESSAGES

- Foreign banks, through their brick-and-mortar operations, have the potential to improve the performance of local banks as well as the degree of competition in the local banking sector and the overall access to credit in the host economy. These benefits are more likely to materialize when the proper regulatory and supervisory frameworks are in place in both the host and home countries, and when financial liberalization is accompanied by institutional reforms that strengthen the information environment and contract enforcement of the host economy.

- Although foreign banks can help smooth credit flows during local financial crises, they also can import shocks from abroad. Cross-border cooperation between authorities from both the home and host countries can help minimize the propagation of shocks. In addition, host economies can opt to allow the entry of foreign banks from home countries with stricter bank regulations, or to diversify the roster of foreign banks by the home country in order to mitigate the impact of shocks from a specific country.

- The composition of foreign banks is evolving rapidly. Since the global financial crisis, most bank exits have been by banks with headquarters in high-income countries, whereas South–South entry has been increasing and greater regionalization in the roster of foreign banks has been observed. These trends could affect who gets credit because South–South banking may be better at overcoming the challenges of lending to the smaller and more informationally opaque clients common in developing countries. Nevertheless, greater South–South banking may also entail additional risks from hosting foreign banks from less regulated and institutionally weaker home countries.

- More intensive cooperation is needed between home and host countries, going beyond international agreements and the exchange of information. Under the current cooperation arrangements, host country authorities have limited ability to properly supervise international banks, and supervisors from home and host countries do not fully consider the effects of their decisions beyond their borders.

- New technologies in the finance area are bringing new competitors and altering the way banks do business. These changes are likely to impact access to financial services as well as the efficiency and stability of the financial sector. Financial technology can increase access and improve the delivery of financial services, thereby reshaping competition among financial providers. Large international banks that can afford to increase investment in research and development are likely to play an important role in this area. A key challenge for policy makers will be to closely monitor the risks of a new, rapidly developing industry without hindering its potential.

2

Brick-and-Mortar Operations of International Banks

An extensive body of literature is devoted to studying the role of foreign banks in the domestic banking sectors that host their brick-and-mortar operations and their impact on local bank competition, financial stability, and access to credit. The bulk of the research published from the late 1980s to the early 2000s found that a foreign bank presence had generally positive effects on banking sector competition, efficiency, and stability, with more mixed results on access to credit. But this generally positive assessment was, at least in part, a reflection of the types of banks that chose to go abroad during this period—that is, they were mostly well-established banks from developed countries. And their effects on domestic banking sectors depended crucially on the extent of development of the host country's banks, with greater gains in competition and efficiency in host countries with less developed banking sectors. Indeed, foreign banks found it much harder to compete effectively when entering many developed countries (Berger and others 2000; Chang, Hasan, and Hunter 1998; DeYoung and Nolle 1996; Hasan and Hunter 1996; Miller and Parkhe 2002; Peek, Rosengren, and Kasirye 1999). Also, banking crises generally emanated from less developed host countries, and

the entry of foreign banks helped them restore financial intermediation. Moreover, the foreign banks that were already present in those countries (again, largely the affiliates of parent banks in developed countries) were often able to help stabilize the credit supply.

A wider reading of the literature, especially in light of new research since the global financial crisis and euro area crises, makes it clear that international banking has always been accompanied by both risks and opportunities. The balance between benefits and costs has depended on the roster of foreign participants, the health of their home country banking sectors, and, perhaps most important, the institutional and legal environments of the host country. Global evidence indicates that the relationship between the presence of foreign banks and private credit levels is negative in low-income countries and in countries where contract enforcement is costly and access to credit information is limited (Claessens and van Horen 2014b).

New evidence also reveals that a foreign bank presence fosters higher rates of business formation, but that these effects are much stronger in economies with tougher legal enforcement. Foreign bank entrants from developed economies are especially dependent on strong legal frameworks to foster business formation (Alfaro, Beck, and Calomiris 2015). Further findings indicate that the competitiveness of the domestic banking sector at the time of liberalization affects how domestic banks respond to the added competitive pressures imposed by foreign banks. Post-liberalization gains in the aggregate supply of credit, increases in growth, and declines in the volatility of growth are more likely to occur if countries have domestic banking sectors that are already relatively competitive (Behn and others 2014).

The impact of foreign banks on banking sector stability clearly depends on financial conditions in the countries in which their parents are headquartered as well as the conditions in the banking sector of the countries that host them. International banks can offer the host economy a risk-sharing arrangement in which, on the one hand, they can help to stabilize credit flows during local crises, while on the other hand, they may more easily spread foreign shocks to the local economy (Chava and Purnanandam 2011; Morais and others forthcoming; Peek and Rosengren 1997, 2000; Schnabl 2012). Nevertheless, evidence suggests that the transmission of shocks varies substantially across foreign banks, and it is greatly influenced by conditions in the home and host countries, as well as the characteristics of the parent bank (Buch and Goldberg 2015). In the wake of the global financial crisis, the differing business strategies pursued by foreign banks implied that not all of them responded to financial shocks in the same way. Even in emerging Europe, which was hard-hit by the crisis, a number of large foreign banks remained committed to their host countries, in effect treating them as a second home market (Bonin and Louie, forthcoming).

The impact of foreign banks largely depends, then, on the actions taken by the host country before and after financial liberalization. On their own, foreign banks are no panacea for guaranteeing financial development and stability. Host countries should, therefore, aim to create the conditions needed to reap the benefits of international banking. Regulators should adopt a strong financial regulatory and supervisory framework, accompanied by institutional reforms that strengthen the local banking sector and thus prevent foreign banks from capturing enough market power to force out domestic banks (Demirgüç-Kunt, Beck, and Honohan 2008). As for institutional factors, host countries should improve their information environment and the quality of contract enforcement, which can enable foreign banks to further develop the domestic banking sector. Host country authorities can also minimize the risks associated with foreign bank participation, by, for example, having their regulators strive for a diversified roster of foreign banks, which would limit the exposure to shocks from a particular country.

Regulators should also be aware of the increase in South–South banking. Although the overall levels of foreign presence have remained steady since the global financial crisis, the composition of foreign banks is changing. The network of foreign bank subsidiaries from emerging markets and developing economies operating in other developing countries increased substantially over the last decade (map 2.1). Banks from developing countries represented about two-thirds of the new entries postcrisis, and banks from high-income member countries of the Organisation for Economic Co-operation and Development (OECD) were responsible for most of the exits from markets (Claessens and van Horen 2015). Greater South–South entry has also coincided with regionalization in the roster of foreign banks in many host countries (Claessens 2016). These trends could affect who gets credit. For example, a foreign bank presence is more strongly linked to higher rates of business formation when those banks are headquartered in developing countries, although banks from developing countries are mainly able to spur business formation in industries characterized by simpler production processes, where agency conflicts are lower (Alfaro, Beck, and Calomiris 2015). However, South–South banking may also bring additional risks in terms of stability because the home economies of the new foreign banks are more likely to have weaker institutional environments and more lax regulations.

Alternative delivery mechanisms are another aspect to monitor closely because they are reshaping who has access to banking services, and foreign banks are likely to play an important role in providing those services. In principle, digital financial services, and in particular those provided via mobile telephony, hold the promise of deepening financial inclusion to market segments that have been underserved (Ahmed and others 2015; Demirgüç-Kunt and Klapper 2012). But even though deeper financial inclusion likely improves household welfare, it also exposes newly served households and firms to risks, mainly in the credit market, which could have implications for overall financial stability.[1] More broadly, financial technology (fintech) is likely to affect the way banks compete with each other (and other nonbank providers of financial services) for all market segments, which could again have implications for access, efficiency, and financial sector stability.

The greater regionalization in foreign bank presence and the increasing reliance on alternative delivery mechanisms for digital banking services will pose challenges for bank regulation and supervision. Responsibility for the supervision and resolution of the affiliates of international banks is a burden largely borne by the host countries. Greater regionalization in foreign bank participation could open the door to more effective cooperation and information sharing between supervisors across host countries. But a general supervisory approach—as dictated by, for example, the Basel Committee on Banking Supervision—could be poorly suited to some countries, especially in light of the substantial increases in South–South foreign bank entry.[2] The regulation of nonbank providers of digital financial services also remains an important challenge.

The remainder of this chapter is structured as follows. It begins with a discussion of the conditions and drivers that determine the entry of foreign banks in an economy. It then discusses three standard aspects of the performance of foreign banks and their influence on host country banking sectors—competition and efficiency, financial volatility, and access

MAP 2.1   **South–South Banking Subsidiary Networks, 2005 and 2014**

a. 2005

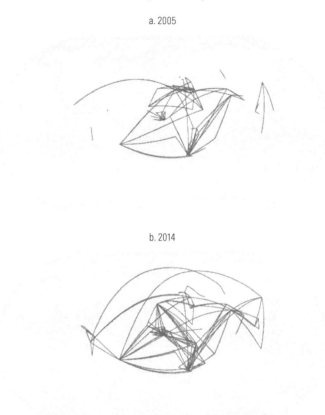

b. 2014

Source: Visualization based on Bertay, Demirgüç-Kunt, and Huizinga 2017.
Note: The maps show the location of foreign bank subsidiaries to and from developing countries. The connections reflect majority ownership.

to credit—but through the lens of the recent developments and trends just described. The chapter closes with a review of the most recent cross-border approaches to supervising and regulating international banks and a series of recommendations for policy makers.

DETERMINANTS OF FOREIGN BANK ENTRY

By identifying the factors that drive foreign banks into a host economy, regulators can better assess ways to attract international banks. The banking sectors of many developing countries and emerging economies have experienced a significant increase in foreign bank entry since the 1990s (Cull and Martínez Pería 2010). The experiences of financial liberalization have differed greatly from country to country, and they have increased understanding of the factors that attract foreign banks to a host economy. Overall, foreign banks expand abroad to pursue profitable opportunities by either following their home customers or seeking new clients. Expanding abroad also allows them to diversify their business. However, the entry of foreign banks is greatly dependent on the information environment of the host country. Thus, foreign banks find it easier to operate in countries in which the proper mechanisms to reduce the information costs of doing business abroad are in place. Barriers to entry and restrictions on the operations of foreign banks also matter. This section reviews these drivers in more detail.

Following Home Country Customers and Profit Opportunities in Host Countries

Two of the main reasons that foreign banks expand abroad are to follow their international clients and to seek new profit opportunities in host countries. Studies from the 1990s found that foreign banks are more likely to enter host economies with higher foreign direct investment (FDI) from or higher bilateral trade with their home country in relation to other countries, which is indirect evidence that banks follow home clients across borders.[3] Using granular data, Seth, Nolle, and Mohanty (1998) document that a substantial fraction of the lending of foreign banks operating in the United States goes to clients from their home countries. Other studies, however, also show that foreign banks are interested in expanding their business to new clients. Analyzing the international location choices of Japanese banks, Yamori (1998) confirms that these banks have pursued local banking opportunities in host countries. Indeed, some cross-country studies have positively related a host country's economic activity and financial depth to higher foreign bank participation (Focarelli and Pozzolo 2000), suggesting that international banks look for profitable markets when making their internationalization decisions.

International Diversification

Benefits from prospective diversification are also among the most important motivations for bank internationalization. The literature on portfolio optimization in an international setting dates back to the late 1960s, but only during the last decade have researchers begun looking at the benefits of international diversification in banking. Hayden, Porath, and Westernhagen (2007) find evidence that such diversification tends to be associated with reductions in German banks' returns, even after controlling for risk, whereas García-Herrero and Vázquez (2013) suggest that the risk return gains from the foreign subsidiaries of international banks from eight high-income countries are potentially substantial and not entirely exploited. Buch, Driscoll, and Ostergaard (2010) compute optimally diversified international asset portfolios for banks using the mean-variance portfolio model and compare them with the actual cross-border asset positions of banks to show that there are effective impediments to international diversification.

Entry Barriers and Other Restrictions

Barriers and regulatory restrictions are important determinants of foreign bank entry. In the last few years, several studies have deepened understanding of how the entry decisions of banks may be motivated by cross-country differences in banking regulation. A few theoretical papers in the 2000s tried to model the "race to the bottom" in the presence of regulatory arbitrage opportunities. Acharya (2003) shows, in a two-economy model of financial integration, how more regulatory forbearance in one country induces banks to assume more risk abroad. This factor reduces the competitive advantage of banks in countries with less forbearance, and, because it forces some banks to exit the market, the regulators of these countries adopt greater forbearance.[4] The empirical evidence suggests that regulatory differences in both home and host countries influence cross-border bank mergers and acquisitions (M&As) and lead to a reallocation of international banks' activities. Karolyi and Taboada (2015) and Dong, Song, and Tao (2011) find that cross-border acquisitions primarily involve acquirers from countries with more regulation, and that the takeover premium tends to increase for banks located in less regulated countries. Analyzing the European context, Carbo-Valverde, Kane, and Rodriguez-Fernandez (2012) find evidence validating the hypothesis of a race-to-the-bottom form of arbitrage. However, in a similar context, Hagendorff and others (2012) find contradictory results, in that less regulation in the host country does not mean that bidders are willing to pay a premium for less regulated regimes. A more recent study that analyzes the activities of U.S. banks operating

abroad also finds evidence that regulation in the host country relative to the home country matters for location decisions. Using a bank-level data set of the most active American banks operating in 82 foreign countries from 2003 to 2013, Temesvary (2015b) shows that U.S. banks are more likely to open subsidiaries in host economies with laxer capital requirements and disclosure rules and where banking activities are less restricted than those in the United States. Similarly, the closure of U.S. banks abroad is more likely to occur if the host economy has stricter deposit insurance schemes and more restrictions on bank activities than those in the United States. As box 2.1 further discusses, the legal structure of foreign banks is also influenced by regulation.

BOX 2.1   How Do Banks Expand Abroad? Branches or Subsidiaries?

In practice, there are two different ways in which international banks can expand abroad: as subsidiaries or as branches.

Branches are legally integrated with the parent bank. Capital requirements are generally waived because the parent bank remains responsible for the regulation and the liabilities of its operations in the host country. Deposits tend to be insured by the deposit insurance agency of the foreign bank's home country. *Subsidiaries* entail setting up or acquiring a separate legal entity, and thus they tend to operate like independent foreign banks. They are capitalized separately, they are subject to host country regulation, their deposits can be insured by the host country's deposit insurance agency, and they can even fail separately from their parent bank (Calzolari and Loranth 2011).[a]

In both scenarios, the host country authorities should exchange relevant information with the home country authorities because the banking group is regulated and supervised on a consolidated basis. Fiechter and others (2011) point out that under the home–host supervisory accord of the Committee on Banking Supervision, the responsibilities of host countries are far greater for subsidiaries, whereas home countries have much greater control over branches.

Several factors, such as the levels of legal restrictions on their operations as well as entry require-

ments and corporate taxes, are crucial in the choice of operation of cross-border banks. Based on their analysis of a database on the operations of cross-border banks in Latin America and Eastern Europe, Cerutti, Dell'Ariccia, and Martínez Pería (2007) provide evidence of the importance of these elements. They find that foreign banks are less likely to operate as branches in countries that limit financial activities or when there are barriers to the entry of new banks. They are more likely to open branches in host countries with high corporate tax rates or where foreign operations are smaller.

Many of the factors that affect entry decisions can be seen as forms of ex ante ring-fencing on the part of host countries. Ring-fencing refers to the geographical separation of part of a cross-border banking group from its parent institutions or other affiliates—an approach that aims to protect domestic financial markets, but typically makes a host market less attractive to multinational banking groups.[b] Ex ante ring-fencing often takes the form of higher capital or liquidity requirements, tighter dividend restrictions, and limitations on liquidity flows.

More generally, although host country regulatory authorities may have strong incentives to impose ex post ring-fencing measures—for example, to preserve banking sector liquidity after the onset of a crisis—

(box continued next page)

BOX 2.1   **How Do Banks Expand Abroad? Branches or Subsidiaries?** *(continued)*

---

these measures should be distinguished from the ex-ante measures that are likely to affect the mode of operation of cross-border banks and thus the structure of the banking sector.

The factors that lead foreign banks to enter as either a branch or a subsidiary have implications for their subsequent performance and thus potential implications for how they should be regulated and supervised. For example, Danisewicz, Reinhardt, and Sowerbutts (2015) find that following a tightening of capital requirements in the home countries of their parents, branches of international banks reduce the growth of their interbank lending by 6 percent more relative to subsidiaries of the same banking group. This result suggests that when a branch operates within the capital requirements of its parent, it cuts lending activities in the host country significantly in response to an increase in the capital requirement in the home country of the parent bank. As a result, a policy change in the home country will affect the host country differently, depending on the legal structure of the foreign operation.

Studies suggest that the mode of entry of foreign banks can also affect credit procyclicality. Albertazzi and Bottero (2014) analyze the contraction of credit of Italian banks during the collapse of Lehman Brothers, and find that the difference in the contraction of credit between foreign and domestic banks was mainly explained by the credit contraction of branches, rather than subsidiaries, of foreign banks.

However, the legal structure of foreign banks cannot by itself protect banks from systemic shocks. When the global financial crisis hit, contagion in some countries happened very quickly, no matter how the foreign operations were legally organized. Iceland, for example, had structured its foreign operation using both subsidiaries and branches, and the detrimental impacts were similar, no matter how the activities of foreign banks in Iceland were organized. This experience provides potentially important lessons for emerging market supervisors because it indicates that the financial, operational, and reputational ties between home and host operations can override legal and ownership structures in governing the responses of foreign banks to a crisis.

a. See Hoggarth, Hooley, and Korniyenko (2013) and Fiechter and others (2011) for detailed explanations.
b. A report by the International Monetary Fund (IMF 2015a) emphasizes the perspective of the regulator rather than that of the banking group, defining ring-fencing as "measures imposed by prudential supervisors with the objective of protecting the domestic assets of a bank so they can be seized and liquidated under local law in case of failure of the whole or part of an international banking group." See also D'Hulster and Ötker-Robe (2015) for a detailed explanation of ring-fencing.

More evidence is provided by research looking at how global banks tend to reallocate their activities between domestic and international locations when regulation tightens. According to Ongena, Popov, and Udell (2013), in Europe foreign banks incur greater risk abroad when bank regulation and supervision in the home country tighten, suggesting that they try to compensate for a lower charter value or a restriction on certain risky activities at home. Aiyar, Calomiris, and Wieladek (2014) and Danisewicz, Reinhardt, and Sowerbutts (2015) obtain similar results in the context of the United Kingdom. Meanwhile, regulatory arbitrage could conceivably be curbed by adopting

a level playing field in international bank regulation (such as the Basel Accords). Morrison and White (2009) show theoretically, however, that such efforts are not without cost; the better-regulated economy suffers in favor of the weaker one, but multinational banking helps to reduce the damage. Nevertheless, harmonizing and enforcing effective regulation and supervision across countries with different incentives and degrees of financial, legal, and economic development have proved to be extremely difficult. This was particularly evident in the recent global financial crisis.

Since the crisis, although entry has not generally been restricted, the activities of foreign banks have been curtailed. As discussed in more detail in the last section of this chapter, other, sometimes more informal measures have been adopted to limit the influence of cross-border financing as a response to the financial crisis. Common measures that countries have adopted are macroprudential policies, countercyclical buffers, or even ring-fencing in an effort to constrain capital flows (box 2.2). Meanwhile, the regulation and supervision of global banks have become stricter and more intense. These increased restrictions may induce global banks to shift their activities to other countries (Berlin 2015) or to replace activities regulated at the host country level with those regulated at the home country level (Temesvary 2015a). In general, the arbitrage practices revealed in different studies highlight the challenges presented by cross-country differences in banking regulation and the need for international coordination to regulate and supervise the activities of international banks.

High fixed costs may be a barrier to entry for some banks, depending on their size and productivity. Buch, Koch, and Koetter (2011, 2014) investigate theoretically and empirically whether the size pecking order documented for manufacturing firms in the international trade literature holds for global banks—that

is, whether banks have to be large to compete in international markets. They test their hypothesis using microdata within the universe of German banks and learn that only the largest and most productive banks have a commercial presence abroad. This finding confirms the importance of scale in international operations. However, in contrast to the predictions of recent trade models, the smallest banks also hold foreign assets, and some unproductive banks have an international presence. Galema, Koetter, and Liesegang (2016) focus on relative cost advantages instead, and find that less profitable, riskier, and larger banks are more likely to operate abroad.

Financial safety nets may also play a role in banks' internationalization decisions because home country authorities may be less likely to intervene when the bank holds considerable international assets. Bank size in both absolute and systemic (relative to national economies) terms affects the market discipline applied to a bank. This market discipline, which can be defined as the response of depositors, or more broadly bank funding costs, to changes in bank risk, depends on the strength of the financial safety net (that is, the capacity of national economies to bail out banks in trouble). Thus banks that are too large systemically, especially in countries suffering public

---

BOX 2.2   Macroprudential Policies to Manage Credit Growth

Cerutti, Claessens, and Laeven (2015) examine the effect of macroprudential policies on credit growth in 119 countries from 2000 to 2013. They find that emerging economies are more likely to adopt such policies than others. Although borrower-based macroprudential tools such as limits on loan-to-value and debt-to-income ratios are associated with slower credit growth in all countries, the relationship is stronger for developing countries. Similarly, institution-based tools such as dynamic provisioning, limits on leverage, and countercyclical capital requirements are negatively associated with credit growth in

developing economies. Finally, limits on foreign currency lending are negatively related to credit growth in all countries, but especially in emerging markets and developing economies. The patterns suggest that macroprudential policies can help countries manage financial cycles, though the evidence also indicates that they are more effective in boom than bust phases. These policies are also associated with increased cross-border lending, suggesting that some lending that would otherwise occur in host countries is diverted to avoid them.

deficits, can be too big to save and therefore are subject to more intense market discipline (Demirgüç-Kunt and Huizinga 2013).

Financial safety nets, and more specifically the incentive for national authorities to bail out a bank in trouble, can also be related to bank internationalization because cross-border resolution proved to be problematic during the recent crisis period. Beck and others (2013) develop a model that they then test in the data, highlighting the incentives that national authorities have to intervene in a troubled cross-border bank. Because intervention is costly and national supervisors are mainly interested in protecting domestic stakeholders, the incentives for intervention are stronger if the share of domestic assets and deposits is high. Likewise, if the share of domestic bank equity is high, the incentives to intervene will be low because the national authorities will align with the interests of domestic shareholders, who will prefer to let the bank continue operating and avoid the costs of bank failure. In line with the financial safety net and distorted incentives of national authorities' arguments, Bertay, Demirgüç-Kunt, and Huizinga (2016) show that internationalizing banks face greater market discipline via increased funding costs—a result that is especially driven by banks in countries with large public deficits.

Conditions That Mitigate Asymmetries of Information

Geographical, cultural, and institutional distances are important determinants of banks' entry decisions because they affect information asymmetries. Buch (2003) reveals how information costs, proxied by geographical distance and cultural and legal system similarities, drive the international investment decisions of banks.[5] Moreover, van Horen (2007) suggests that developing country foreign banks are more likely than their developed country counterparts to invest in small developing countries with weak institutions, suggesting a role for institutional proximity.[6] These results may help shed light on the recent trends in international banking, where the entry of foreign banks from developing countries into other developing economies has been steadily increasing. One example, outlined in box 2.3, is Ecobank, an African bank that has expanded its operations across more than 30 countries in Africa.

BOX 2.3   **Foreign Banks in Africa: The Case of Ecobank**

The banking industry in Africa has traditionally been dominated by European banks because of its economic and legal legacies. Over the last decade, the rise of South–South banking has gained importance globally, and it has significantly affected finance in Sub-Saharan Africa (Beck, Fuchs, and others 2014).

Compared with developing countries elsewhere, Sub-Saharan economies tend to be characterized by shallower and less efficient financial systems (Honohan and Beck 2007) that offer relatively limited basic services (Beck and Cull 2013). Based on common financial access and depth measures, access to traditional banking services in West and East Africa is among the lowest globally (Nyantakyi and Sy 2015). Meanwhile, the synergy of financial liberalization and postcrisis retrenchment of European banks have induced the international expansion of Sub-Saharan banks within the region (Honohan and Beck 2007; Moyo and others 2014). Such developments have opened up possibilities for enhancing banking sector competition, deepening financial systems, and widening financial access.

Ecobank Transnational Incorporated, or Ecobank, is an example of regionalization by an African bank during the last two decades, highlighting both the opportunities and risks related to South–South bank-

(box continued next page)

BOX 2.3   **Foreign Banks in Africa: The Case of Ecobank** *(continued)*

FIGURE B2.3.1   **Distribution of Ecobank's Branches and Offices (2015) and Assets (2011 and 2015)**

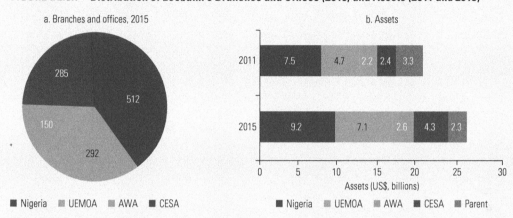

■ Nigeria   ■ UEMOA   ■ AWA   ■ CESA   ■ Nigeria   ■ UEMOA   ■ AWA   ■ CESA   ■ Parent

Source: Ecobank 2017.
Note: The geographical regions are classified according to Ecobank: UEMOA (West African Economic and Monetary Union), Benin, Burkina Faso, Cabo Verde, Côte d'Ivoire, Guinea Bissau, Mali, Niger, Senegal, and Togo; AWA (Anglophone West Africa), The Gambia, Ghana, Guinea, Liberia, Sierra Leone; CESA (Central, Eastern, and Southern Africa), Burundi, Cameroon, the Central African Republic, Chad, Democratic Republic of Congo, Equatorial Guinea, Gabon, Kenya, Malawi, Mozambique, Republic of Congo, Rwanda, São Tomé and Príncipe, South Sudan, Tanzania, Uganda, Zambia, and Zimbabwe.

ing. Founded in 1985 when foreign- and state-owned entities controlled West African banking industries, Ecobank had by 1990 expanded to five countries in West Africa from its home country of Togo; and by 2001 it had further extended its reach to 12 countries across Africa to become a regional bank. Traditionally serving wholesale customers, by around 2005 Ecobank had gradually transformed itself into a full-service, pan-African bank. A decade later, Ecobank is among the few multinational financial institutions operating extensively beyond their home countries in Africa (Beck, Fuchs, and others 2014). With 1,239 banking offices in 33 countries across the continent (see figure B2.3.1), Ecobank has a footprint in Africa that surpasses that of any bank in the world.[a]

Since 2011, Ecobank has been rebalancing its presence in neighboring Nigeria (Nigeria is the home of Ecobank's largest subsidiary, holding 40 percent of the group's assets) in order to further grow into central, eastern, and southern Africa. The redistribution of its activities to different regions is aimed at obtaining more profitability and efficiency as well as reevaluating its business model. The group also has established representative offices in finan-

cial centers such as Paris, Beijing, Dubai, Johannesburg, and London, thereby gaining access to global and regional financial markets—a common move by internationalizing developing country banks.

Ecobank is particularly notable for the relatively small size of its domestic operations; 12 percent of its total revenue of $2.1 billion in 2015 originated in Togo. Furthermore, its share of Togolese assets fell from 16.5 percent in 2011 to 9.2 percent in 2015, suggesting significant expansion into the wider African economy.

However, Ecobank's achievements as a sizable regional bank in Africa have not been without challenges. In 2013, the bank went through turmoil related to corporate governance issues, which also produced judiciary and political tensions among home and host countries. Given the complexity of international banks, this experience has highlighted the importance of strong legal institutions in empowering supervision and regulatory enforcement. Furthermore, it shows that the increasing geographical reach of international banks also warrants deepening cross-border information sharing and coordination mechanisms for banking supervision.

---

a. Ecobank relies extensively on a network of subsidiaries, as opposed to parent-reliant branches.

Recent studies have found that the location decisions of foreign banks are influenced not only by the bilateral distance between their home country and the host economy, but also by how close other competing foreign banks are to the host economy. The farther away its competitors, the more likely it is that a foreign bank will enter a host economy. Claessens and van Horen (2014a) introduce this concept as "competitor remoteness"—defined as the weighted average distance of all competing banks from a host country—to account for the fact that the closest country for a foreign bank might not be the most attractive one if the bank's competitors are already closer to this country. Using bilateral data on 1,199 foreign banks from 75 home countries present in 110 host countries, the authors find that closer distance and greater competitor remoteness increase the likelihood that a foreign bank will enter a host country. The impact is stronger for home and host countries that are not members of the OECD, for banks from countries that have engaged relatively more in FDI, and for host countries in which foreign banks dominate. The richness of their data allows Claessens and van Horen (2015) to further examine some patterns related to the recent growth of South–South banking and the dynamics of foreign bank retrenchment after the global financial crisis (see box 2.4).

IMPACTS OF FOREIGN BANK PARTICIPATION

Competition and Efficiency

Evidence suggests that although foreign banks are less efficient than domestic banks in high-income countries, they perform better than their domestic counterparts in developing countries. Foreign banks may bring superior technologies and processes to a host economy, but they face the extra cost of doing business abroad. Part of this cost may arise from operating in a different environment in which foreign banks may have to familiarize themselves with the institutional development, regulatory frameworks, financial markets, or credit risk of the host economy. Whereas most studies in high-income countries find that domestic banks are more efficient than foreign banks (Berger and others 2000; Chang, Hasan, and Hunter 1998; DeYoung and Nolle 1996; Hasan and Hunter 1996; Miller and Parkhe 2002; Peek, Rosengren, and Kasirye 1999), studies focusing on developing countries find the opposite pattern: foreign banks tend to be more efficient than domestic banks in terms of cost and profits.[7] Indeed, consistent with the evidence from country case studies, empirical work that exploits large panels of countries finds that, although in developed countries foreign banks tend to be less efficient than domestic ones, in developing countries the pattern is reversed (Claessens, Demirgüç-Kunt, and Huizinga 2001; Demirgüç-Kunt and Huizinga 1999).

The performance of foreign banks in a host country depends on various factors, such as home country characteristics, geographic and cultural determinants, and market structure. In developing countries, foreign banks have lower overhead costs, higher interest margins, and higher profitability, which may suggest that foreign banks, in general, bring better technologies to less developed banking sectors (Claessens, Demirgüç-Kunt and Huizinga 2001; Demirgüç-Kunt and Huizinga 1999; Micco, Panizza, and Yañez 2007). But foreign banks may not have that technological edge in more developed banking markets. More recently, Claessens and van Horen (2012) find that foreign banks are relatively more profitable when coming from a high-income country, when the competition in the local banking sector is limited, and when the foreign bank is larger. Foreign banks become more profitable over time, especially when the host economy shares similar geographical and cultural backgrounds with a bank's home country.

In principle, the higher efficiency of foreign banks in developing countries can improve the performance of local banks and the degree of competition in the system. Foreign banks can improve the performance of domestic banks in several ways. For one thing, the increased competition from new foreign players puts pressure on local banks to increase their efficiency by, for example, reducing their

BOX 2.4   Dynamics of Postcrisis International Bank Retrenchment: From Globalization to Regionalization?

Several major international banks headquartered in high-income member countries of the Organisation for Economic Co-operation and Development, such as Deutsche Bank, recently announced plans to drastically reduce the number of countries in which they operate. The general view has been that financial markets have been fragmenting since the global financial crisis. However, as Claessens (2016) argues, fragmentation of the financial systems has been observed more in cross-border claims than in foreign bank presence.

A comparison over time of the number and size of subsidiaries of foreign banks reveals that retrenchment has not been that severe. Even though the number of foreign banks headquartered in high-income countries declined after the crisis (Claessens and van Horen 2015), in terms of their assets, foreign banks from high-income countries that continued to operate abroad grew, widening the gap (in terms of assets) between them and foreign banks from developing countries (see figure B2.4.1).

Nevertheless, the dynamics of entry and exit among foreign banks reveal some interesting trends (see figure B2.4.2). Greenfield entries have been similar for high-income and developing country foreign banks (panel c), but closures have been mainly by the foreign banks of high-income countries (panel d). In terms of foreign acquisitions of domestic banks, in the precrisis period most domestic banks were acquired by banks from high-income countries. After the crisis, the number of foreign acquisitions dropped drastically (panel a), and of those acquisitions that did take place, most were by foreign banks from developing countries. In some regions, the retrenchment of global banks has been accompanied by an expansion of regional players. As panel b shows, most ownership transferals of foreign banks have been from high-income foreign banks to banks from developing countries. All in all, even though the overall number of foreign banks has remained stable, significant changes in the composition of banks have been observed in recent years.

FIGURE B2.4.1   **Growth over Time of Foreign Banks by Number of Subsidiaries (2000–13) and Average Assets (2005–13)**

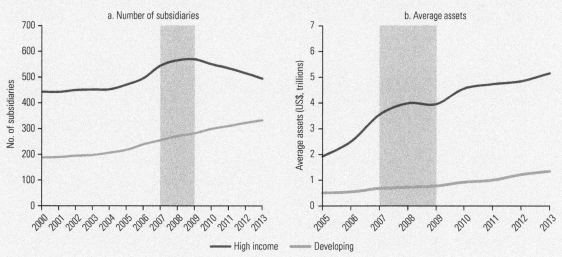

Source: Analysis based on Claessens and van Horen's Foreign Bank Ownership Database, matched with consolidated Bankscope statements (Claessens and van Horen 2015).
Note: "High income" and "developing" categories correspond to banks headquartered in high-income and developing countries, as defined by the World Bank. The gray area indicates the global financial crisis period.

(box continued next page)

BOX 2.4 **Dynamics of Postcrisis International Bank Retrenchment: From Globalization to Regionalization?** *(continued)*

FIGURE B2.4.2 **Acquisitions, Transferals, Greenfield Entries, and Closures of Foreign Banks, 2000–13**

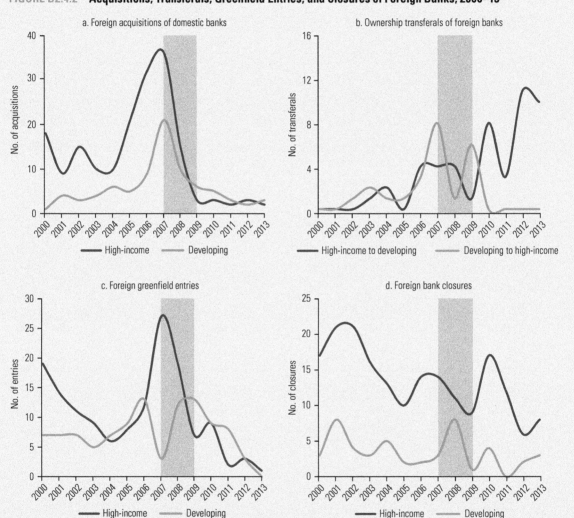

Source: Analysis is based on Claessens and van Horen's Foreign Bank Ownership Database, matched with consolidated Bankscope statements (Claessens and van Horen 2015).
Note: "High-income" and "developing" categories correspond to banks headquartered in high-income and developing countries, as defined by the World Bank. The gray area indicates the global financial crisis period.

costs and offering products of higher quality. In particular, the greenfield entry of foreign banks increases the number of banks in the host economy, induces more competition, and could lead to lower market concentration (Claeys and Hainz 2014; Lehner and Schnitzer

2008). For another, through spillovers local banks can learn from foreign banks about new financial services, better practices, or more sophisticated techniques (such as risk management, personnel training, or data processing) that make them more efficient, even without directly competing with their foreign peers (Lehner and Schnitzer 2008; Zhu 2012).

The empirical evidence mostly indicates that foreign bank participation is positively related to bank competition and efficiency in host countries. Analyzing a panel of 80 countries over time, Claessens, Demirgüç-Kunt, and Huizinga (2001) find that in developing countries, a larger foreign ownership share of banks is associated with the lower profitability and margins of local banks. The effects of foreign bank entry are apparent shortly upon entry, and they do not increase as foreign banks gain market share. More recent cross-country studies confirm a positive link between foreign bank entry and competition. Using bank-level data over time across 17 developing countries, Jeon, Olivero, and Wu (2011) demonstrate that when foreign bank penetration increases, competition in the banking sector of the host economy improves,

particularly when more efficient and less risky foreign banks enter markets with less concentrated banking sectors.

Recent empirical studies have attempted to quantify the role of knowledge spillovers from foreign to domestic banks. Besides the direct impact of foreign banks on competition, a host economy might experience further gains as it opens up to foreign bank entry (Goldberg 2009). These gains can take the form of technology transfers, institutional change, productivity enhancements, and wage spillovers from foreign banks. Such spillover effects are documented by Zhu (2012), who finds that the managerial performance of domestic banks in Eastern Europe and Latin America is positively linked to foreign bank presence. The gap in managerial efficiency between foreign and local banks not only narrows over time but also does so even when competition is low. Box 2.5 presents a case study of such

---

BOX 2.5   Improving Rural Finance in Albania through Knowledge Exchange

In Albania, as in many developing countries, the financing needs of households and firms in rural areas are largely met by cooperative financial institutions (CFIs). Although CFIs have an extensive information network in local areas, their governance and technological and institutional capacity tend to be weak, and their regulation is usually not well defined.

In 2014 the Albanian Savings and Credit Union (ASCU) approached the European Fund for Southeast Europe (EFSE) and Rabobank, an international bank with vast experience in providing financial services to small and unbanked clients, for help in designing and implementing a structural reform that would allow it to professionalize and organize its operations on a par with commercial banks. The ASCU, a CFI that was established in 1992, provides microloans to over 30,000 rural families in Albania (Rabobank 2015). It has built a strong local presence and a healthy asset portfolio, but further growth has been hampered by a weak institutional capacity, a lack of information technology, and limited funding.

The reform was a collaborative effort among regulators, ASCU, and Rabobank, a large Dutch cooperative bank with subsidiaries in 23 develop-

ing countries. They targeted smallholders, small and medium-sized enterprises, and individuals who lacked access to banking services. Their strategy consisted of merging several small savings and credit associations (SCAs) into a one-tier operational structure, with a multitier governance model that would provide the new institution with greater economies of scale in terms of products and services and would improve its access to financial markets, yet with continued bottom-up member involvement.

As part of the reform, the cooperative legal and judicial framework was amended to provide room for the sector to grow and consolidate under a stronger regulatory regime. A more inclusive deposit insurance agency was also designed in order to include financial cooperatives. As a result, by the end of 2015, 70 out of the 84 rural SCAs were merged into one large SCA, even before the new cooperative law was ratified. It was a unique achievement because very few CFIs have leapt forward to welcome a one-tier operational structure. In February 2016, the new financial institution, called FED, was licensed by the Bank of Albania. The EFSE and Rabobank will continue to support FED for three years by providing technical assistance for the restructuring process.

knowledge transfers from the experience of a large Dutch bank operating in Albania.

Evidence suggests that the role that foreign banks play in a host economy is also determined by the mode of entry. When foreign banks expand abroad, one decision they face is the mode of entry—that is, through greenfield investments or acquisition of existing banks. Some theories suggest that this decision is largely influenced by the efficiency of the entering bank in screening potential clients. If the bank is inefficient (for example, if information about clients in the local market is nonexistent or too costly), then the bank may choose to enter through acquisitions and make use of the information already possessed by the acquired bank. With increasing efficiency, greenfield entry becomes more attractive for a foreign bank (Lehner 2009).

The type of entry will affect not only the number of competitors in the host economy but also the way in which information is distributed among foreign and domestic banks, which in turn will influence the degree of competition in the domestic banking sector (Claeys and Hainz 2006). Empirical work has found that foreign bank entry via greenfield investments has a stronger positive effect on competition than entry via M&As—see Claeys and Hainz (2014) and Jeon, Olivero, and Wu (2011). Exploiting a large sample of countries over time, Delis, Kokas, and Ongena (2014) confirm these results, but they also find that as the share of foreign banks in a host economy increases, the market power of the average bank in the industry also rises. This occurs because the primary mode of entry of foreign banks is through M&As. And yet, even though foreign banks are more efficient, that efficiency does not translate into more competitive pricing. Meanwhile, even though greenfield investments are associated with higher levels of competition, they are not necessarily associated with greater access to financial services.

Financial Stability

International banks play a risk-sharing role in the host economy in which, on the one hand, local shocks may be better diversified, but, on the other, shocks from abroad may be more easily imported. Studies of financial stability find that the degree of risk sharing is mixed because it depends on conditions in both the host and home countries. The impact of foreign banks on the stability of host economies has been studied widely. Foreign banks have been found to adjust their lending when financial or macroeconomic factors in the home or host country change, which may have ambiguous effects on the stability of the host economy. Foreign banks may enhance the stability of a domestic banking system exposed to local shocks because they have access to liquidity and capital from their parent companies. In addition, because foreign banks are typically more diversified than domestic ones, they should be less affected by local shocks. And yet foreign banks could also destabilize host economies by transmitting shocks from their home country or other countries where they operate.[8] Destabilization of the domestic banking sector may also occur through competitive pressure if, for instance, foreign banks push local banks to riskier segments or even to exit the market. Alternatively, as box 2.6 discusses, foreign banks may hinder the stability of the domestic banking sector by increasing the foreign exchange risk of the host economy.

Countries with a higher foreign bank presence appear to have fewer crises. Analysis of bank-level data across 80 developed and developing countries suggests that greater foreign bank participation is associated with a reduced probability of financial crises in the host country (Demirgüç-Kunt, Levine, and Min 1998). Barth, Caprio, and Levine (2004) compare the performance and stability of the banking sectors in a sample of over 100 countries with those countries' regulatory and supervisory practices. They find that countries that impose official barriers to foreign bank entry tend to have more fragile banking sectors and, in particular, tend to have a higher likelihood of a major banking crisis.

Meanwhile, credit growth from foreign banks can be more resilient during local financial turmoil. Using bank-level data for over 300 foreign and domestic banks operating in 10 Eastern European countries, De

BOX 2.6   Foreign Exchange Risk: The Case of Latvia

In the absence of a well-developed local currency deposit base, most of the funding for international banks may be in a foreign currency, either from their parent entities, international capital markets, or international financial institutions. Foreign exchange risks pose a problem when banks lend in a foreign currency to households and firms with incomes and assets denominated in the local currency. While borrowers may find debt contracts in a foreign currency attractive due to lower interest rates, they are unable to protect themselves against future exchange rate fluctuations. Concerns are even greater when longer-term loans, such as mortgages, are extended in a foreign currency.

During the global financial crisis, Latvia showcased the negative consequences that foreign currency lending can bring (IEG 2012). In 2008, Latvian subsidiaries of Nordic banks accounted for 60 percent of total banking sector assets. Their increased presence also brought a rise in the proportion of loans denominated in a foreign currency, which rose from 50 percent in 2001 to more than 85 percent in 2007 (Blanchard and others 2013). By 2007, the IMF warned that rapid growth in credit in foreign currencies was leading to large currency mismatches on the balance sheets of firms and households and a boom in housing prices (Cordero 2009).

According to Weisbrot and Ray (2010), one important driver of the financial crisis in Latvia was

its pegged exchange rate. They argue that the fixed exchange regime was widely believed to be permanent, encouraging borrowers and lenders to issue and obtain debt in euros, assuming no exchange rate risk. However, once the global recession hit and foreign banks began retrenching, exchange rate uncertainty substantially impacted the economy. The Latvian authorities decided to maintain the fixed exchange rate, and thus allow the adjustment in the real exchange rate to take place via declining prices and wages. Even though the nominal exchange rate was left untouched, increasing numbers of borrowers were not able to pay off their loans due to falling incomes and unemployment.[a] In the third quarter of 2010, NPLs in Latvia were 19.4 percent of total loans (Škarica 2014).

Foreign exchange risk is not exclusively attached to foreign currency loans. Collecting deposits in a foreign currency may also distort local credit markets, as funding in the local currency may drop. This was the case in Azerbaijan, where foreign banks received a high share of their deposits in a foreign currency. When the government banned foreign currency loans to unhedged borrowers, banks had to curb total lending because their local currency funds were insufficient to support it. Moreover, once devaluation hit, foreign currency deposits became extremely costly for foreign banks.

a. Beck, Jakubik, and Piloiu (2013) note that even though the foreign exchange rate was kept fixed during the crisis, since interest rates had to increase to defend the fixed exchange rate, higher lending rates were one of the factors that contributed to the large increase in NPLs among households and firms.

Haas and van Lelyveld (2006) study the responses of banks to changing business cycle conditions and to domestic financial crises. Their findings show that during financial crises, domestic banks contract their credit and deposits, whereas foreign banks continue lending at the same level. Similar findings are drawn from a study analyzing banks across 20 Asian and Latin American countries from 1989 to 2001 (Arena, Reinhart, and Vazquez 2007). The study documents that, compared with those of local banks, the lending and deposit rates of foreign banks have a smoother pattern in times of financial distress. De Haas

and van Lelyveld (2010) analyze data from multinational banking groups to examine the extent to which parent banks manage the credit growth of their subsidiaries abroad. Consistent with previous findings, their evidence confirms that when a host economy is hit by a banking crisis, parent banks can inject funds in their subsidiaries in order to maintain their levels of credit supply.[9] In line with this research, Cetorelli and Goldberg (2012b) show that internal capital markets are active in international banks and that parent support makes foreign bank subsidiaries more resilient than local banks. Finally, a recent study by Demirgüç-Kunt and others (2017) reveals how a greater foreign bank presence in an international sample of countries makes cross-border lending (through syndicated loans) more stable and less destabilizing in response to international monetary policy shocks.[10] The study also illustrates the interaction between brick-and-mortar activities—the focus of this chapter—and cross-border lending, which is examined in chapter 3.

The stabilizing role of foreign banks during local financial crises is further confirmed in several studies at the country level. Only a few studies at the country level have examined the role of foreign bank participation during periods of financial crisis. Overall, the findings from these studies support the previously discussed cross-country results; foreign banks appear to have a stabilizing effect in times of financial distress. Goldberg, Dages, and Kinney (2000) analyze the experiences of Argentina and Mexico in the 1990s by examining bank-level quarterly loan data for each country. Their findings reveal that in both countries, foreign banks were more stable lenders than local banks. The authors argue that having diverse ownership in the banking system is important because it, in turn, diversifies the sources of foreign funding in the banking system. Crystal, Dages, and Goldberg (2001, 2002) also analyze Latin American foreign and local banks in the late 1990s, which was a period characterized by both the large entry of foreign banks in the region and significant macroeconomic stress. They find that throughout this period, foreign banks had consistently stronger credit growth, were more aggressive in addressing asset quality deterioration, and were better able to absorb losses. More nuanced evidence from Malaysia highlights the importance of diversification among foreign banks. Detragiache and Gupta (2006) compare the performance of local and foreign banks in Malaysia during the Asian crisis of the late 1990s, distinguishing foreign banks that specialize in Asia from those that have more diversified operations outside Asia. The study finds that diversified foreign banks were crucial in helping the banking system

throughout the crisis period. The more diversified foreign banks continued lending and had substantially higher profits and fewer nonperforming loans than both local banks and foreign banks specializing in the region.

Evidence suggests that the stabilizing role of foreign banks is greatly dependent on the characteristics of their parent banks. Analyzing the lending patterns of a large sample of domestic and foreign banks, a report by the IMF finds that the lending behavior of foreign subsidiaries during financial crises varies (IMF 2015c). Foreign subsidiaries of better-capitalized parent banks and parent banks with more stable funding sources tend to be more stable lenders. This heterogeneity across foreign banks may help explain why some studies see more nuanced results when analyzing the lending procyclicality of foreign banks. In some studies, the lending from foreign banks is shown to be more procyclical than that of domestic banks. If lending from foreign banks accentuates the business cycles of host economies, then financial instability can increase. In good times, lending from foreign banks may fuel lending booms, possibly associated with the lower lending standards of banks (Dell'Ariccia and Marquez (2006b); and in bad times, it may worsen the credit crunch.[11] Albertazzi and Bottero (2014) find the latter for Italy after the collapse of Lehman Brothers. Notably, their results are driven by foreign banks with a lower local presence, proxied by loans over local deposit funding. Box 2.7 describes further empirical evidence of a higher lending cyclicality for foreign banks.

As South–South banking and bank regionalization expand, the stabilizing role of foreign banks may change. On the one hand, closer geographical proximity to the host country could limit the potential of foreign banks to diversify shocks because shocks are more likely to be correlated between host and home countries. On the other hand, greater proximity (physical, institutional, or cultural) may facilitate communication and coordination between host and home country authorities. Moreover, differences in the funding sources of the new generation of foreign banks (such

BOX 2.7   The Lending Cyclicality of Foreign Banks

Bertay, Demirgüç-Kunt, and Huizinga (2015) compare cyclicality in lending across different types of banks (private versus state-owned, and domestic versus foreign-owned) for a yearly panel spanning 1999 to 2010 and consisting of 1,633 banks from 111 countries.

In their sample, 52.8 percent of bank-year observations correspond to private domestic banks, followed by 35.8 percent to private foreign banks and 11.4 percent to state-owned banks. To examine cyclicality in lending, they analyze how the credit growth of the different types of banks in a given period is associated with the growth rate of the gross domestic product (GDP) per capita (as a measure of the business cycle).

Their results confirm that, although lending from state banks is essentially insensitive to GDP per capita growth, lending from private banks increases as GDP rises, and it increases even more strongly for foreign banks. Specifically, a 1 percent increase in GDP per capita growth leads to credit growth of 1.0–1.1 percent for private domestic banks and 2.1 percent for private foreign banks.

Overall, the authors find evidence that the lending of foreign banks is more sensitive to macro developments in the host country (and thus more procyclical) than that of their domestic counterparts (see figure B2.7.1), which may have consequences for financial stability. One explanation may be that, with funding from their international parents, foreign banks are more likely to take advantage of local lending opportunities during economic booms. The authors are not able to identify the parents of the foreign banks they study, and thus are unable to test this conjecture directly.

However, evidence from other sources indicates the substantial heterogeneity in the cyclicality of lending among foreign banks. For example, Cull and Martínez Pería (2013) find that foreign banks in Eastern Europe were better able to maintain credit growth during the global financial crisis if their parents were profitable and liquid (although the same patterns did not hold in Latin America, where the solvency of the subsidiaries themselves proved more important). Bonin and Louie (forthcoming) find simi-

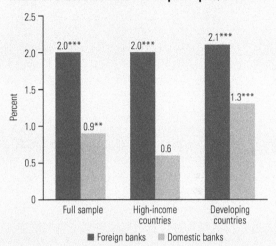

FIGURE B2.7.1   Change in Bank Lending Associated with a 1 Percent Increase in GDP per Capita, 1999–2010

Source: Recalculated from Bertay, Demirgüç-Kunt, and Huizinga 2015.
Note: The figure shows the marginal effects of a regression of bank lending on GDP per capita growth and other control variables, estimated using a sample of 1,633 banks from 111 countries. Developed economies are defined as high-income countries based on the World Bank classification, and the rest of the countries are defined as developing economies. ** and *** indicate statistical significance at the 5 and 1 percent levels.

lar lending behavior during the crisis among domestic banks and the six multinational European banks (the "Big Six") that were operating in Bulgaria, Croatia, the Czech Republic, Hungary, Poland, Romania, the Slovak Republic, and Slovenia. By contrast, the lending of other foreign banks operating in these countries was much more procyclical than that of domestic banks. These authors speculate that the Big Six treated these countries as something akin to a second home market.

As noted, during many of the crisis episodes in the banking sectors of developing countries, foreign banks were better able to maintain lending than domestic banks. A report by the IMF (2015a) provides bank-level evidence across countries that foreign-owned subsidiaries, and in particular those with well-capitalized parent banks, lend less procyclically than domestic banks during domestic crises.

as local deposits versus equity, and short-term funding versus long-term funding) may also influence the stability of their credit behavior. As figure 2.1 shows, South–South subsidiaries are increasingly being funded by local deposits, which during the global financial crisis proved to be a more stable source of funding, enabling foreign banks to better smooth their lending throughout the crisis. During that period, local deposits accounted for 57 percent of funding for South–South subsidiaries and 47 percent for North–South subsidiaries.

Although foreign banks can attenuate local shocks in a host country, they also can spread shocks from one country to another. The literature also suggests that, as with any other risk-sharing scheme, foreign banks can pass external shocks to the host economy. Among the first studies to employ a rigorous methodology to causally identify that shocks can be transmitted across countries via foreign banks was that by Peek and Rosengren (1997, 2000). This study exploited the collapse in Japanese stock prices in the late 1980s as an exogenous shock to the supply

of credit in the United States that was independent of the demand for credit in the United States. The authors found that Japanese banks operating in the United States significantly reduced their supply of credit as a result of the collapse of stock prices. Using a similar event, Chava and Purnanandam (2011) and Schnabl (2012) examine how the 1998 Russian crisis was transmitted via foreign banks to borrowers in the United States and Peru, respectively.

There is growing evidence for the transmission of foreign monetary policies to host economies via foreign banks. In recent years, policy makers and scholars have been concerned that the foreign monetary policy of developed countries may have substantial spillovers into the credit cycles and financial stability of developing countries (Fischer and others 2014; Rajan 2014; Rey 2015). A recent study of Mexico by Morais and others (forthcoming) uncovered rigorous evidence that foreign banks transmit the monetary policy of their home countries through the lending of their subsidiaries in host economies. The

FIGURE 2.1   Contribution of Local Deposits, Equity, and Short-Term and Long-Term Funding to Total Bank Funding, 2000–14

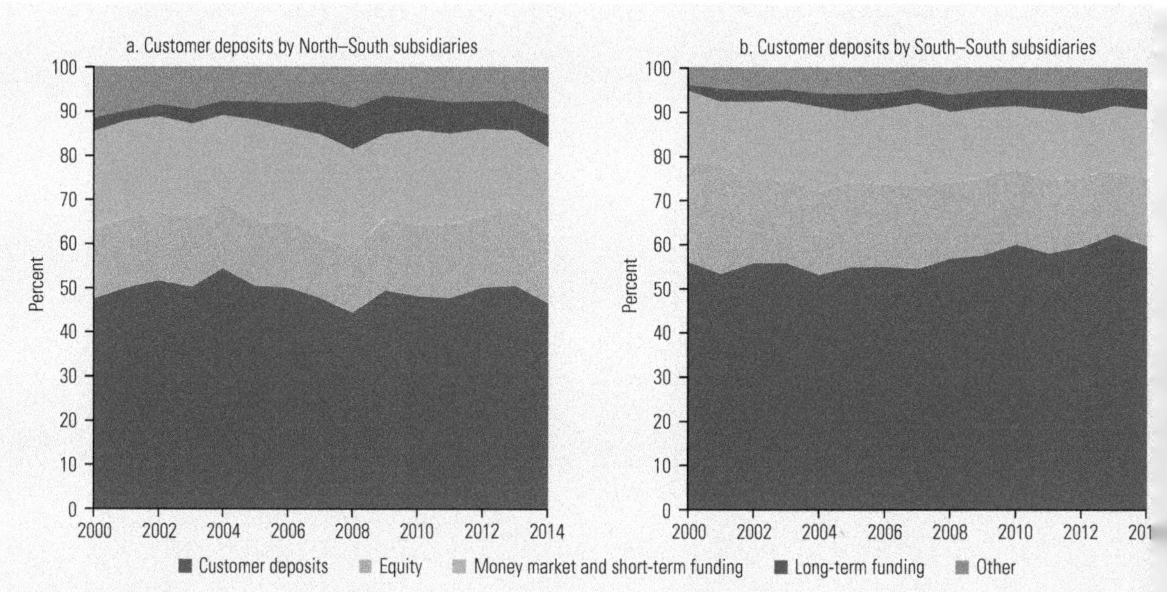

Source: Bertay, Demirgüç-Kunt, and Huizinga 2017.

authors found that the credit supply of foreign banks increases when the monetary policy of their home country softens. The future defaults on these loans also increase, suggesting that foreign banks may be engaging in more risk taking abroad when their home country policy rates are low. Box 2.8 presents a more detailed discussion of this study, and chapter 3 discusses the international transmission of foreign monetary policies at greater length.

Since the global financial crisis, a large number of studies have examined in greater depth the ways in which foreign banks contribute to cross-border contagion. The vast majority of studies use microdata to disentangle the effects of supply and demand. The evidence is consistent with the fact that during the crisis, foreign banks contracted their lending earlier and faster than domestic banks. Aiyar (2012) finds that in the United

---

BOX 2.8   **The Transmission of International Monetary Policy via Foreign Banks in Mexico**

Morais and others (forthcoming) analyze the impact that foreign monetary policy, transmitted via banks' lending channels, has on Mexican firms. Over a 10-year period, using the universe of new and outstanding commercial bank loans, they examine monetary policy shocks in the form of interest rates and nonstandard quantitative easing (QE) transmitted from three regions: the United States, the United Kingdom, and the euro area. The main foreign banks operating in Mexico have their headquarters in these regions.

One of the main challenges in identifying the impact that foreign monetary policy has on the supply of credit is that both the supply and demand for credit may change in response to a monetary policy shock. Morais and colleagues overcome this challenge in two ways. First, they compare loans offered in the same period to the same firm by different foreign banks exposed to different monetary policies, thereby allowing them to hold the demand for credit constant. Second, because only 21 percent of all firms borrow from multiple banks in the same period, they also compare loans offered by different foreign banks in the same period with firms from the same state and industry—an alternative way to hold the demand for credit constant.

To identify whether the transmission of foreign monetary policy through bank credit leads to real effects on firms, they examine the dynamics of firms' assets, employment, and total credit from any source. Analyzing these variables is important because firms may switch from foreign bank credit to credit from other banks or other sources when their credit condi-

tions change. In other words, firms could neutralize international shocks by replacing bank credit from foreign banks with other sources of finance. If firms find it costly to change banks and thus cannot protect themselves from the shocks transmitted by their banks, foreign monetary policy shocks could have real effects on the performance and operations of firms.

The study results indicate that a softening of foreign monetary policy increases the supply of credit that foreign banks extend to Mexican firms. Consistent with the evidence on the transmission of monetary policy from home to host countries, each type of regional policy shock affects supply via each region's foreign banks. For example, U.S., U.K., and euro area monetary policies affect the credit supply to Mexican firms via those regions' banks in Mexico. All loan terms are affected (loan volume, maturity, loan interest rate, and collateral rate), but the effects are substantially weaker for loan rates. Moreover, the international monetary policy channel implies strong real effects, with substantially stronger elasticities from monetary rates than from QE.

A decline in foreign monetary policy rates and an expansion of QE lead to a higher credit supply for borrowers with higher ex ante loan rates (consistent with a reach-for-yield) and substantially higher ex post loan defaults, which suggests that foreign banks increase their risk taking when their country's monetary policy softens. Furthermore, foreign QE is found to bring about greater risk taking in emerging markets through an expansion of credit to riskier firms rather than improving the real outcomes of firms in those markets.

Kingdom, the shock to external bank funding caused by the crisis led to a substantial reduction in banks' credit supply, driven mainly by branches of foreign banks. In the Russian Federation, foreign banks reduced their lending more than other banks (Fungáčová, Herrala, and Weill 2013).[12] One conclusion from a review of the literature is that the responses of foreign banks to shocks vary substantially, depending on country and bank-level characteristics. The evidence suggests that the transmission of shocks is stronger when regulation is lax in the home country (Bertay 2014) or in host countries (Anginer, Cerutti, and Martínez Pería 2017). The transmission of shocks also appears to be stronger among host countries that are more financially open and that have more competitive banking sectors (Jeon, Olivero, and Wu 2013). As for bank-level characteristics, the transmission of shocks is stronger for foreign banks that have lower levels of capital, are less profitable, and are more dependent on their parent banks (Anginer, Cerutti, and Martínez Pería 2017; Choi, Gutierrez, and Martínez Pería 2014; De Haas and van Lelyveld 2014; De Haas and others 2015; Jeon, Olivero, and Wu 2013; Popov and Udell 2012). In addition, the transmission of shocks is stronger if foreign banks entered host markets via greenfield investment rather than M&As (Jeon, Olivero, and Wu 2013).

Recent studies have furthered understanding of how foreign banks can lead to cross-border contagion. Cetorelli and Goldberg (2012a, 2012b, 2012c) and Jeon, Olivero, and Wu (2013) reveal the existence of an active cross-border internal capital market whereby global banks reallocate funds across their branches and subsidiaries to buffer shocks to the parent bank's balance sheet. These studies show how a monetary policy shock in the home country can spill over to other countries through a reduction in lending by global banks' subsidiaries. Global banks also contribute to the transmission of shocks via interbank lending. The authors of a recent study construct a network of direct and indirect bilateral exposures using detailed data on loan transactions in the syndicated interbank

market and show that greater exposure to banks in crisis-affected countries reduces profitability and the supply of new credit (Hale, Kapan, and Minoiu 2016).

There are, however, ways to reduce the international transmission of shocks from home to host countries. By analyzing the Vienna Initiative, in which some parent banks committed to supporting their subsidiaries in emerging Europe, De Haas and others (2015) show that cross-border coordination efforts can reduce cross-border transmission and make foreign subsidiaries relatively stable lenders without imposing negative externalities on the other countries in the region. Since the global financial crisis, other initiatives, such as alternative cross-border resolution schemes, have been put in place with the objective of reducing the cost of future financial crises. A comprehensive review of the different approaches that have been followed for the regulation, supervision, and resolution of global banks is presented later in this chapter.

Foreign banks may also transmit shocks from their host countries to their home countries, hindering the home countries' stability (Cetorelli and Goldberg 2012b). Buch and others (2012) look at the impact of the internationalization of German banks on the structure and risk taking of Germany's banking sector. They find that bank internationalization is weakly related to bank risk. Some recent studies, however, imply that bank internationalization leads to higher bank risk for the (internationalizing) parent bank—see Berger and others (2016) focusing on U.S. banks and Gulamhussen, Pinheiro, and Pozzolo (2014) for an international sample of banks. Nevertheless, evidence from the recent financial crisis suggests that the parent banks, especially those with liquid foreign subsidiaries, were better able than their domestic counterparts to protect their home country operations (De Haas and van Lelyveld 2014).

Foreign banks may also experience systemic risk consequences because of their size and complexity. The associations between bank size and bank performance and activity mix and funding strategy have been documented for an international sample of banks by Bertay, Demirgüç-Kunt, and Huizinga (2013), who differentiate between absolute and relative (to national economies) size. They find that bank returns increase with absolute bank size but decrease with systemic size (proxied by bank size with respect to national GDP), and that returns are uncorrelated with bank risk measured by the Z-score. Focusing on bank holding companies in the United States, Hughes and Mester (2013) provide evidence of economies of scale for both small and large banks, and they argue that those economies are not driven by too-big-to-fail subsidies. Nevertheless, banks, especially in advanced economies, suffered very large losses during the crisis, and regulators have taken steps to end the too-big-to-fail problem. Indeed, recent regulatory changes may have important implications for bank internationalization because larger banks are increasingly tending to become international. Large, internationally active banks that face regulatory scrutiny of their risk capital allocation in both home and host countries may decide to reduce their international operations (as discussed in box 3.5 in chapter 3 or, as observed anecdotally, from Deutsche Bank's exit from many markets).

One other crucial dimension of large banks is their complexity. Cetorelli and Goldberg (2014) propose measures to capture two aspects of the complexity of global banks: "organization" complexity, accounting for the number and geographic spread of an institution's affiliates; and "business" complexity, capturing the type and variety of activities of an institution. These measures reveal a substantial degree of diversity in complexity within the universe of U.S. banks and prompt a call for further research on the positive and negative externalities generated by complexity. In a recent study, Carmassi and Herring (2015) analyze the corporate complexity of global systematically important banks (G-SIBs), finding a significant increase in complexity (proxied by the number of majority-owned subsidiaries) through 2011.

Access to Credit

The impact that foreign bank participation can have on overall access to credit is greatly dependent on host country factors. On the one hand, the advantages that foreign banks could bring to a host economy, such as superior technology, better supervision practices, or achievement of larger economies of scale, may allow these banks to overcome the costs of doing business abroad, and they may materialize in more widespread access to credit. In principle, these advantages could give foreign banks an edge with segments of the population that are underserved by domestic banks. On the other hand, the cost of acquiring information about new clients may be too high for foreign banks, forcing them to lend exclusively to the largest, safest firms. Access to credit may be hindered if foreign banks not only limit their lending to the largest customers but also, by their entry, force domestic banks out of the market. Aggregate credit in the host country may then contract, particularly among the smaller and more informationally opaque clients that previously were dependent on credit from domestic banks. Detragiache, Tressel, and Gulpta (2008) and Gormley (2014) develop theoretical frameworks to illustrate that only under certain conditions does the entry of foreign banks increase access to credit. One implication of these models is that foreign banks are more likely to have a negative effect on credit access in host economies where obtaining information is costly (Gormley 2014).

Consistent with theory, empirical research reveals a negative association between foreign bank entry and access to credit in host countries with less competitive banking sectors or weak institutional and legal environments.[13] Behn and others (2014) analyze a sample of 26 developing countries around the time of bank liberalization and find that in countries with more competitive local banks, foreign bank entry resulted in a greater supply of credit. By contrast, host countries with less competitive banking sectors experienced a reduction in aggregate lending, whereby foreign lending mostly crowded out lending from domestic banks. Similarly, exploiting India's commitment to the World Trade Organization (WTO) to allow a greater foreign bank presence during the 1990s, Gormley (2010) presents further evidence of a negative effect of foreign banks on access to credit in the country.[14] In a sample of 137 countries over 1995–2009, Claessens and van Horen (2014b) find a negative correlation between the presence of foreign banks and the ratio of private credit to GDP in low-income countries, in countries where contract enforcement is costlier and access to credit information is limited, in countries where the share of foreign banks is smaller, and in countries where parent banks are located far away.[15] These findings are consistent with the theoretical implications that highlight the importance of the information environment (as modeled in Dell'Ariccia and Marquez 2004) and contract enforcement in reaping the benefits of increased access to credit from foreign banks.

In countries with a more competitive banking sector, one way in which foreign banks can expand overall access to credit is by pushing domestic banks to lend to smaller clients. Even though foreign banks may have more funding sources or better screening technologies than domestic banks, local banks have better information about the quality of local borrowers, and in particular about the more informationally opaque ones, which gives them a comparative advantage in serving these segments (Dell'Ariccia and Marquez 2004). By offering more competitive services, foreign banks may attract the best clients in the host economy, pushing domestic banks to improve their services to prevent good clients from switching banks. Alternatively, domestic banks may also be pushed to expand their operations to SMEs and other previously underserved clients. Several studies from different regions have corroborated that foreign banks lend in general to the largest and safest borrowers.[16] Thus for those domestic banks trying to compete with foreign banks for the large, more informationally transparent firms, it may be preferable to expand their business to smaller, more opaque customers. This, in turn, may

lead to an overall increase in credit supply in the host economy. Several studies provide evidence in favor of this mechanism. Clarke, Cull, and Martínez Pería (2006), analyzing a sample of firms from developing and transition countries, reveal that foreign bank participation is associated with better financing conditions for all firms, even though the firms that benefit most are the largest ones. Similar evidence from Eastern Europe also indicates that, even though foreign banks target larger firms, access to credit for small and medium-sized enterprises (SMEs) is not reduced by the presence of foreign banks (De Haas, Ferreira, and Taci 2010; Giannettia and Ongena 2012).

Alternatively, foreign banks may adopt new lending technologies to expand their business to SMEs. Even though relationship lending is challenging and costly for foreign banks, these banks have found alternative technologies that rely on hard information and allow them to lend to more opaque firms (Berger and Udell 2006). In this way, even when customers do not have formal financial statements, they may have other types of hard information that allow banks to calculate their repayment probability. Some of the technologies targeted to more informationally opaque customers are credit scoring, asset-based lending, factoring, leasing, and fixed-asset lending. Public policies aimed at improving the informational, legal, and regulatory environments in which financial institutions operate could make it possible to use these technologies, and thus, affect access to credit for more informationally opaque customers. Box 2.9 provides more detail on these alternative lending technologies and foreign banks' approach to SME lending.

Foreign banks can also affect governments' access to finance. Home bias in sovereign debt involving domestic banks is well-documented (Hesse, Bakhache, and Asonuma 2015; Horváth, Huizinga, and Ioannidou 2015). Sometimes called the "doom loop," home bias is a problem because it ties a government's default to banks' defaults (Reuters 2013).[17] One possible explanation for this home bias in sovereign debt is moral suasion by the government toward domestic banks. Indeed,

BOX 2.9   Lending Technologies of Foreign Banks and Their Approach to SME Lending

Typically, studies comparing foreign banks with domestic banks point to the screening technologies used to assess credit risk as one of their main differences. Because local banks have better information on domestic customers, they can rely on soft information to evaluate these customers' creditworthiness. In the absence of soft information, foreign banks need to rely more on the hard information offered by credit bureaus and found in collateral registries and audited balance sheets and income statements (Cull, Martínez Pería, and Verrier 2017).

Indeed, large financial institutions and foreign banks have developed and implemented innovative business strategies and technologies that, by relying on hard information, facilitate arm's-length lending to more informationally opaque firms (Berger and Udell 2006; De la Torre, Martínez Pería, and Schmukler 2010). These strategies and technologies include credit scoring, in which banks use hard information from credit registries or bureaus to determine the likelihood of loan repayment; asset-based lending, which relies on assets pledged as collateral; factoring, in which banks purchase a firm's accounts receivable at a discount; and leasing/fixed-asset lending, in which banks rely on valuations of a firm's fixed assets that are either owned by the firm (in the case of leasing) or pledged as collateral (in the case of fixed-asset lending). This effort of foreign banks to develop and implement new screening and lending technologies is consistent with evidence

from Clarke and others (2005), who find that large foreign banks in four Latin American countries lend as actively to small and medium-sized enterprises (SMEs) as large domestic banks. Similarly, Beck, Ioannidou, and Schäfer (2012) use detailed credit registry data on the terms and pricing of loans to show that foreign banks in Bolivia are able to serve the same clientele as domestic banks by requiring collateral, imposing shorter maturities on loans, and basing their pricing on credit ratings and collateral pledges.

De la Torre, Martínez Pería, and Schmukler (2010) surveyed 48 banks across 12 countries to document to what extent banks are engaged in SME lending. Their findings suggest that most banks, including large and foreign ones, are not only interested in the SME segment but also find it profitable. Banks rely on various transactional technologies to screen the creditworthiness of their SME customers. Large international banks have several comparative advantages in dealing with the SME segment, such as economies of scale or superior business models and risk management systems. The authors argue that the ability of foreign banks to serve many SMEs in different countries using superior business and risk management technologies gives them a competitive edge over other banks because they can compensate more easily for the costs of developing new products geared toward SMEs while exploiting larger economies of scale and scope.

Ongena, Popov, and van Horen (2016) show that during the European sovereign debt crisis of 2010–12, domestic banks were more likely to increase sovereign debt holdings than foreign banks when governments had to roll over large amounts of debt. This finding suggests a role for foreign banks in breaking the harmful sovereign bank loop.

On the technology side, today fintech is reshaping who has access to banking services, and foreign banks are likely to play an important role in this process. Initially, fintech helped financial institutions to speed up transactions at a lower cost, whereas the most recent technologies include a variety of services such as

data security, risk management, mobile banking, and alternative currencies. In principle, digital financial services, especially those provided via mobile telephony, hold the promise of deepening financial inclusion to market segments that have been underserved (Ahmed and others 2015). Fintech is likely to facilitate the provision of financial services and affect the ways in which banks compete with each other (and with other nonbank providers of financial services) for all market segments and across geographical boundaries, which could have broader implications for access, efficiency, and financial sector stability (see a more in-depth discussion of fintech in chapter 3).

Although fintech could significantly alter the financial inclusion landscape, it also could entail new risks. A key challenge going forward is how to regulate and monitor an industry with such exponential growth. If regulation is redundant or excessive, the potential that fintech has to promote overall financial inclusion may be hindered. And yet, policy makers need to adopt and monitor regulation that will keep pace with the fast speed at which fintech is growing. The full set of risks, which are explored in detail in chapter 3, are not yet understood. They range from data security and cyber risk to regulatory arbitrage from rules that are not consistent across countries or even companies (World Economic Forum 2016a).

Another recent development that can change the role of foreign banks is the increasing importance of South–South banking. Since the global financial crisis, the roster of international banks in developing economies has been changing. Although foreign banking assets in developing economies continue to grow as financial systems deepen, the presence of developed economy banks, as measured by the number of local bank subsidiaries, has been in decline since 2009, according to the Foreign Bank Ownership Database (Claessens and van Horen 2015). In the wake of this retrenchment, banks from regional financial centers (Hong Kong SAR, China and Singapore) as well as emerging economies (China, Colombia, Russia, and South Africa) have steadily expanded into developing markets (box 2.10 discusses the expansion abroad of the largest Chinese banks).

Even though foreign banks from emerging economies tend to be smaller than their high-income country counterparts, their overall performance has been similar since the global financial crisis. In terms of profitability, the return on assets of foreign banks from emerging economies has followed closely those of banks from high-income countries over the years.[18] As for the size of their credit portfolios, since the global financial crisis foreign banks from developing countries have been growing their lending at faster rates than their high-income competitors (see panels a and b of figure 2.2).

Meanwhile, the ratio of debt to liabilities (measured by local deposits to total liabilities) has remained higher for foreign banks from developing countries over the past decade (panel c). And whereas before the crisis, foreign banks from emerging economies earned a higher share of income from interest than foreign banks from developed countries, this pattern reversed starting in 2007 (panel d). As for the health of their portfolios, although the nonperforming loan (NPL) ratio of foreign banks from developing countries improved over time, during the crisis years NPLs increased substantially for all banks, particularly for foreign banks from developing countries. Interestingly, in recent years the NPLs of foreign banks from developing countries have declined, even to levels lower than those of banks from high-income countries (panel e). By contrast, the Z-scores of foreign banks from high-income countries have been catching up to the levels of developing country foreign banks (panel f).

The recent trends in South–South banking will likely influence who gets credit. Since the global financial crisis, the composition of foreign banks has changed substantially. Whereas banks from developing economies have been increasing their presence abroad, most of the exits from markets have been by banks from OECD countries. These trends may have an impact on who gets credit; relative to a "North–South" foreign bank, a "South–South" foreign bank may be more familiar with the cultural, legal, political, and economic environments of the host country and thus may be better suited to overcome the common challenges that foreign banks face when lending to smaller and more informationally opaque segments (Mian 2006). A recent cross-country study using firm-level data finds that a foreign bank presence is more strongly linked to higher rates of business formation when those banks are headquartered in developing countries. However, banks from developing countries are better able to spur business formation in industries that rely on standardized inputs, which potentially have fewer agency conflicts (Alfaro, Beck, and Calomiris 2015).

BOX 2.10   The Global Expansion of Chinese Banks

With commercial banking assets totaling $24.2 trillion in 2015, China is home to one of the largest banking systems in the world.[a] As trade and investment ties strengthen in the global economy, Chinese banks are beginning to create a global financial services network that supports domestic clients and contributes to the financial development of host countries.

Data collected from the annual reports of the five largest commercial banks (LCBs) in China reveal a steady increase in their brick-and-mortar operations abroad from 2005 to 2015.[b] As figure B2.10.1 illustrates, the LCBs had by 2015 established 153 branches and subsidiaries in 50 overseas jurisdictions, 35 of which were located in 19 developing countries.[c] The bank branch presence in developed countries has rebounded sharply since a temporary setback after the global financial crisis in 2007–09. Subsidiaries have increasingly penetrated markets in Latin America and the Caribbean, in addition to those in Europe and Asia and the Pacific. The number of subsidiaries in developing countries more than tripled during these years.[d]

Because of its cultural similarity, political connectedness, and geographical proximity, as well as its established financial industry, Hong Kong SAR, China has been host to many of the earliest affiliated overseas offices of Chinese banks. Around the time of the Great Depression, the Bank of China entered global financial centers to gain access to foreign currency clearance and security trading. Its banking offices in London, Luxembourg, New York, Singapore, and Tokyo would in the following decades become regional hubs of Chinese banking operations. Following China's accession to the World Trade Organization (WTO) in 2001, its banking presence expanded from regional host countries (such as Australia, the Republic of Korea, and Russian Federation) to Western Europe, Turkey, the Gulf Cooperation Council (GCC) countries, Latin America, and several countries in Sub-Saharan Africa. In recent years, commensurate with China's fundamental role in global trade, the internationalization of Chinese banks has facilitated the use of

FIGURE B2.10.1   Chinese Banks in the World: A Snapshot of Chinese Large Commercial Banks, 2005–15

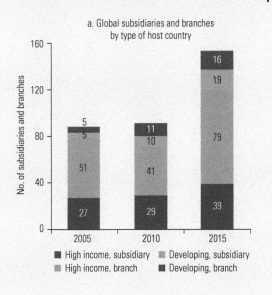

a. Global subsidiaries and branches by type of host country

■ High income, subsidiary   ▨ Developing, subsidiary
▨ High income, branch   ■ Developing, branch

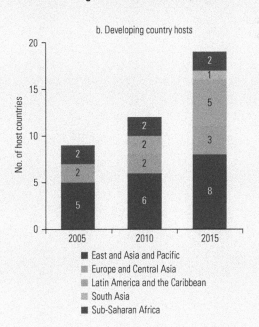

b. Developing country hosts

■ East and Asia and Pacific
▨ Europe and Central Asia
▨ Latin America and the Caribbean
▨ South Asia
■ Sub-Saharan Africa

(box continued next page)

BOX 2.10   The Global Expansion of Chinese Banks *(continued)*

FIGURE B2.10.1   Chinese Banks in the World: A Snapshot of Chinese Large Commercial Banks, 2005–15
(continued)

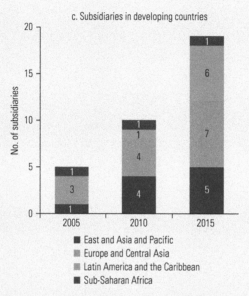

c. Subsidiaries in developing countries

■ East and Asia and Pacific
■ Europe and Central Asia
■ Latin America and the Caribbean
■ Sub-Saharan Africa

Sources: 2016 Annual Reports of Agriculture Bank of China; Bank of China; Bank of Communications; China Construction Bank; Industrial and Commercial Bank of China.

the yuan as an increasingly important currency for settlements (Eichengreen, Walsh, and Weir 2014).

Associated with $1.5 trillion in overseas assets (out of a gross total of $12.1 trillion), in 2016 the overseas business portfolio of Chinese LCBs included investment loans, project loans, trade finance, and financial consulting (CBRC 2016a).[e] In addition, the LCBs participated in lending syndications and cross-border security issuances for clients in the infrastructure, energy, natural resources, and telecommunication sectors, undertaking major international endeavors. Altogether, the overseas business contributed to 7.5 percent of the aggregate pretax profit of LCBs as a group (PwC 2016).

a. Including large commercial banks, joint stock commercial banks, urban and rural commercial banks, and foreign banks.

b. Large commercial banks, as categorized by the China Banking Regulatory Commission (CBRC), include the Industrial and Commercial Bank of China, China Construction Bank, Agricultural Bank of China, Bank of China, and Bank of Communications. They represent the majority of the international Chinese banking presence. In 2015 joint stock commercial banks as a group established seven branches in Luxembourg; Hong Kong SAR, China; Singapore; and the United States.

c. Argentina, Brazil, Cambodia, India, Indonesia, Kazakhstan, Lao People's Democratic Republic, Malaysia, Mexico, Myanmar, Panama, Peru, the Philippines, Russia, South Africa, Thailand, Turkey, Vietnam, and Zambia.

d. In a regulatory and supervisory context, home countries exert more control over overseas branches than subsidiaries. This is often one consideration when banks expand abroad. Box 2.1 offers further discussion on foreign bank entry via branches and subsidiaries.

e. A 2016 assessment of global systemically important banks (G-SIBs) by the Basel Committee on Banking Supervision indicated that the LCBs' consolidated cross-jurisdictional activities in 2015 amounted to $1.1 trillion in claims and $1.6 trillion in liabilities (BCBS 2016).

FIGURE 2.2   **Trends over Time of Foreign Bank Subsidiaries in Developing Countries by the Type of Country in Which Each Bank Is Headquartered, 2001–13**

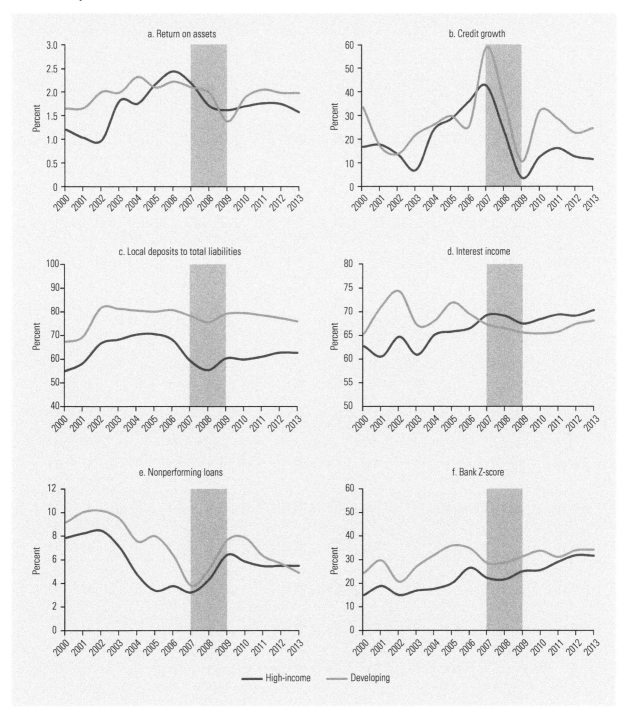

Source: Analysis is based on Claessens and van Horen Foreign Bank Ownership Database, matched with consolidated Bankscope statements (Claessens and van Horen 2015).
Note: "High-income" and "developing" categories correspond to bank subsidiaries in developing countries headquartered in high-income and developing countries, as defined by the World Bank. Figures present averages of the indicators weighted by bank assets. The gray area indicates the global financial crisis period.

Meanwhile, more lax regulation in the home countries of South–South banks may bring higher risks to the host country. In terms of stability, the home country of a foreign bank matters. Although foreign banks can spread shocks from their home countries to a host economy, this transmission has been found to be stronger among foreign banks from home countries with lax financial regulation and weaker institutional environments, and those banks are more likely to be headquartered in less developed countries. Foreign banks from developing countries may bring better knowledge on how to operate in a weaker and more informationally opaque environment, but they may be poorly supervised in their home country, which could translate into more instability for the host economy (Claessens and van Horen 2007).

Other Real Effects

Foreign banks also play an important role in the trade sector of the host economy. Several empirical studies show that firms in countries with a higher level of financial development are not only more likely to export but also more likely to export in sectors that are more dependent on external finance (Beck 2002; Manova 2013). Moreover, in less developed economies, firms in sectors with more external financial dependence tend to export more as the share of foreign banks in the economy increases, and particularly when foreign banks are headquartered in the importing country (Claessens, Hassib, and van Horen 2014). This finding suggests that foreign banks may have an edge in supplying specific financing needs to exporting firms. This edge may be a result of the more advanced lending technologies that foreign banks tend to use or of the ability of foreign banks to diversify risks (because of their scale and global nature), which may allow them to specialize in specific trade-related products such as letters of credit. This finding also indicates that foreign banks can facilitate trade through an information channel (see box 3.2 in chapter 3). Foreign banks, particularly if they are headquartered in the importing country, may be better able than domestic banks to anticipate trade risks from both importers and exporters. This could allow them to better overcome information asymmetries and contracting problems.

Studies have also found that a foreign bank presence enables and fosters FDI in a host economy. In developing countries, FDI may be limited by the lack of information about the local market, or by the absence of bank financial expertise. Foreign banks, with expertise in global transactions and plausibly more sophisticated lending technologies than local banks, can help overcome these barriers and thus enable FDI in a host economy. Recent studies have shed light on the role of foreign banks in promoting FDI. Ongena, Qi, and Qin (2014) collected data on FDI and the presence of foreign banks by source economy for 12 regions in China over a period of 14 years, and they found that the level of FDI in a region indeed increases as the network of foreign banks expands. Using the instrumental variables approach, they show that their results are robust to instrumenting for the presence of foreign banks with the timing of the regional phasing out of the local limits for foreign banks on local currency business.[19] Foreign banks may also facilitate investment by firms from their home economy in which they operate. Poelhekke (2015) finds evidence supporting this view. Using data on FDI and exploiting the large differences in the deregulation of banking sectors across economies and time, Poelhekke shows that the entry of foreign banks in a host economy was followed by an expansion in nonfinancial FDI from firms in the same home economy.

Foreign banks may also have a direct effect on firm innovation. Bircan and De Haas (2015) find that Russian firms that receive credit from foreign banks are more innovative. Innovation is not only higher in localities with a greater number of foreign banks, but also conditional on borrowing; firms that borrow from a foreign bank innovate more than firms that borrow from domestic banks.[20]

Although the presence of foreign banks may have long-term effects on the economy of their host country, studies have found mixed results. Many studies have analyzed the indirect links between foreign banking and long-term growth, but very little attention has been devoted to the direct links between banking openness and economic growth. Early studies that investigated the relationship between foreign bank presence and growth at the macro level were inconclusive. Demirgüç-Kunt, Levine, and Min (1998) regressed real GDP per capita growth on foreign assets (or foreign bank presence) while controlling for other factors associated with growth, and they found no significant direct effects. Later studies tried to address the endogeneity issues present in these studies by refining the estimation techniques. Employing dynamic panel estimators on a sample of 28 countries between 1994 and 2003, Bayraktar and Wang (2008) reveal that the asset share of foreign banks has a significant positive effect on GDP per capita growth. Other studies have analyzed the causal impact of the liberalization of intrastate branching in the United States by exploiting the differentiated responses across states and time. For example, Beck, Levine, and Levkov (2010) look at the consequences for the distribution of income and find boosted incomes for the lower part of the distribution, whereas Huang (2008) studies economic growth, finding limited evidence of higher growth. Using an international panel, Bremus and Buch (2014) analyze whether financial openness may affect economic growth through "granularity" in the banking sector—that is, the propensity of idiosyncratic shocks affecting large banks to affect in turn the aggregate economy.[21] The results suggest that financial openness is negatively associated with economic growth (but this is mostly driven by countries with low financial depth), and they find evidence that granular effects exist and are stronger in financially closed economies.

CROSS-BORDER APPROACHES TO REGULATION, SUPERVISION, AND RESOLUTION

Authorities face a complex challenge when it comes to regulating, supervising, and, especially, resolving a global bank. One key difficulty is that national sovereign countries operate within globalized and international markets (Goodhart 2013). In these interconnected markets, bank failures in one country may result in substantial externalities in other countries. For example, when a bank with a high share of foreign deposits fails, depositors abroad may be at risk. However, such costs may not be considered by domestic supervisors, leading to inefficient decisions (Beck, Todorov, and Wagner 2013).[22] This is where the value of international regulation lies. To avoid these distortions and externalities, the regulation, supervision, and resolution of global banks should occur at a supranational level.

However, there is a basic trade-off when selecting the optimal international financial architecture. As Beck, Silva-Buston, and Wagner (2015), discuss, if all countries were identical, it would be easy to agree on the right model for international regulation. However, the greater the differences among countries (for example, in their legal and regulatory systems, or in their exposure to costs in bank failure), the higher is the cost of closer cooperation. Therefore, the larger these differences across countries, the less desirable and less effective supranational supervision becomes. Beck, Silva-Buston, and Wagner (2015) argue that as externalities become more important and failure costs are more similar between countries, the more likely it is that supranational supervision is preferred over national supervision. As discussed later in this section, this basic trade-off can serve as a general framework for assessing the effectiveness and suitability of different forms of cross-border integration of bank supervision.

Until now, international supervisory cooperation has been the preferred way to deal with the geographic mismatch between global banks and national supervision. For more than 40 years, supervisors have cooperated not only by harmonizing regulations and supervision standards but also by exchanging information on individual cross-border financial institutions. Exchanging information on financial institutions helps the host country to evaluate the risk profile of a foreign bank based on its activities in the home country, and such information enables it to take the actions needed to deal with potential risks. Exchanging information is also crucial for preventing significant operational risks, such as money laundering and terrorism financing.

The Basel Committee on Banking Supervision has been the primary global standard-setter for bank regulation and supervision. Its mandate is to improve the regulation, supervision, and practices of internationally active banks, and thus seeking to increase global financial stability. Supervisory cooperation, designed by the Basel Committee, is based on an agreed-on division of responsibilities among prudential supervisors. Specifically, supervisors in the home country are responsible for consolidated supervision, and supervisors in the host country are responsible for supervision on an individual or subconsolidated basis for financial institutions operating in their country. Cooperation should take place at all stages of supervision (prevention), early remediation (recovery), and resolution (crisis management). It can take different forms, including supervisory colleges, bilateral cooperation, regulatory harmonization, and more recently established crisis management groups.[23]

Nevertheless, coordination across countries is challenging, and the resolution of global banks is extremely complex. Effective coordination across countries of regulation and supervision as well as intervention in case of financial distress are very difficult to achieve because countries have different policy preferences and incentives.[24] When foreign banks are systemic in host countries but not large in their home country, as in many developing countries, the incentives of foreign authorities to cooperate may be low (Claessens 2016).[25] The reason is simple: even when the risks associated with weak supervision are high, if the costs are largely borne by the host country then regulators in the home country, may have little incentive to act.

The need to improve the current arrangements for cooperation was clear during the global financial crisis, particularly in the resolution phase, when distress, chaos, and improvisation were common. During the crisis, supervisory cooperation broke down, and many banks had to be resolved along national lines. The reasons for these breakdowns are complex, and a large body of literature has analyzed them. One lesson from the financial crisis is that the existing cooperation arrangements seemed appropriate in normal times, but they failed in times of crisis, when rapid, collaborative responses were needed. The international rules of cooperation laid out in memoranda of understanding between authorities were, and remain, nonbinding. These nonbinding approaches clearly did not suffice during bad times, when cooperation was significantly reduced and most cross-border resolutions were poor (Claessens 2016). One example was the resolution of Fortis, the largest Belgian bank with significant operations in the Netherlands and Luxembourg. Regulators from the Netherlands, Luxembourg, and Belgium decided to inject capital into the failing bank, until the Dutch government nationalized its Dutch assets, which led to an uncoordinated resolution along national borders (Wiggins, Tente, and Metrick 2014). The sale of Belgian Fortis to BNP Paribas was challenged in court by its shareholders, postponing finalization of the deal (IMF 2010).

Another important reason for the breakdown in international cooperation was the lack of coordinated resolution mechanisms that could minimize the impact of distressed financial institutions on global financial stability. A core feature of a stable system is that financial institutions must be able to fail in an orderly fashion, which means without excessively disrupting the financial system; without interrupting, when possible, the critical functions that banks provide; and without exposing taxpayers to losses. Because of the absence of specific instruments to resolve systemically important banks in an orderly way, the tools used to resolve cross-border banks were last-minute, ad hoc interventions involving public support.[26] Global banks that failed or ran into trouble during the global financial crisis were largely supported by the governments of host economies. As Beck, Todorov, and Wagner (2013) document, supervisors were more likely to intervene if banks' equity was in the hands of foreigners, and incentives to intervene were lower if the deposits or assets of a bank were held abroad (that is, by nonlocals).

Since the global financial crisis, policy makers have been addressing this lack of enforceable and effective mechanisms for crisis resolution of cross-border banking groups in various ways. Since the crisis, regulation of cross-border flows has become more restrictive, and informal barriers in the form of ring-fencing have increased. A report by the IMF (2015) emphasizes that the destabilizing effects of cross-border lending during shock episodes are best confronted by mutually compatible resolution frameworks that could provide a global safety net, preventing the ad hoc imposition of ex post ring-fencing by prudential supervisors. Regulators and supervisors should also be aware that ex ante ring-fencing measures are likely to affect the operational structures and the roster of foreign banks that operate in a host country.

The greater focus on crisis management and resolution is reflected in the policy response by the Group of 20 and the Financial Stability Board (FSB). Significant progress has been made in strengthening cooperation by establishing crisis management groups, which have been set up for systemically important institutions, and by creating recovery and resolution plans. Another example is "bail-in" mechanisms, which consist of writing off banks' liabilities or converting them to equity, allowing the institution to continue as a going concern while giving the authorities' time to reorganize or wind down parts of the business in an orderly manner without the need for taxpayer support. Claessens (2016) describes specific regulations passed after the global financial crisis and intended to better regulate and supervise international banks. More intense monitoring of large global banks and their risks is now in place, and preventive measures, such as total loss absorbing capacity (TLAC) in case of financial distress, have been implemented. Box 2.11 discusses in detail other initiatives aimed at reducing the cost of future financial crises.

Structural banking reform measures can be used to limit activities that are too risky or whose risks are too complex to measure. Because price-based regulations such as capital requirements or leverage ratios may be inadequate for measuring the risks associated with certain activities, structural reforms have been proposed that move risky, complex businesses into stand-alone subsidiaries or prohibit these activities altogether. An important aim of these measures is to limit contagion from financial markets and thus limit the benefits of public guarantees to core banking services, such as deposits, lending, and payments (Viñals and others 2013). U.S. approaches have favored the outright separation of investment banking and trading activities, whereas European approaches to ring-fencing entail subsidiarizing them.[27] Although structural separation may be warranted for some activities, regulators should also recognize that this may curtail the ability of banks to diversify risks across activities to some extent and, perhaps more importantly, could push risks outside the formally regulated financial sector to shadow banks whose regulation and supervision would need commensurate improvement.

But more importantly, the global financial crisis highlighted the need to improve the cross-border regulation and supervision of global banks, as well as their resolution in case of stress. The existing cross-border resolutions and cross-country cooperation were poor because of the so-called financial trilemma. According to Schoenmaker (2013), a trilemma entails the incompatibility of pursuing financial stability and financial integration while maintaining national resolution authority. Any two of these policy objectives can be combined, but not all three. Thus, taking into account these trade-offs, regulators need to decide on a supervisory cooperation model that maximizes welfare. There is a wide spectrum of supervisory cooperation models, which can be positioned along a continuum of increasing loss of sovereignty.

BOX 2.11   Decentralized Global Banks and Multiple-Point-of-Entry Resolution

One key challenge arising from the recent financial crisis that has not yet been solved is how to deal with global systemically important banks (G-SIBs). The failure of such too-big-to-fail institutions could be devastating for the financial system and the economy as a whole. However, bailing out institutions entails large costs and may give them an incentive to increase their risk taking and grow ever larger (Bolton and Oehmke 2015).

In the aftermath of the global financial crisis, regulators decided to put in place a new bank resolution framework aimed at reducing the cost of future banking crises. This framework requires shareholders and creditors to absorb losses while avoiding the use of taxpayer money (the European Union's Bank Recovery and Resolution Directive is one example of this arrangement). One of the main challenges of this new way of handling crises is the cross-border dimension, in particular for global banks, which would be reflected in the resolution strategy selected by regulators.

The resolution strategy for global banks should be consistent with the way in which they operate. Broadly speaking, global banks tend to follow either a centralized business model or a decentralized one.

Under the decentralized model, global retail banks operate abroad with legally independent subsidiaries with autonomous capital and liquidity management, relying mainly on local currency–denominated deposits. The subsidiaries are supervised by the local authorities and protected by the host country deposit guarantee scheme. The parent provides group strategy guidelines, such as setting the global risk appetite framework, as well as a common culture, governance, and control. Intragroup connections are very limited. Although support from the parent to the subsidiaries is possible, it is exceptional, temporary, and at market prices.

Recent studies—such as those by Kamil and Rai (2010) and Feyen and others (2014)—uncovered the resilience of decentralized banking during the global financial crisis and highlighted its stabilizing role in limiting contagion from connected countries. In the 2011 deleveraging episode, for example, Latin American subsidiaries of European banks suffered relatively little liquidity contraction, in contrast to their counterparts in Europe and Central Asia (ECA), which were more reliant on parent funding (see figure B2.11.1). The vulnerability of the subsidiaries in the ECA region to contagion necessitated the Vienna Ini-

FIGURE B2.11.1   **Liquidity and Cross-Border Funding of European Bank Subsidiaries in Europe and Central Asia and Latin America and the Caribbean Regions**

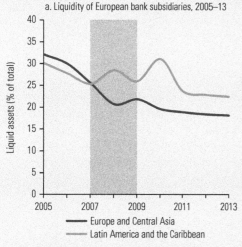

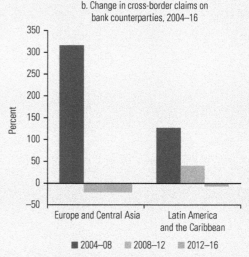

Sources: Staff calculations, based on Bankscope (database).
Note: The gray area in panel a indicates the global financial crisis period.

Sources: Álvarez, García, and Gouveia 2016, based on Bank for International Settlements International Banking Statistics.

(box continued next page)

BOX 2.11   Decentralized Global Banks and Multiple-Point-of-Entry Resolution (continued)

tiative, which was given the goal of improving home-host coordination and safeguarding financial stability in emerging Europe. Cerutti and others (2010) argue, however, that such a decentralized model may also lead to inefficiencies, such as reducing the ability to relocate bank capital internationally and increasing the size of capital buffers at the subsidiary level.

The Financial Stability Board (FSB) has defined two resolution approaches for global banks:

- *Single point of entry* (SPE). Resolution power is exercised at the top level by the supervisory authority of the parent, with losses absorbed within the banking group. To reassure host banking authorities, this strategy normally requires total loss-absorbing capacity (TLAC) to be internally prepositioned by the parent bank.
- *Multiple point of entry* (MPE). Resolution power is distributed to different authorities relevant to the entire banking group, along dimensions of geographic location or business line. Each subsidiary is then resolved by the local authority according to the applicable resolution frameworks.

Using a simple model, Bolton and Oehmke (2015) highlight the trade-offs that arise in cross-border resolutions of global banks, including the political constraints faced by national regulators. Their main results suggest that even though an SPE resolution is in principle more efficient than an MPE solution,

such an arrangement may be incompatible with the interests of national regulators because they would prefer to ring-fence their national financial systems. The authors' analysis shows that the more decentralized the operations of a global bank, the more efficient the MPE resolution is relative to the SPE one.

The MPE resolution strategy is better adapted to decentralized banks funded with local deposits under the legal structure of subsidiaries, with little or no intragroup positions and decentralized capital and liquidity management.[a] Local authorities that already supervise the local subsidiary on a business-as-usual basis would retain this feature when the bank is failing or likely to fail. Local authorities would also be the leaders in any resolution. The home authority would mainly act as a coordinator in case several subsidiaries have to be resolved at the same time, which is very unlikely because of the diversification inherent in this model.

Although there is no unique foreign bank business paradigm, the MPE resolution strategy is more appropriate in the ring-fencing context, where the bail-in paradigm still faces the test of practical implementation. It is important that regulations acknowledge the specificities of the MPE model and do not penalize it by requiring internal TLAC (which complicates the functioning of this model by increasing intragroup positions) or by imposing consolidated requirements over and above those decided by local authorities.

a. See, for example, Faia and Weder di Mauro (2015) for a recent theoretical approach to optimal resolution design.

At one end of the spectrum is the universal approach, with legally binding frameworks, loss of sovereignty, and centralized decision making. An example of this approach is the European banking union (box 2.12). At the other end of the spectrum is a more territorial approach, consisting of a noncooperative solution whereby each unit of a global bank is resolved according to local regulations (Claessens 2016). Although there is no international burden sharing under the latter approach, it would be costlier for global banks to allocate

capital and liquidity globally, potentially hindering the benefits that global banks may bring to the host economy.

An alternative model for supervisory cooperation is a more intermediate approach. In the years before the onset of the global financial crisis, countries were moving toward a more universal approach to supervisory cooperation. Since the crisis, a more territorial view has prevailed. Countries have adopted barriers to limit cross-border finance, such as macroprudential measures

BOX 2.12 The European Banking Union

The European Union's (EU's) banking union was launched in 2012 in response to the deterioration of credit conditions during the European debt crisis. Under this arrangement, the responsibility for banking policy passes from the national level to the euro area level. As of 2016, the union had two main pillars, the Single Supervisory Mechanism (SSM) and the Single Resolution Mechanism (SRM). A third pillar, European Deposit Insurance, is currently under development.

The Single Supervisory Mechanism is part of the European Central Bank (ECB). Its main goals are ensuring the safety and soundness of the European banking system, increasing financial integration and stability in Europe, and conducting consistent supervision across participant banks. It directly supervises some 130 significant banks, which account for about 85 percent of the total banking assets in the euro area, and it is empowered to intervene directly in less significant institutions. The SSM licenses all banks in the euro area. It works with national authorities, and it currently is limited to the euro area. The SSM relies on local supervisors to collect information and perform on-site inspections.

The Single Resolution Mechanism was put in place to ensure that the resolution of credit institutions facing financial difficulties is carried out efficiently, thereby reducing its costs to the real economy. In the resolution of a systemically important institution, the costs of failure should not be borne by taxpayers. Instead, the EU's banking union will set up a Single Resolution Fund (SRF) that has no national elements either in the calculation of its fund-ing or in the use of the fund itself. The fund will be built up over a 10-year period by contributions reaching the target funding level of at least 1 percent of covered deposits. During an eight-year transition period, national contributions are still earmarked and held in national compartments, after which the SRF will be set up as a truly European fund. Even though the fund will be small, it can help to meet the unavoidable costs of resolution, and the main capital deficiency can be borne by the total loss-absorbing capacity (TLAC) liabilities.

In November 2015, the European Commission adopted a legislative proposal for a European Deposit Insurance Scheme (EDIS), which will be fully operational by 2024. EDIS would create a centralized euro area–wide deposit insurance scheme that would comprise national deposit guarantee schemes plus a European deposit insurance fund built over eight years. The existing national deposit guarantee funds would remain in place as part of EDIS, which would be built up by coinsuring national deposit guarantee schemes and pooling the available funds for payouts over time without requiring an overall increase in bank contributions. EDIS would be developed in three stages: (1) a reinsurance scheme for the first three years, providing liquidity assistance and limited loss absorbance of the national schemes; (2) a coinsurance scheme for four years, until 2024, under which EDIS would absorb a progressively larger share of losses of the national schemes; and (3) a final stage, in which EDIS would fully insure deposits and cover all liquidity needs and losses in the event of a payout or resolution procedure and protect deposits below €100,000.[a]

a. At the time this chapter was drafted, political resistance to EDIS was continuing, and implementation had not yet been scheduled.

and countercyclical buffers. However, the intended impact of these measures is difficult to achieve without coordination with authorities in the countries in which foreign banks are headquartered.[28] Nevertheless, an intermediate model of cooperation, in which some elements of the universal approach are adopted (such as resolution procedures), may be the preferred model for many countries. Looser, often bilateral and nonbinding cooperation models, such as the Association of Southeast Asian Nations (ASEAN) or the West African Economic and Monetary Union (WAEMU), are examples of the intermediate approaches discussed in boxes 2.13 and 2.14. As Claessens (2016) suggests, the intermediate approach could aim to have a "concordat," an international agreement with a framework

BOX 2.13   Intermediate Cooperation Approaches: The ASEAN and Australia–New Zealand Cases

A recent, looser form of cooperation is the ASEAN Economic Community, which was established at the end of 2015. The 10 member states of the Association of Southeast Asian Nations (ASEAN) entered the ASEAN Banking Integration Framework in March 2015.[a] Member states may enter bilateral agreements that allow qualified ASEAN banks to operate in partner countries on the same terms as domestic banks. The criteria and reciprocal terms for bank access are negotiated bilaterally. This agreement is part of ASEAN's efforts to create a single economic market. It grants ASEAN banks greater market access than non-ASEAN banks, but it remains based on a network of bilateral agreements. The ASEAN Banking Integration Framework is fundamentally different from the European Union's "single passport regime." Their main similarity is that they both seek to make market access for banks less burdensome.[b]

Another example of legally binding cooperation is the supervisory cooperation between Australia and New Zealand. The largest Australian banks dominate the financial system of New Zealand.[c] As a result, both countries have a very close home–host relationship. The cooperation and information sharing between the Australian Prudential Regulation Authority (APRA) and the Reserve Bank of New Zealand (RBNZ) are extensive. This cooperation has been further reinforced by a 2006 amendment to the RBNZ Act that legally obliges the RBNZ to cooperate and consult with the financial supervisory authorities in Australia to try to avoid actions that may negatively affect financial stability in Australia. The Australian Banking Act contains similar provisions.

a. ASEAN is a political and economic organization comprising Brunei, Cambodia, Indonesia, Lao People's Democratic Republic, Malaysia, Myanmar, the Philippines, Singapore, Thailand, and Vietnam.
b. The European passport principle allows a bank that is licensed in one EU member state to open branches in other member states by simply notifying the host country before opening the branch. The relevant host authorities do not have the right to refuse the establishment of the branch if it has been authorized by the home country and cannot force the branch to take another legal form.
c. Australia's big four banks—the ANZ, Commonwealth Bank, National Australia Bank, and Westpac—control almost 90 percent of the assets of New Zealand's banking system.

similar to that of the Basel Committee on Banking Supervision but focused on crisis management and, importantly, with explicit incentives for collaboration, credible resolution processes, and clarity on cost sharing in a resolution.

Nevertheless, obstacles to cross-border resolution, particularly among developing countries, continue to exist. For cross-border cooperation agreements to work, both host and home authorities need to cooperate fully and commit to legislative action as necessary to empower resolutions. As noted by the Financial Stability Board (FSB 2013), emerging and developing countries may not have adequate supervisory expertise, capacity, or resources to respond to postcrisis global regulatory incentives. Moreover, many developing

countries and emerging markets do not have much representation in the relevant bodies and forums, which creates problems for them in the design and implementation of regulation and supervision arrangements (FSB 2011). These obstacles are particularly important because of the growing trends in regionalization and South–South banking.

In the years to come, South–South entry and more regionalization of foreign banks will substantially shape cross-border supervisory and regulatory arrangements. As South–South banking and bank regionalization continue to develop, the benefits and risks of international banks may also change, with important consequences for their regulation and supervision. The new generation of foreign banks from other developing countries,

BOX 2.14   Intermediate Cooperation Approaches: The WAEMU Case

Cross-border banking has been increasing in Africa. As of 2014, there were 104 active cross-border banks with at least one branch or subsidiary outside their home countries.[a] The recent growth of pan-African banks has transferred the risks and benefits of cross-border banking from European to African policy makers. Regional integration of African banks brings many benefits but also a cost of contagion, hence the need for increased supervisory cooperation. That is, potential instabilities arising from pan-African banks will need to be handled collaboratively rather than by individual supervisors.

The West African Monetary Union Banking Commission, founded in 1990, is overseen by the governor of the Central Bank of West African States (BCEAO). As a further step for supervisory cooperation, the treaty for the West African Economic and Monetary Union (WAEMU, also known by its French acronym, UEMOA) was signed in 1994. The member states are Benin, Burkina Faso, Côte d'Ivoire, Guinea-Bissau, Mali, Niger, Senegal, and Togo. The focus of the WAEMU and its Banking Commission has been the banking sector, but this is evolving rapidly with the emergence of transnational banking groups and microcredit institutions. As of 2015, the WAEMU banking sector included 127 credit institutions, including 114 commercial banks and 13 other quasi-bank financial institutions.[b] This amounts to more than 90 percent of all financial assets in the region and more than half of regional GDP. The WAEMU aims to maintain a common legal and regulatory framework for the regional banking system. Considering the political and regional characteristics of these countries, addressing these issues requires different approaches than in developed countries. More specifically, the political and institutional characteristics of these countries are more heterogeneous than in European countries. In addition, financial deepening and access, supervisory capacity, and financial infrastructure are different in Africa than in developed economies. As a

result, the standards set by the Basel Committee may not be appropriate for African banking cooperation. As noted by the Financial Stability Board (2013), these countries may not have adequate supervisory expertise or resources to respond to postcrisis global regulatory incentives. When compared to the level of cooperation in the European or Australia–New Zealand examples, WAEMU is at its early steps. Beck, Fuchs, and others (2014) discuss that information exchange is still very weak in Africa, and it would be a first step to create a basic data set, and hence facilitate better supervisory cooperation.

Member countries of the WAEMU are affected by frequent and often idiosyncratic shocks, such as natural disasters or political instabilities. The macroeconomic volatility makes the domestic financial sector more unstable. Hence, policies must be based on bilateral or subregional agreements rather than being unique across all countries in the region. In the case of West Africa, an increasing level of financial integration coexists with these heterogeneities across countries. More specifically, financial systems have developed differently in the countries with Anglophone and Francophone cultures. This may suggest a more detailed framework within subregions. Another aspect of the heterogeneity is the ownership structure of banks in African countries. African countries that are mostly dominated by European banks, for instance Mozambique, may need considerations within the subregions. Security risks may also yield delays in reforms, which creates another problem for the harmonization goals of WAEMU. Another concern is that less developed business conditions, asymmetric information, and weak judicial environments impose difficulties for an effective union in the region. Finally, despite the centralized structure of WEAMU, supervisory decisions made by the WAEMU Banking Commission are mostly subject to the approval of national agencies. This aspect of the African case differs from the EU's banking union model.

---

a. Some of these influential banks of African origin that operate in many African countries outside their home country are Ecobank, United Bank for Africa, Standard Bank Group, Banque Marocaine du Commerce Extérieur, Banque Sahélo-Saharienne pour l'Investissement et le Commerce, and Attijariwafe Bank.
b. European Investment Bank, "Recent Trends in Banking in Sub-Saharan Africa: From Financing to Investment," July 2015.

with more proximity to host countries in terms of culture, economic conditions, and even physical distance, may facilitate communication and coordination between host and home country authorities. The rise of foreign banks from developing countries also implies that the developing countries that host them need to be more engaged with the international financial agenda and need to better monitor the activities of their foreign banks. Regulators should also be cautious about the regionalization of foreign banks because this trend could lead to financial repression, ring-fencing, and fragmentation, which could in turn adversely affect the financial stability of the host economy (Claessens 2016).

Regulators must also pay close attention to fintech and the way it is revolutionizing the banking sector. Fintech may bring new challenges to the already-complex supervision and regulation of foreign banks. Regulators need to keep pace with the rapid speed with which nonbank providers enter the market and digital services are rolled out and the potential risks that these changes may entail.

CONCLUSIONS AND POLICY IMPLICATIONS

The brick-and-mortar operations of international banks can have important benefits for the higher financial development of a host economy. The entry of foreign banks into a host economy can increase competition in the banking sector, the performance of local banks, and overall access to credit. Foreign banks also can provide the host country with a risk-sharing scheme, but, as in all risk-sharing schemes, it is not a one-way relationship; the two sides (parent banks and foreign affiliates, or home countries and host countries) must support each other during difficult times. The experience of international banks over the last few decades offers valuable policy lessons for reaping the benefits of international banking while keeping the costs at a minimum for both sides.

Studying the drivers of bank internationalization and its consequences reveals good and bad ways of attracting international banks. Opening host economies to foreign nonfinancial firms and providing foreign firms with profit opportunities will attract foreign banks looking for profits and diversification. Host countries should, however, avoid offering foreign banks these profit opportunities via weak regulation and supervision because this approach will tempt parent banks to incur excessive risk in host economies, such as through regulatory arbitrage. Thus, for host economies, the best way to avoid being exploited as a risk-taking haven is to adopt a strong financial regulatory and supervisory framework and ensure that foreign subsidiaries are self-sufficient (with high capitalization requirements and a high share of funding through retail deposits). Because foreign branches are mostly under home country regulation, host country authorities should prefer subsidiaries as the mode of entry for international banks. Moreover, a mix of greenfield and foreign bank subsidiary takeover investment should be welcomed. Because they are better integrated with the parent bank, greenfields may help more during local downturns, whereas investment through acquisitions may yield greater benefits in response to home country or global shocks. Finally, some diversification of foreign banks' business models may shield host economies from the negative outcomes associated with a specific type of activity (for example, a negative shock to fee-based, noninterest, income-generating activities).

Strong regulation and supervision are not possible in a weak institutional environment. Financial liberalization should be accompanied by institutional reforms that prevent foreign banks from crowding out incumbents without increasing the competitiveness and efficiency of the banking sector in the host economy. Financial liberalization should also be introduced gradually to allow domestic banks to adapt and better compete with new foreign banks. During home country or global downturns, foreign banks will be less likely to retrench from host countries that have solid institutional environments and competitive banking systems. Moreover, host economies with a good information environment and effective contract enforcement are likely to reap more benefits from foreign banks, as improved information sharing—through, for example, credit registries—can help foreign banks to lower average lending interest rates and increase average loan quality.[29]

When possible, such as in a privatization process, host country authorities should consider choosing among foreign parent banks as prospective owners. They could try to diversify the roster of home countries and ensure that the prospective parent banks are also diversified and not overly dependent on wholesale funding so they can provide liquidity and other support to their subsidiaries even during bad times at home. Host countries can try to pick parent banks from home countries with effective banking regulations and some proximity to the host country (culturally, institutionally, or in physical distance) to increase the stability of the foreign bank subsidiary or branch. Host country authorities may also diversify across other characteristics of foreign banks, such as their business models. This strategic diversification may be planned at the level of financial sector strategies, rather than at the more ad hoc stage of the licensing process. Finally, a core position in the banking group—in terms of relative size or profitability—lowers the chances that a foreign bank will run for the exit in response to a shock. Any efforts to shape the roster of foreign banks must be consistent with a country's obligations under multilateral and preferential service trade agreements. A country that pursues this approach would likely need to identify a set of objective criteria for evaluating prospective entrants to ensure that provisions in trade agreements precluding discrimination against other countries are not violated.

The regulatory and supervisory failures during the recent global financial crisis led to an intensive effort to redesign the regulatory landscape. Two extreme approaches influencing the ongoing policy discussions entail territoriality—ring-fencing of activities under a particular authority's domain, which inhibits

an open financial system—and universalism—the equitable distribution of bankruptcy costs involving cross-border burden sharing. The European SRM is a prospective example of the latter approach (Claessens 2016). Although these two approaches may be too extreme for many countries, an intermediate model of cooperation that includes some elements of the universal approach may be feasible. Ideally, this intermediate model would adopt an international agreement on crisis management that explicitly outlines responsibilities and processes to follow in a resolution.

Ring-fencing is how some local regulators seek to limit the potentially negative consequences of having foreign banks. Host authorities request local liquidity and capital to minimize the impact of external shocks. In terms of advantages, this approach provides better incentives for local supervision and no burden-sharing requirements. Ring-fencing, however, is less efficient for financial institutions because it reduces the benefits of cross-border banking in the first place, potentially imposing costs in times of stress through possible runs and liquidity problems. This approach also undermines any cross-border regulation and supervision incentives, thereby hurting the general openness of financial systems.

NOTES

1. See Čihák, Mare, and Melecky (2016) on the trade-offs between the pursuit of deeper financial inclusion and financial stability.
2. Even though most emerging economies and developing countries have strengthened their banking supervision and regulation, they still face various challenges, such as supervisory capacity constraints or incomplete legal frameworks (Financial Stability Board 2011).
3. See, for example, Goldberg and Johnson (1990) for the U.S. case and Focarelli and Pozzolo (2000) for an international analysis. Also see Cull and Martínez Pería (2010) for a literature review on foreign bank participation in developing countries.
4. Another example is from Dell'Ariccia and Marquez (2006a), who develop a race-to-the-bottom model in which they show that com-

petition among regulators reduces regulatory standards, creating competition in laxity in order to promote their domestic banks.

5. See Mian (2006), who relates various distance measures to information, agency, or enforcement costs in a developing country environment.

6. As highlighted by Claessens (2016), foreign banks are likely to select host countries that have income levels and institutional development similar to or lower than that in their home countries.

7. An extensive number of studies in developing countries, at both the regional and country levels, find evidence that foreign banks are more efficient than domestic banks (see, for example, Bonaccorsi di Patti and Hardy 2005; Detragiache and Gupta 2006; Havrylchyk and Jurzyk 2011; Isik and Hassan 2002; Matoušek and Taci 2004; Weill 2003). However, other studies find a more ambiguous pattern. For example, in countries with a limited foreign bank presence, such as India and China, differences in efficiency between domestic and foreign banks are not very large (Berger, Hasan, and Zhou 2009; Bhattacharya, Lovell, and Sahay 1997; Sensarma 2006; Wu, Chen, and Lin 2007). In other studies from Latin America, the findings differ, depending on the efficiency measure used (Barajas, Steiner, and Salazar 2000; Berger and others 2005; Crystal, Dages, and Goldberg 2001; Goldberg, Dages, and Kinney 2000).

8. Morgan, Rime, and Strahan (2004) illustrate this ambiguous relationship with a simple model in which they compare the impact of collateral and bank capital shocks under a regime in which banks can allocate their capital freely across states versus a regime with restricted interstate bank capital flows. Although these shocks are contractionary in both environments, their magnitudes vary. If banks are allowed to move their capital freely, bank capital shocks in the host economy may be less intense because international banks can import capital from abroad. However, international banks may help amplify collateral shocks in the host economy because they can lend away their capital.

9. A substantive share of the entry episodes of foreign banks in emerging markets and developing countries occurred after a financial cri-

sis (and were not just as the result of removal of entry barriers).

10. Evidence on the transmission of international monetary policy via foreign banks in a particular country such as Mexico is discussed in box 2.8.

11. See, for example, De Haas and van Lelyveld (2006), who confirm the procyclicality of foreign banks for Eastern Europe.

12. Other empirical studies analyzing the lending of foreign banks during the global financial crisis are those by Choi, Gutierrez, and Martínez Pería (2014); Claessens and van Horen 2015; De Haas and van Lelyveld (2014); De Haas and others (2015); and Mihaljek (2011).

13. Using individual-level data across 123 different countries, Allen and others (2012) analyze the association between financial inclusion measures and different individual and country characteristics, and they find that the share of foreign banks is not significantly correlated with financial inclusion. This finding, however, may mask the fact that the impact of foreign banks in a host economy is not homogeneous across countries and largely depends on the institutional context of the host economy.

14. Also see Detragiache, Tressel, and Gupta (2008) for a focus on poor countries showing similar results.

15. Although a foreign bank presence is negatively associated with credit access in low-income countries, it is not necessarily true that a foreign bank presence causes reductions in lending. As Cull and Martínez Pería (2010) show, the context surrounding the entry of foreign banks is likely to affect the relationship between their presence and credit levels. In this way, the negative relationship between foreign bank presence and credit levels could be driven by the nonrandom entry of foreign banks into banking markets that were in crisis or had experienced large drops in credit levels prior to their entry.

16. This pattern has been found especially in developing countries, where foreign banks overwhelmingly lend to the safest, largest already-banked customers such as large firms, corporations, and public firms (Beck and Brown 2013; Beck and Martínez Pería 2010; Berger, Klapper, and Udell 2001; Berger and

others 2008; Bonin and Wachtel 2003; Gormley 2005; Mian 2003, 2006).

17. Gennaioli, Martin, and Rossi (2014) provide a theoretical model and empirical evidence on how public defaults relate to the financial system and on how this relationship has a disciplinary effect on governments in countries with good market institutions.

18. Similar trends are observed when comparing the returns on equity of both types of foreign banks.

19. Although the phasing out of limits strongly encouraged foreign bank participation, it was driven by compliance with the original WTO commitments.

20. The conclusions of this study are robust to a series of tests that rule out that firms that borrow from local banks are statistically different from firms that borrow from foreign banks.

21. Both the de jure and de facto dimensions of financial openness are examined. The de jure dimensions are measured using Chinn and Ito (2006, 2008), and Schindler (2009). The de facto dimensions are (1) the sum of total foreign assets and total foreign liabilities relative to GDP, (2) the sum of cross-border bank loans relative to GDP, and (3) FDI in banking.

22. Evidence from Beck, Todorov, and Wagner (2013) shows that during the global financial crisis, the incentives of supervisors to resolve failing banks were distorted by the type of cross-border activities of these banks.

23. Supervisory colleges are composed of the supervisors of both the home and host countries of a foreign bank. Crisis management groups are integrated by the various home and host authorities of all global and large systemic banks (such as central banks and supervisory authorities) with the objective of increasing the ability to act quickly and effectively in a crisis situation.

24 According to the Financial Stability Board (FSB 2015), it is important that host supervisors not represented in coordination groups for different reasons (for example, because they supervise a part of the banking group that is not considered material to the global bank) still have access to relevant information about the bank using bilateral contacts.

25. Consider, for example, two Portuguese banks operating in Mozambique that were authorized to merge by Banco de Portugal in 2000. Although this merger did not represent a dramatic change in the financial sector of Portugal, it significantly affected the banking sector of Mozambique, where a new foreign banking entity with substantial market power was created. After the merger, almost 50 percent of banking assets in Mozambique were owned by this new institution.

26. One example is Landsbanki, an Icelandic bank that collected deposits from Dutch and British households through its online branch, Icesave. When the bank went bankrupt during the global financial crisis, Icelandic deposit insurance should have applied to the Icelandic, Dutch, and British depositors of Icesave. The Icelandic authorities, however, decided to honor the insurance for only domestic depositors, a decision that was later approved by a European court (*The Economist* 2013b). The British government then used an antiterrorism law to freeze the assets of the failed bank. Eventually, the losses of foreign depositors were covered by the British (fully) and Dutch governments (up to €100,000)—see Zeissler, Piontek, and Metrick (2015).

27. For example, in the United States the Volcker rule mandates the separation of proprietary trading, hedge fund investments, and private equity fund investments because they "generate a risk culture that is fundamentally at odds with banks' client-facing activities, particularly deposits, lending, and wholesale banking" (Viñals and others 2013).

28. Claessens (2016) discusses the various types of externalities and negative spillovers that these measures could create when coordination across countries is not in place.

29. See Claeys and Hainz (2006) for a theoretical discussion.

CHAPTER 3: KEY MESSAGES

- Banks have globalized in part through their cross-border lending activity, which doubled from 2001 to 2014 and has become a substantial part of international capital transactions. The stock of cross-border bank claims around the world in 2012 was larger than that of cross-border portfolio holdings and foreign direct investment.

- Whereas Japan, the United States, and Western Europe have historically accounted for most cross-border banking activity, economies in the "South" (mainly developing countries) have been gaining ground since the early 1990s. The South, as a source and destination of cross-border bank funds, increased from representing 28 percent of the world's cross-border bank claims in 2001 to 33 percent in 2014, and from 21 percent of syndicated loans in 2001 to 31 percent in 2014.

- The growing participation of the South in global financial transactions has allowed these economies to not only diversify their investments but also obtain financing from abroad, complementing domestic markets and widening their available funding choices.

- As part of the risk-sharing arrangement, cross-border banking also tends to act as a transmission mechanism for external shocks. This tendency was observed during the global financial crisis, when cross-border bank flows collapsed after having risen during the early 2000s.

- Because the largest global banks were mostly located in high-income countries hit by the global financial crisis, the shock to their balance sheets affected both their domestic and cross-border activities, spilling over to developing countries.

- Firms reacted to the decline in the supply of cross-border banking activity during the global financial crisis by switching to different sources of financing. In high-income and developing countries, firms moved toward bond markets. In developing countries, firms also switched to domestic banks. Because of these switches, global financial activity during the crisis declined to less than the collapse in cross-border loans. The change in debt composition then continued during the postcrisis period. The substitution and compositional effects were also observed at the aggregate level. Whereas before the global financial crisis, North–South lending grew faster than South–South lending, this situation reversed after the crisis.

- The postcrisis period has also been characterized by the emergence of a broad set of technology-driven nonfinancial companies acting in parallel with traditional banking services. These so-called fintech companies have been adding solutions to different segments of the banking value chain, such as payments, cross-border transfers, and savings vehicles. Although the new players are ramping up competition and pushing digital transformation in the global financial sector, to date the level of disruption has seemed low, and their services appear highly complementary to the ones provided by the more established banking sector.

3

Cross-Border Lending by International Banks

Cross-border bank credit has expanded rapidly in recent decades, and has become an important part of global banks' business activities. Cross-border bank claims worldwide doubled during the period 2001–14. An important part of this growth was transactions involving developing nations as a source and destination of funds. For example, cross-border bank claims to developing economies expanded by a factor of three during the same period. The rise in cross-border bank credit to and from economies in the South occurred in parallel with the rapid growth of other financial transactions, deepening developing countries' integration into global financial markets.

This expansion has not been monotonic; cross-border lending has been characterized by boom-and-bust patterns. Of special importance, because of its scope and length, was the across-the-board retrenchment observed during the global financial crisis. Although cross-border lending to developing economies primarily originated with global banks located in high-income countries, the period since the crisis has been characterized by increased South–South lending. Moreover, as bank credit to and from high-income countries has declined, the postcrisis years have been characterized by greater use of alternative sources of finance, such as bond markets

and domestic loans, and also by the emergence of new digitally enabled businesses providing financial services outside the traditional banking sector. These developments have allowed firms to diversify their funding sources, but they also have exposed them to new types of risks. This chapter studies these developments, which have shaped the global financial landscape in recent decades.

THE PROS AND CONS OF CROSS-BORDER LENDING

Cross-border credit can provide both lenders and borrowers with important benefits. Through cross-border banking, savings can be channeled toward countries with more productive investment opportunities, so that capital is allocated more efficiently globally. It also allows global banks to achieve better international risk diversification and to hedge against country-specific risks (De Haas and van Lelyveld 2010; Goldberg 2009). From the borrowers' perspective, global banks can ease financial constraints in host economies by providing access to alternative sources of external financing and compensating for the volatility of domestic credit (Allen and others 2011). In turn, the presence of foreign capital may pressure policy makers in host countries to adopt good policies and better governance practices so they can attract foreign lending and to maintain those policies to avoid capital flight (Gourinchas and Jeanne 2009). Foreign capital also intensifies competition among the different providers of financing, thereby creating a threat of "flight to quality" that can improve the efficiency of the domestic banking system (Agenor 2003).

And yet, cross-border banking can also pose threats to financial stability through financial spillovers or contagion. An inevitable consequence of international risk diversification is that global banks could cut foreign lending to accommodate adverse balance sheet conditions at home, among other reasons (Peek and Rosengren 2000). This is just part of the bargain; an economy open to international transactions benefits from more lending when times are good in the source economy, and it receives less when times are bad. For example, some banks in Western Europe cut back credit to their Eastern European subsidiaries during the global financial crisis (Popov and Udell 2012). Global banks' balance sheets were severely affected by the crisis, and they reacted by pulling back from their international investments. Countries that relied heavily on foreign lending during the precrisis years were hit harder (Milesi-Ferretti and Tille 2011). Schnabl (2012) reveals how the 1998 Russian default crisis was transmitted to Peruvian banks by reduced cross-border lending to that country from global banks. According to Feyen and others (2014), credit growth in many countries is highly sensitive to cross-border banking shocks. Cross-border bank flows are also more volatile than other types of cross-border flows (Levchenko and Mauro 2007) and local lending by foreign affiliates (Buch and Goldberg 2014; De Haas and van Lelyveld 2004; García-Herrero and Martínez Pería 2007; McCauley, McGuire, and von Peter 2010; Peek and Rosengren 2000; Schnabl 2012).

Country-specific *pull factors*—such as macroeconomic conditions, sound institutions, and the nature of the regulatory framework—are important drivers of cross-border

banking. Capital flows are highly heterogeneous across countries and regions, reflecting the relevance of a country's idiosyncratic, or pull, factors as drivers of capital flows. For example, the literature has found macroeconomic conditions in the recipient countries to be important pull factors of cross-border flows (Buch, Carstensen, and Schertler 2009; Jeanneau and Micu 2002; Müller and Uhde 2013). Sound institutions are another important driver. Using a large panel of financial flow data from banks, Papaioannou (2009) finds that the protection of property rights, legal efficiency, and expropriation risk are important determinants of bank capital flows. Siregar and Choy (2010) find that political instability and weaknesses in the legal, judicial, and bureaucratic systems help to explain the continued stagnation in lending after the Asian financial crisis. Conversely, Kalemli-Ozcan, Papaioannou, and Peydró (2010) show that in the European Union, the convergence in the legislative and regulatory frameworks with the adoption of the euro has spurred cross-border financial transactions. The literature also finds evidence of regulatory arbitrage. Cross-border bank flows are positively correlated with regulatory restrictions in the source country and negatively correlated with restrictions in the recipient country (Aiyar, Calomiris, and Wieladek 2014; Houston, Lin, and Ma 2012). Moreover, gravity models applied to international finance suggest that the geographical and cultural distances between countries are also important factors explaining the volume of bank flows (Brüggemann, Kleinert, and Prieto 2011; Buch, Carstensen, and Schertler 2009; Heuchemer, Kleimeier, and Sander 2009).

As financial globalization has increased, push factors have also become key drivers of capital flows. *Push factors* refer to conditions outside the recipient economy. These conditions can originate in one particular economy or in several economies (involving a whole region or group of economies). Decades ago, Calvo, Leiderman, and Reinhart (1993, 1996) pointed to global external factors as opposed to country-specific pull factors as the driving forces behind cross-border flows. As the world has become more financially integrated, these global factors have gained importance over time, and cross-border flows have become more dependent on global financial and monetary policy circumstances, generally linked to conditions in core financial centers (Bruno and Shin 2015a, 2015b). The term *global liquidity,* defined as ease of funding for global banks, has been used to determine how much global banks are willing to lend abroad (Cetorelli and Goldberg 2011; Herrmann and Mihaljek 2013; IMF 2014; Landau 2013; Rey 2015). Empirical studies have commonly proxied global liquidity by bank leverage and health conditions (Avdjiev, Kuti, and Takats 2012; Bruno and Shin 2015a; Chui and others 2010; Düwel, Frey, and Lipponer 2011; Hoggarth, Mahadeva, and Martin 2010; McGuire and Tarashev 2008). Although most studies typically focus on funding conditions in the United States, Cerutti, Claessens, and Ratnovski (2016) find that cross-border bank flows are also driven by conditions in other financial centers, in particular the euro area and the United Kingdom.

As the role of push factors has intensified over time, countries have become more vulnerable to foreign shocks, as witnessed during the global financial crisis. In fact, global factors were the main reasons behind the decline in cross-border flows during the crisis, as opposed to financial and economic conditions in recipient countries (Fratzscher 2012). In particular, the shock to some U.S. banking institutions in 2008 was rapidly transmitted to the balance sheets of other global financial institutions, which reacted by deleveraging and retreating from their international activities. During the postcrisis years, global banks continued to shrink from risk and reduce cross-border activities as regulators imposed new rules, such as Basel III, involving tighter capital and liquidity requirements (the liquidity coverage ratio, LCR, and the net stable funding ratio, NSFR), macroprudential policies, and stricter stress tests, among others (Claessens 2016). The realization that cross-border bank operations were an important channel

of contagion during the global financial crisis and the sovereign debt crisis in Europe also prompted some regulators around the world to attempt to ring-fence their banking systems (Cerutti and Schmieder 2014; D'Hulster 2014; IMF 2015c).

The rest of this chapter focuses on three important developments that are shaping the present and future of cross-border banking and global banking more generally: the rise of the South, the substitution across markets, and the emergence of fintech. It begins by describing the process of integrating the South economies into global financial markets, with particular emphasis on their participation in cross-border bank flows. It then uses the example of the global financial crisis to illustrate how such a shock can be transmitted across borders and produce changes in the sources of finance at the global level, highlighting some of the problems that arise when countries become financially integrated. And it concludes by documenting how global banks are facing growing competition from new technology companies that are providing alternative types of financial services and pushing transformation in the financial system as a whole.

THE RISE OF THE SOUTH

Several papers and reports have discussed the growing role of the South in the global banking system.[1] Typically, studies have looked at two different types of information: (1) the asset and liability banking positions across economies compiled by the Bank for International Settlements (BIS) and (2) the cross-border flows of syndicated loans provided by private companies. For bank claims, this chapter relies on BIS Locational Banking Statistics data used by Broner and others (2017). These data capture all reported gross cross-border positions between any two economies transacted via the global banking system.[2] The syndicated loan flows data from Thomson Reuters's Securities Data Corporation (SDC) Platinum database consist of direct cross-border lending through which a group of financial intermediaries provides funds to a single borrower. Recent studies estimate that, on average, syndicated loan exposures represented up to a third of the total cross-border loan claims from 1995 to 2012 (Cerutti, Hale, and Minoiu 2015). However, these different data sets are not directly comparable in terms of volume. Bank claims are stocks at a given point in time, whereas syndicated loans data reflect flows based on transaction-level information.[3] To offer a more complete picture of the role of the South in the global financial system, this section provides evidence and discusses studies that use both types of data, which reveal two different but complementary perspectives.

Since the 1990s, many developing economies have undertaken significant efforts to liberalize and expand the scope and depth of their financial systems. A wide range of indicators shows better performance in *de jure* measures of financial openness and

integration for the average developing economy over time (figure 3.1). In addition to the unilateral reduction of formal restrictions on international capital mobility (both on capital inflows and outflows), developing economies have relied on other cooperative initiatives to boost their integration in global financial markets. Some examples of such initiatives are the ASEAN Comprehensive Investment Agreement (ACIA), signed in 2009 by the Association of Southeast Asian Nations (ASEAN), the ASEAN Capital Market Forum (ACMF), established in 2004; and the more than 4,000 bilateral investment treaties signed by South economies between 1990 and 2013.[4] These financial liberalization policies have promoted the integration of the South into the global financial scene.[5]

Partly as a result, South economies have become increasingly connected with the rest of the world in terms of cross-border bank lending. Cross-border bank claims and syndicated loans to and from the South expanded the most rapidly from 2002 to 2014 (compared with North–North lending).[6] Indeed, South–South lending has grown faster than North–North, North–South, and South–North lending. When considering cross-border bank claims, South–South lending grew from representing 5 percent of global claims in 2001 to 9 percent in 2014. As for syndicated loans, South–South lending grew from an average of 2 percent of total world lending in 1996–2001 to 6 percent in 2002–14. However, these shares are still small when compared with the volume of North–North lending, which accounted for 68 percent of world cross-border bank claims in 2014 and an average of 71 percent of world syndicated loans in 2002–14 (figure 3.2). Alternative analyses that exclude China and the largest 20 economies in the South reveal that these trends are not dominated by these economies.[7] As the South has gained weight in terms of value (intensive margin), the number of its bilateral financial connections has also expanded (extensive margin). Connections involving South economies have increased in all directions (North–South,

FIGURE 3.1 Restrictions to Capital Flows: Average across Economies of the South, 1990–2013

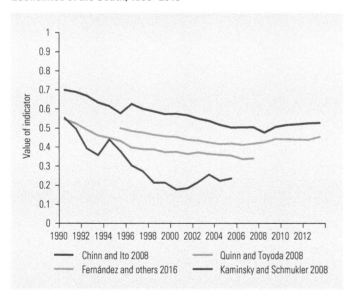

Sources: Chinn and Ito 2008; Fernández and others 2016; Kaminsky and Schmukler 2008; Quinn and Toyoda 2008.
Note: This figure shows the average across economies of the South for several capital account and current account restriction indicators. All the indicators consider restrictions to both capital inflows and outflows. The degree of restrictions is rescaled 0–1, where 0 means fully open and 1 means fully closed. The North comprises the G-7 economies and 15 other Western European economies. The South comprises the economies not included in the North. Offshore financial centers are excluded from the sample.

FIGURE 3.2   **Direction of Cross-Border Bank Lending, Selected Years**

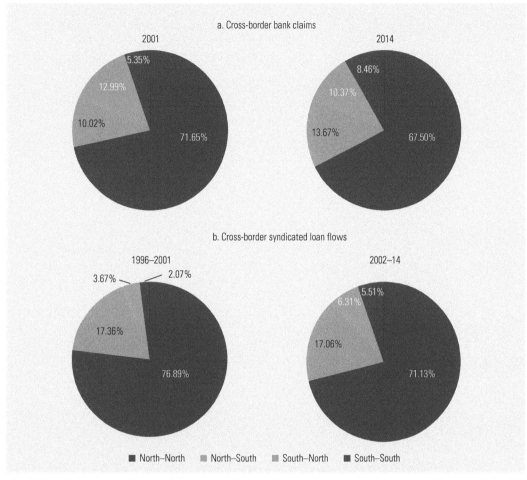

a. Cross-border bank claims

2001

5.35%
12.99%
10.02%
71.65%

2014

8.46%
10.37%
13.67%
67.50%

b. Cross-border syndicated loan flows

1996–2001

3.67%   2.07%
17.36%
76.89%

2002–14

5.51%
6.31%
17.06%
71.13%

■ North–North   ■ North–South   ■ South–North   ■ South–South

Source: Broner and others 2017.
Note: This figure shows the value of the stocks of cross-border bank claims scaled by worldwide cross-border bank claims and the value of flows of syndicated loans scaled by worldwide syndicated loans. Data are aggregated for all economies within a source region to all economies within a receiver region. For cross-border bank claims, end-of-the-year statistics are shown. For syndicated loans, the statistics are calculated year by year and then averaged over time. The North comprises the G-7 economies and 15 other Western European economies. The South comprises the economies not included in the North. Offshore financial centers are excluded from the sample.

South–North, and South–South), but the new South–South connections have expanded the fastest (map 3.1).

However, the South is not a homogeneous group; notable differences can be found across regions in their inter- and intraregional lending patterns. Regarding interregional lending, there is substantial heterogeneity in the net debtor-creditor positions with respect to the rest of the world. In particular, the East Asia and Pacific (EAP) region stands out as the only net capital exporter region in the

South.[8] The remaining regions in the South are net capital importers, whereas the North stands as the major counterpart to these flows to the South and is thus a net creditor to the rest of the world (figure 3.3). Therefore, the EAP region is not a typical South region, and its lending patterns are more similar to those of the North, which could be interpreted as a manifestation of the persistent current account surpluses run over the years by many economies in this region (Didier, Llovet, and Schmukler 2017).

MAP 3.1 **South–South Lending Connections**

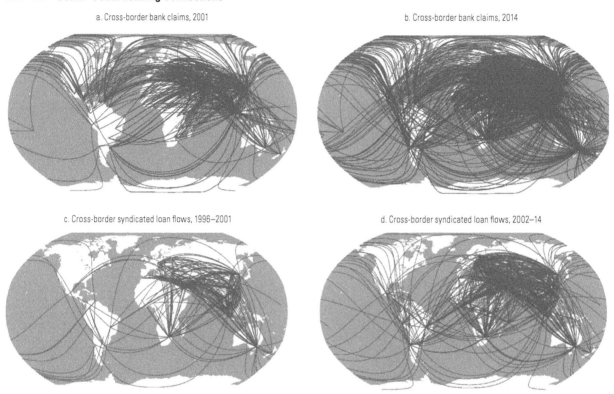

a. Cross-border bank claims, 2001

b. Cross-border bank claims, 2014

c. Cross-border syndicated loan flows, 1996–2001

d. Cross-border syndicated loan flows, 2002–14

Source: Broner and others 2017.
Note: The maps show only the connections between South economies. The lines in each map represent the active connections—that is, the country pairs for which the stock or the flow is positive. For syndicated loans, the lines in each map represent any connection that was positive during at least one year of the period analyzed. The North comprises the G-7 economies and 15 other Western European economies. The South comprises the economies not included in the North. Offshore financial centers are excluded from the sample.

As for intraregional lending, EAP and MENA are the most financially integrated regions in the South. On the one hand, there are regions such as South Asia (SAR) where intraregional syndicated loans only accounted on average for less than 1 percent of cross-border syndicated loans (intra- and interregional loans) in 2001–14. On the other hand, in the EAP and MENA regions, intraregional syndicated loans accounted on average for 19 and 16 percent of cross-border loans, respectively. In the MENA region, intraregional syndicated loans were driven mainly by the economies in the Gulf Cooperation Council, which originated about 90 percent of the total syndicated lending within the region in 2001–14 (Cortina, Ismail, and Schmukler 2016).[9] In the EAP region, the largest intraregional lenders were China and

the region's financial centers of Hong Kong SAR, China and Singapore. These three EAP economies accounted for 60 percent of EAP intraregional syndicated lending in 2001–14. An extreme case of regional clustering is the North, where intraregional syndicated loans captured about 76 percent of the North's total cross-border syndicated lending during the same period (figure 3.4).

This period of increasing globalization was not monotonic—in fact, it came to a sudden halt during the global financial crisis. A general view is that the crisis put an end to a trend of increasing financial globalization, leading to a fragmentation of the global banking sector (*The Economist* 2013a). Economies reacted to the crisis by raising restrictions to capital mobility to reduce contagion (figure 3.1). Cross-border bank claims

FIGURE 3.3   **Average Net Syndicated Loan Outflows by Region, 2001–14**

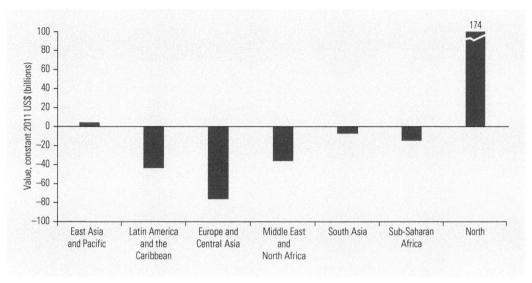

Source: SDC Platinum.
Note: This graph shows the average value of net syndicated loan outflows to the rest of the world for the period 2001–14. Net outflows are calculated as the difference between the value of the flows that a region sends to the rest of the world and the value of the flows that a region receives from the rest of the world. The data do not account for intraregional flows. The North comprises the G-7 economies and 15 other Western European economies. The South comprises the economies not included in the North. Offshore financial centers are excluded from the sample.

declined from about $36 trillion in 2007 to $32 trillion in 2009, leading to a change in the nature of cross-border banking during the postcrisis period (Claessens 2016; IMF 2015c). The reduction in the exposure of banks in the North to some regions left a gap that has been filled in part by banks located in developing economies.

After the retrenchment in cross-border banking activity during the global financial crisis, cross-border lending changed its composition; in particular, South–South transactions grew the fastest, replacing the leading role of North–South lending in the precrisis years. The period before the crisis was characterized by fast growth in North–South lending. During 2003–07 North–South bank claims grew at an annual average rate of 19 percent (33 percent for North–South syndicated loans). However, the crisis led to a change in the global financial scene. After the retrenchment in bank credit during 2008–09, cross-border lending transactions began to recover in almost all directions (North–North, North–South, South–North,

FIGURE 3.4   **Average Share of Intraregional Syndicated Loans of Total Cross-Border Syndicated Loans, by Region, 2001–14**

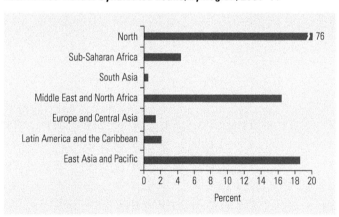

Source: SDC Platinum.
Note: This figure shows the average share of intraregional cross-border syndicated loan flows in a region's total cross-border syndicated loan flows for the period 2001–14. The North comprises the G-7 economies and 15 other Western European economies. The South comprises the economies not included in the North. Offshore financial centers are excluded from the sample.

and South–South). Nevertheless, the fastest increase took place in South–South lending, which quickly overtook its precrisis levels—see figures 3.5 and 3.6. Specifically,

South–South bank claims grew at an annual average rate of 11 percent (28 percent for syndicated loans) between 2010 and 2014. These rates are much higher than those for North–South lending, which grew at an annual rate of 4 percent during the same period (17 percent for syndicated loans). The faster growth of South–South credit after the crisis

can be attributed to the expansion in the value of both old and new connections.[10]

As a consequence, South economies have increased their role as providers of funds to other economies in the South since the global financial crisis. Although the North's economies are still the main lenders to developing economies (the value of North–South lending

FIGURE 3.5   **Evolution of Cross-Border Bank Claims by Partner Economy, 2001–14**

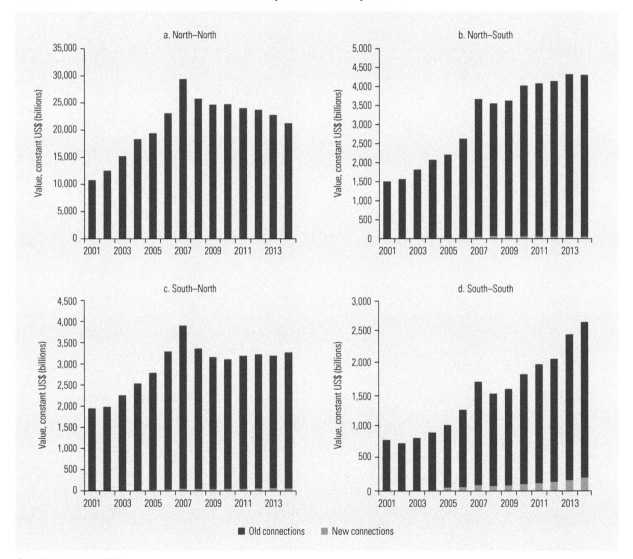

Source: Broner and others 2017.
Note: This figure shows the evolution of the value of cross-border bank claims over time by type of connection. Old connections are represented by the total value of country-pair links that were established in 2001, and new connections are represented by those that were established later. By definition, there were no new connections in the year 2001. The North comprises the G-7 economies and 15 other Western European economies. The South comprises the economies not included in the North. Offshore financial centers are excluded from the sample.

is still larger than that of South–South lending), their participation in cross-border lending to the South has decreased over time,
giving way to economies in the South as
providers of funds (figure 3.7). This increasing trend of the South accelerated after the
crisis. The share of South economies in cross-
border bank credit channeled to the South

increased from 31 percent in 2009 to 38 percent in 2014. The same pattern is observed
for syndicated loans, where the South's shares
grew from 26 percent in 2009 to 36 percent
in 2014. However, this trend has been dominated by the EAP region, which accounts for
the bulk of South–South transactions. The
participation of EAP as a lender of syndicated

FIGURE 3.6   **Evolution of Cross-Border Syndicated Loan Flows by Partner Economy, 1996–2014**

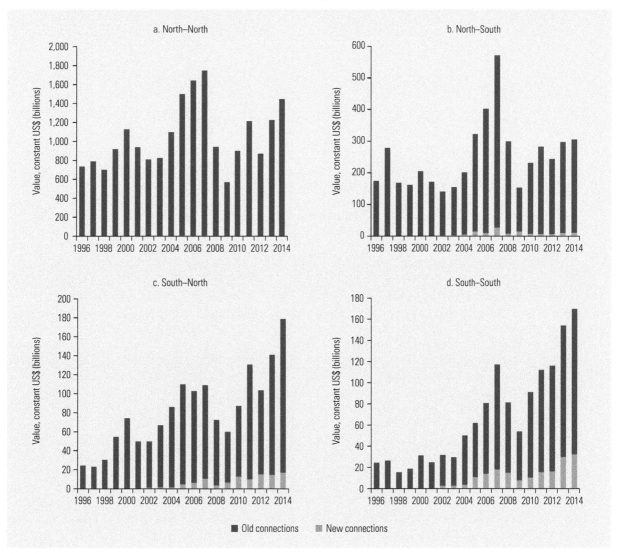

Source: Broner and others 2017.
Note: This figure shows the evolution of the value of syndicated loan flows over time by type of connection. Old connections are represented by the total value of country-pair links
that were established during the period 1996–2001, and new connections are represented by those that were established later. By definition, these were no new connections in
the years 1996–2001. The North comprises the G-7 economies and 15 other Western European economies. The South comprises the economies not included in the North. Offshore
financial centers are excluded from the sample.

FIGURE 3.7   **Share of Lending to the South from the North and the South**

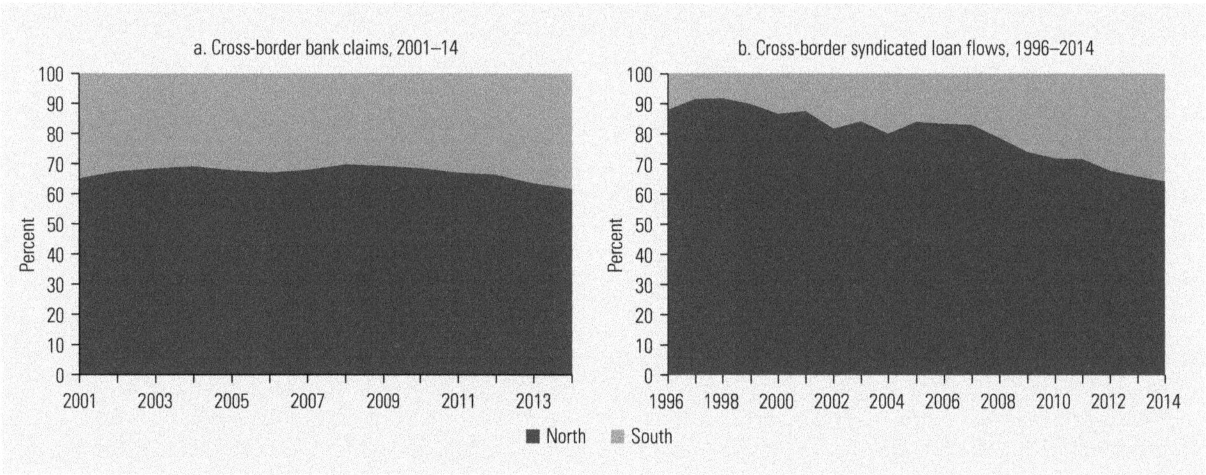

Sources: Bank for International Settlements Locational Banking Statistics and SDC Platinum.
Note: This figure shows the role of economies in the North and South as providers of funds to the South. The North comprises the G-7 economies and 15 other Western European economies. The South comprises the economies not included in the North. Offshore financial centers are excluded from the sample.

loans to South economies after the global financial crisis more than doubled its precrisis level, originating on average 25 percent of the total cross-border syndicated loans to the South during 2009–14, up from 12 percent during 2002–07.

An important part of the expansion in South–South bank credit since the global financial crisis has been associated with a trend toward regionalization. Although both inter- and intraregional lending have played a role in the expansion of South–South syndicated lending since the crisis, intraregional lending has dominated this trend. In particular, intraregional syndicated lending accounted on average for 75 percent of South–South lending during 2010–14, up from 70 percent during 2003–07. This pattern held across most South regions, except for Latin America and the Caribbean (LAC) and MENA. For example, EAP's intraregional syndicated lending accounted for 78 percent of total EAP lending to the South during 2010–14, up from 71 percent during 2003–07.[11] The same applies to the Europe and Central Asia (ECA), Sub-Saharan Africa (SSA), and South Asia (SAR) regions, where the share of intraregional syndicated lending increased from 81 to 89 percent, from 1 to 6 percent, and from 26 to 67

percent, respectively, between the precrisis and postcrisis periods.

The rise of the South in global banking is part of a broader trend involving different types of cross-border financial transactions. Broner and others (2017) document that economies in the South have been gaining market shares in global cross-border portfolio investments and foreign direct investment (FDI) as well. During 2001–12, South–South portfolio investments increased from $93 billion to $1,067 billion, and FDI increased from $518 billion to $2,845 billion (box 3.1).

The increasing presence of the South in global financial transactions has been accompanied by its growing influence in international trade. Although the theoretical literature is inconclusive about the relationship between trade and capital flows, empirical studies seem to support the idea of complementarity between them. A number of researchers have used gravity models to document that country financial investments are strongly biased toward trading partners (Aviat and Coeurdacier 2007; Dailami, Kurlat, and Lim 2012; Daude and Fratzscher 2008; De Santis and Gerard 2009; Forbes 2010; Lane and Milesi-Ferretti 2008; Portes and Rey 2005). Among the channels relating

BOX 3.1   The Big Sur: Beyond Banking

In a recent paper, Broner and others (2017) use bilateral data on international investments to document the importance of South economies in cross-border portfolio investments, bank credit, and foreign direct investment (FDI). They show that the South has captured an increasingly sizable share of all types of financial transactions. Although the North still accounts for a significant share of international financial activity, the South has been growing faster than the North, in particular South–North and South–South investments. They also find that the expansion of the South, relative to the North, accelerated in the aftermath of the global financial crisis.

The authors argue that the faster expansion of the South in cross-border financial transactions is only partially explained by the faster growth of the South's gross domestic product (GDP). Results show that the South still expands faster than the North in general, although at a more moderate rate when investments are scaled by GDP.

The authors report the growth of the South not only in the value of cross-border financial investments but also in the number of financial connections (number of partners). More South economies are becoming connected with each other and with the North.

The patterns found in cross-border bank credit are comparable to those in portfolio holdings and FDI. In particular, the authors report that the share of South–South FDI in the world's total FDI grew from 8 percent in 2001 to 12 percent in 2012. More impressive was the growth exhibited by South–South cross-border portfolio investments, whose share grew from about 1 percent of total cross-border portfolio holdings in 2001 to 3 percent in 2014 (figure B3.1.1).

FIGURE B3.1.1   Direction of Foreign Direct Investment and Cross-Border Portfolio Investments, Selected Years

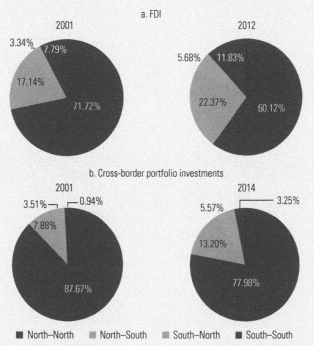

Source: Broner and others 2017.
Note: This figure shows the value of the stocks of cross-border investments scaled by total cross-border world investments for FDI and portfolio investments. Data are aggregated for all economies within a source region to all economies within a receiver region. End-of-the-year statistics are shown. The North comprises the G-7 economies and 15 other Western European economies. The South comprises the economies not included in the North. Offshore financial centers are excluded from the sample.

(box continued next page)

BOX 3.1   The Big Sur: Beyond Banking (continued)

Like South–South investments, North–South and South–North investments have presented an upward sloping trend, although they have been growing at a slower pace. Nevertheless, developing economies do not account for much of global financial transactions. The South's financial investment shares are still small when compared with those of North–North investments. As a benchmark, North–North investments accounted for 60 percent of global FDI in 2012, falling from 72 percent in 2001, and 78 percent of global cross-border portfolio investments in 2014, falling from about 88 percent in 2001.

cross-border trade and finance, there is the role of banks in reducing information asymmetries between trading parties located in different jurisdictions (box 3.2) and the use of trade as collateral to relax borrowing constraints. Thus to the extent that South economies are becoming more connected in trade, one should expect a deepening of their financial connections as well. Hanson (2012) and Iapadre and Tajoli (2014) report how developing economies have been capturing an increasing fraction of international trade

BOX 3.2   Bank-Intermediated Trade Finance

Banks facilitate international trade by generating trade credit, providing liquid working capital loans, and reducing risk in payment settlements for importers and exporters. Bank-intermediated finance supported between $6.5 and $8 trillion of international trade in 2011, or about one-third of the world aggregate (CGFS 2014). Within this subset, $2 trillion was intermediated by 21 large global banks participating in the International Chamber of Commerce (ICC) Trade Register—a volume proportionate to their combined asset sizes in the global banking industry. Nonbank trade finance mostly consists of interfirm credit supplied to factoring companies through open account or cash-in-advance arrangements and receivable discounting. Within the class of financial institutions, banks provide the bulk of trade-related financial services; private insurance companies, for example, covered about $1.7 trillion, or 9 percent, of global merchandise trade in 2011.

Banks finance importers and exporters and reduce their counterparty risks through a multitude of products, which primarily include letters of credit/guarantee, documentary collections, and loans in various forms. A letter of credit, for example, is issued by a bank on the buyer's behalf as an obligation to pay the exporter upon satisfaction of specified terms. More recently, industrial innovations have enabled banks to automate payments and financing across global supply chains for larger retail and manufacturing companies (ICC 2016), as well as to distribute trade-related exposure through securitization and loan sales to third-party, nonbank investors (CGFS 2014).

Among regions, there are important differences in the utilization of bank-intermediated trade finance. In 2011 the Asia-Pacific economies, making up 36 percent of global trade in the aggregate, received more than half of bank trade financial flows, according to the Committee on the Global Financial System (CGFS 2014). By contrast, European economies, which are more dependent on trade credit insurance, shared a quarter of global bank trade finance while generating more than two-fifths of global trade.[a] Bank-intermediated trade finance intensity is found to be higher for exports to countries that have lower levels of financial development or weaker legal frameworks, or are farther away (Niepmann and Schmidt-Eisenlohr 2013). However, as in any other type of cross-border flow, trade finance can also be a channel of regulatory arbitrage in contexts with interest rate or foreign exchange controls or with macroprudential policy differences (Reinhardt and Sowerbutts 2015).

Historically, severe contractions in the supply of trade finance have amplified economic downturns

(box continued next page)

BOX 3.2   **Bank-Intermediated Trade Finance** *(continued)*

FIGURE B3.2.1   **Bank-Intermediated Trade Finance in Emerging and Advanced Economies: Quarterly Trends, 2005–13**

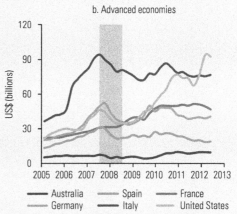

a. Emerging economies

b. Advanced economies

Brazil	India
Hong Kong SAR, China	China (right axis)
Korea, Rep.	

| Australia | Spain | France |
| Germany | Italy | United States |

Sources: International Monetary Fund; and national data adapted from CGFS 2014.
Note: The gray area indicates the global financial crisis period. The series for Italy includes export and import guarantees, which are off–balance sheet items.

in emerging markets, notably during the 1997 Asian financial crisis (IMF 2003). At the height of the global financial crisis in 2007–09, trade finance flows declined sharply in the quarters following 2008:Q3, rebounding quickly as trade regained its pace.[b] As figure B3.2.1 illustrates, banks in China (including Hong Kong SAR, China), India, and the Republic of Korea led the recovery in emerging markets, while in developed economies U.S. banks and their global affiliates overtook the retrenchment of their German and Italian counterparts in the provision of trade finance. For the countries for which data are available, statistical analysis indicates that the reduction in the supply of trade finance accounted for up to 20 percent of the decrease in global trade during the crisis. This effect was secondary compared with that from weakened real activities and reduced prices (CGFS 2014), but nevertheless enormous economically in view of the $3.6 trillion decline in trade.

The postcrisis resilience of bank-intermediated trade finance could be attributed to three factors. First, the general short span of credits and loans—typically a window of 90–120 days during which merchandise receipt and settlement clearance can be processed—means that banks can adjust trade finance exposures relatively quickly, depending on their financial conditions.[c] Second, banks face an inherently lower default risk in trade finance contracts compared with that from other loan products because the merchandise is highly collateralized and transported under standardized procedures. Third, because of the risk levels in trade finance contracts, pricing conditions have generally been favorable for banks (CGFS 2014), although most recently this is being eroded by profuse interbank liquidity, intensifying competition from new market participants, as well as stricter regulatory compliance requirements (Starnes, Alexander, and Kurdyla 2016).

a. The CGFS (2014) report is based on a combination of data sources, including International Monetary Fund, ICC Trade Registry, SWIFT, and national accounts. The regional share of bank-intermediated trade finance is estimated to be between 5 and 10 percent for the Middle East and North America, and about 5 percent for Africa and Latin America.
b. Statistics tracking trade finance volumes in Australia, Brazil, France, Germany, Hong Kong SAR, China, India, Italy, Republic of Korea, Mexico, Spain, and the United States indicated a more than 50 percent decline, from a quarterly aggregate of $850 billion in 2008:Q3 to less than $400 billion in 2009:Q1.
c. Less than 3 percent of bank trade finance exposure is medium to long term, according to Dealogic Loanware, a commercial data source.

over time and are changing global trading patterns. In particular, the South's participation (South–North and South–South transactions) in global exports rose from 27 percent in 1990 to 53 percent in 2014. Although the growth of the South is apparent in North–South, South–North, and South–South directions, trade flows between developing economies (South–South) are the ones that have increased the fastest. The participation of South–South exports in total world exports rose from 9 percent in 1990 to 31 percent in 2014. A similar expansion, though on a minor scale, has been reported by North–South exports (from 16 percent to 19 percent) and South–North exports (from 18 percent to 22 percent). In stark contrast with these trends, the share of North–North exports fell by 50 percent during the same period.

An important aspect of the rise of the South in international finance and trade is associated with the fast growth of its gross domestic product (GDP). Since the early 1990s, economies in the South have been gaining space in the global economic landscape. In fact, the GDP of the South, which was 24 percent of global GDP in 1990, almost doubled, to about 46 percent in 2014. However, South–South bank lending and financial investments still increased after accounting for the growth in the South's real economic activity, albeit at a slower pace. In fact, once GDP growth is taken into account, South–South bank claims and FDI are no longer growing faster than North–North and North–South transactions.

The multidimensional nature of the rise of the South in the global economy helps to reduce concerns about a disproportionate growth of its banking system. In other words, the more prominent role of the South in the global banking system seems to be inevitable because of the South's rapid expansion in real activity and its further diversified financial sector, unlike in, for example, Iceland and Ireland. The banking systems of these countries grew too fast, and the authorities could not respond with their own resources when the global financial crisis struck. By that time, Iceland's and Ireland's banks had become too big

to save, and their governments were incapable of guaranteeing their survival (Buiter and Sibert 2011).[12]

Beyond the typical benefits of financial integration, South–South banking may promote the financial inclusion of previously underserved segments. As with any cross-border financial connection, greater South–South connectivity may allow developing economies to benefit from financial diversification, more efficient resource allocation, access to a wider range of investment projects and funding sources, technology spillovers, and better governance.[13] It may also promote the development of the domestic financial systems through increased competition.[14] But the recent trends in South–South banking may also foster financial inclusion. Because banks tend to be more familiar with the institutions, language, and culture of economies located within their region, most of South–South credit occurs within regions. Consequently, banks in the South may tend to be better at collecting and managing information when serving small and less informationally transparent segments, such as SMEs and households, relative to banks from the North. Furthermore, increasing regionalization may facilitate cross-country regulatory and supervisory coordination, as this tends to be easier to achieve at the regional level.

However, the latest developments in cross-border banking may pose additional risks. Increasing regionalization in the South may limit risk-sharing, which would imply a larger exposure of a country to regional shocks and a faster spread of foreign shocks once they hit one of the countries in the region. Moreover, South–South bank connections may generate financial instability stemming from a laxer regulatory and supervisory environment in the South relative to the North. In other words, to the extent that financial institutions in the South are less tightly regulated than those in the North, the rise of the South as a provider of cross-border lending can negatively affect the stability of the overall financial system (Klomp and De Haan 2014). In line with this argument, Claessens and van Horen (2016) and Mehigan (2016) argue that the regulatory framework prevailing in the lender country is correlated with loan growth in the borrower country, finding that foreign banks from less regulated countries could amplify credit booms in borrower countries. Because it is not possible for policy makers in the borrower countries to regulate financial institutions in the lender countries, their policy agenda has moved toward the use of macroprudential policies to supervise and manage cross-border credit.

SUBSTITUTION EFFECTS DURING THE GLOBAL FINANCIAL CRISIS

Global banks rapidly expanded their lending activities abroad before the global financial crisis, particularly during the 1990s and early 2000s. Between 1991 and 2007, the annual volume of syndicated loan issuances by nonfinancial corporations increased more than seven times in high-income countries and more than eight times in developing ones (figure 3.8).[15] Following the general trend of increasing globalization, a significant part of the loan flows over this period were of the

cross-border type. In particular, about 43 percent of the funds to high-income countries and 86 percent to developing countries were originated overseas during 1991–2007. Banks in high-income countries were at the forefront of not only the cross-border lending to other high-income borrowers, but also most of the flows to developing countries. Western European banks alone intermediated about 53 percent of the cross-border loans to developing nations. The second-largest lender to developing countries was the United States, which originated about 20 percent of cross-border loans.

However, the global financial crisis hit global banks in the developed world especially hard, and these banks reacted by reducing their lending activities worldwide. Specifically, the total volume of syndicated loans issued by firms in high-income countries declined by about 62 percent from 2007 to 2009 (figure 3.8). Developing countries experienced a lower retrenchment in loan financing, with a reduction of about 55 percent during the same period. New loan financing declined relatively more in high-income countries because the banking shock

FIGURE 3.8   Total Amount Raised in Syndicated Loan Markets by High-Income and Developing Countries, 1991–2014

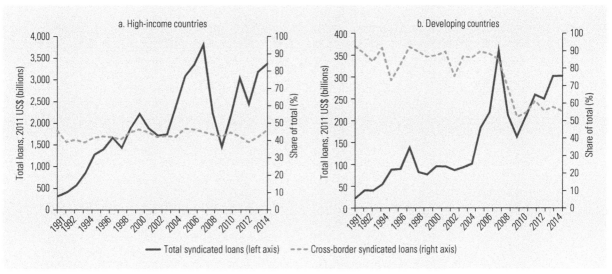

Source: SDC Platinum.
Note: This figure displays the aggregate amount raised per year in syndicated loan markets by high-income (panel a) and developing (panel b) countries. It also shows (right axis) the share of the total volume lent in the form of cross-border loans. Only nonfinancial sector issues are included.

mainly affected financial institutions located in the global financial centers—the United States and Western Europe. As a result, both domestic and cross-border bank flows declined in high-income countries, whereas only cross-border flows did so in developing countries. In fact, for cross-border loans alone, developing countries showed a larger decline than high-income countries. Between 2007 and 2009, cross-border loans to high-income countries declined by 64 percent, and to developing countries by 72 percent.

Although the shock to global banking in high-income economies was largely transmitted to the developing world through the collapse in cross-border lending, recent research suggests that a larger foreign bank presence in borrowing countries can attenuate the transmission mechanism of these types of shocks (box 3.3).

Partially compensating for the cross-border collapse, the issuance of domestic loans in developing countries increased during the crisis. The tightening of lending standards

---

BOX 3.3   Foreign Banks and the International Transmission of Monetary Policy

Since the financial crisis, academics and policy makers have voiced concerns that monetary policies pursued by lending countries can have negative spillover effects on the financial stability of emerging markets (Fischer 2014; Rajan 2014; Rey 2015). Consistent with this concern, recent studies have found evidence of the international transmission of monetary policy through its effect on the aggregate supply of cross-border loans. Using a VAR framework, Bruno and Shin (2015a) show that a contractionary shock to U.S. monetary policy leads to a decrease in cross-border bank lending. Studies using microdata on lending similarly find evidence of the international transmission of monetary policy to borrowing countries (see, for example, Morais and others, forthcoming). Overall, the picture that emerges from these studies is that international banks are frequently sources of financial instability because they transmit monetary policy shocks to borrowing economies.

Demirgüç-Kunt, Horváth, and Huizinga (2017) provide evidence of the role of foreign banks in the monetary transmission process that qualifies this picture. Using data on syndicated loans to 124 countries over the period 1995–2015, they find that a greater foreign bank presence in a borrower country reduces the impact of changes in the lender country's monetary policy interest rates on the provision of cross-border loans. Specifically, column (1) of table B3.3.1 shows that the volume of cross-border loans is related negatively to the policy interest rate, but positively to an interaction of the policy interest rate with the

foreign bank ownership variable, which measures the fraction of borrower country banking assets that are foreign-owned. This finding implies that a reduction in the lender country's policy interest rate increases the volume of cross-border loans less if the foreign banking presence is greater. As shown in columns (2) and (3) of table B3.3.1, this result is robust to controlling for the borrower country's level of economic development, as measured by its gross domestic product (GDP) per capita, and alternatively to the borrower country's level of financial development, as measured by its private credit provision relative to GDP. It is also robust to a range of borrower country and lender country policy variables, including bank regulatory variables.

Foreign bank presence can affect the cross-border loan transmission channel of monetary policy through a lender bank's own experience and local presence in the borrower country, or alternatively through the role played by other foreign banks in the borrower country, by improving the quantity and quality of information available to potential new borrowers. Demirgüç-Kunt, Horváth, and Huizinga (2017) find evidence that the impact of a foreign bank presence on the transmission of lender country monetary policy through cross-border syndicated loans results not only from the lender bank having a subsidiary in the borrower country itself but also from other foreign banks having subsidiaries in the borrower country.

The finding that the impact of lender country interest rate changes on the cross-border loan supply

(box continued next page)

BOX 3.3   **Foreign Banks and the International Transmission of Monetary Policy**
(continued)

TABLE B3.3.1   **Monetary Policy Interest Rates and the Cross-Border Syndicated Loan Volume**

Variable	(1) Volume	(2) Volume	(3) Volume
IR	−1.781***	−2.930***	−2.276**
	(0.605)	(0.716)	(0.914)
IR * foreign-owned banks (borrower)	0.0527***	0.0563***	0.0435**
	(0.0144)	(0.0177)	(0.0169)
IR * GDP per capita (borrower)		0.0000450*	
		(0.0000250)	
IR * private credit (borrower)			0.0112
			(0.00869)
QE	−0.0729***	−0.0668***	−0.0743***
	(0.0224)	(0.0226)	(0.0238)
CPI	0.00671	0.00601	0.00476
	(0.00449)	(0.00407)	(0.00401)
GDP growth	0.00286*	0.00279*	0.00327**
	(0.00165)	(0.00166)	(0.00156)
No. of observations	66,276	64,771	60,034
Adjusted R^2	0.803	0.802	0.801
Borrower*time FE	Yes	Yes	Yes
Lender FE	Yes	Yes	Yes

Source: Demirgüç-Kunt, Horváth, and Huizinga 2017.
Note: The dependent variable is volume, which is the natural logarithm of the U.S. dollar amount of a bank's share of a syndicated loan, aggregated at the borrower-lender-time level. *IR* is the central bank policy rate or the discount rate in the lender country; *foreign-owned banks (borrower)* is the fraction of the banking system's assets in the borrower country that is foreign-owned (in percentage points); *GDP per capita (borrower)* is the GDP per capita in the borrower country; *private credit (borrower)* is the private credit relative to GDP in the borrower country; *QE* is a dummy variable indicating that a quantitative easing program is in place in the lender country; *CPI* is the annual percentage change in the consumer price index in the lender country; *GDP growth* is the annual percentage change of real GDP in the lender country; FE = fixed effects. The sample includes nonfinancial borrowers. The sample period is from January 1995 to March 2015. Standard errors are clustered at the lender country and borrower country levels and are reported in parentheses.
* = 10 percent, ** = 5 percent, *** = 1 percent.

of international banks is reduced by foreign bank presence in the borrower country could well reflect the fact that international banks can mix local and international funding for their loans. Consistent with this, Demirgüç-Kunt, Horváth, and Huizinga (2017) find that the mitigating impact of foreign bank presence on the international transmission of monetary policy to the cross-border loan supply is weaker if the borrower country's monetary policy interest rate is higher because it is likely to reduce the ability of an international bank to substitute borrower country funding for lender country funding.

The evidence of a mitigating impact of foreign bank presence on the transmission of monetary policy shocks through the international syndicated loan market implies that international banks cannot be characterized simply as sources of credit instability in borrower countries that transmit international monetary policy changes in the form of international credit supply shocks. It also suggests that countries that restrict foreign bank presence could benefit from a more stable supply of cross-border credit by allowing foreign bank entry.

FIGURE 3.9   **Volume and Composition of Loan Issuance over Time, 2003–14**

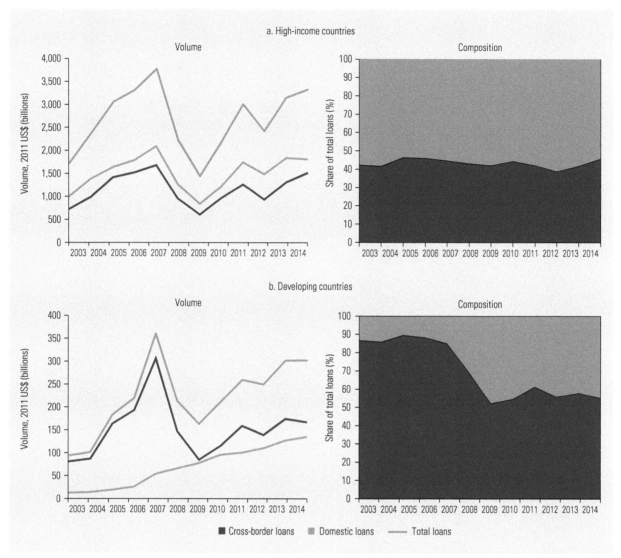

Source: SDC Platinum.
Note: This figure displays the aggregate amount raised per year in domestic and cross-border syndicated loan markets by high-income and developing countries.

and the difficulties in obtaining international bank finance were soon passed on to nonfinancial corporations, which, in some countries, seem to have reacted by changing their debt market composition. For firms in developing countries, a first option was tapping domestic banks instead of the receding international ones (figure 3.9). Indeed, the aggregate issuance of domestic loans increased by 44 percent between 2007 and

2009, which partially compensated for the decline in cross-border inflows. However, it was mainly in Asian economies that domestic lenders seem to have played a compensating role (table 3.1).

Amid the global banking retrenchment during the global financial crisis, the volume of bond issuances experienced an increase worldwide. As the volume of cross-border loans collapsed during the crisis, bond markets

TABLE 3.1   **Debt Issuance Change during the Global Financial Crisis**

Region	Total debt			Corporate bonds		Syndicated loans	
	Δ% total debt	Δ% corporate bonds	Δ% syndicated loans	Δ% domestic bonds	Δ% cross- border bonds	Δ% domestic loans	Δ% cross- border loans
High-income countries	**−38**	**16**	**−52**	**7**	**31**	**−50**	**−54**
Developing countries	**−22**	**56**	**−48**	**135**	**−38**	**33**	**−62**
East Asia and Pacific	10	68	−12	89	0.4	10	−48
Europe and Central Asia	−39	44	−55	43	45	−44	−59
Latin America and the Caribbean	−34	20	−55	55	−39	−26	−56
Middle East and North Africa	−61	−57	−62	59	−64	−44	−65
North America	−46	20	−58	9	20	−62	−46
South Asia	26	26	33	158	−78	137	−68
Sub-Saharan Africa	−51	−87	−37	−64	−90	−25	−39

Source: SDC Platinum.
Note: Table shows the debt issuance change between the global financial crisis (2008–09) and 2007 (peak before the crisis). Each column shows changes within every single market. High-income countries are included in the subgroups according to their geographical location. The region classification is available at https://datahelpdesk.worldbank.org/knowledgebase/articles/906519-world-bank-country-and-lending-groups.

expanded (figure 3.10). In particular, bond issuance increased by 48 percent in high-income countries and by 106 percent in developing countries between 2007 and 2009. This expansion partially compensated (in volume) for the collapse of syndicated loans in high-income and developing countries. Importantly, the use of corporate bonds rose in most regions (table 3.1). In this sense, bond markets fulfilled to some degree the "spare

FIGURE 3.10   **Composition of Debt Issuance over Time, 2003–14**

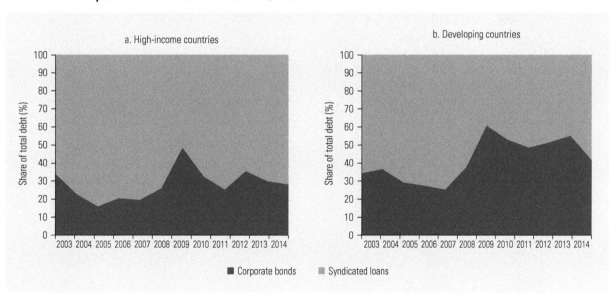

Source: SDC Platinum.
Note: This figure displays the share of funds raised through corporate bond and syndicated loan markets over the total amount raised in debt markets by high-income (panel A) and developing countries (panel B).

tire" function advocated for capital markets (Greenspan 1999a, 1999b). However, only very large corporations can access bond markets (Didier, Levine, and Schmukler 2015), and they do it largely through international issuances (Gozzi and others 2015). Therefore, it is not surprising that bond issuance activity increased even in those regions and countries without sophisticated domestic corporate bond markets.

It is difficult to determine from the aggregate data whether the changes in debt composition during the global financial crisis were driven by within-firm market substitutions or by a compositional change in the set of firms raising new debt. It is also challenging to determine whether such substitutions are caused by shifts in the supply of or demand for capital. For example, Kashyap, Stein, and Wilcox (1993) study relative movements in bank loans and commercial paper to identify the bank lending channel of monetary transmission. But, as highlighted by Oliner and Rudebusch (1996), the heterogeneity of firms in the aggregate data makes it difficult to disentangle supply from demand effects. Intending to solve these issues, recent research has analyzed whether firms in the United States substitute loans for bond financing during bank crunches, thereby providing evidence of the credit supply transmission channel (Adrian, Colla, and Shin 2013; Becker and Ivashina 2014). This research studies firm decisions to issue bonds vis-à-vis loans when they are hit by a credit shock such as the global financial crisis.[16] Because issuing firms reveal a demand for financing, the focus is on the market choice given this demand. For example, conditional on positive debt issuance, a within-firm switch between syndicated loans and bonds during a bank credit crisis is interpreted as evidence of a negative bank credit supply shock. Building on that type of methodology, Cortina, Didier, and Schmukler (2016) study a wider and more heterogeneous set of firms from all around the world. The global dimension of the data allows them to analyze how firms react to domestic and external financial crises by moving across markets. Therefore, they provide evidence

of firm-level substitution at the global level (beyond the United States) not only between bonds and loans but also between domestic and international markets.

The reported aggregate changes in debt composition during the global financial crisis took place at the country and firm levels (within firms). By using discrete logit models with country and firm fixed effects, Cortina, Didier, and Schmukler (2016) analyze firms' decisions to issue bonds versus syndicated loans in domestic and international markets during crises versus normal times.[17] The logit estimates indicate that the issuance of corporate bonds relative to syndicated loans increased during the crisis within firms in both high-income and developing countries. Conditional on debt issuance, during the crisis the probability of firms issuing bonds to obtain new financing increased by 11.5 percentage points in high-income countries and by 8.9 points in developing countries, for a 12 percent and 22 percent increase over the precrisis average, respectively.[18] The estimates also indicate the increasing use of domestic markets relative to international markets during the crisis, especially in developing countries. The probability of issuing domestic bonds (relative to international bonds) increased by 37 percent with respect to the precrisis average in developing countries. Similarly, firms that raised funds in syndicated loan markets during the crisis saw a fourfold increase in the probability of doing so domestically (rather than internationally). Because different markets provide different types of debt financing, these movements across markets provoked by market-specific supply-side shocks directly affect the nature of the new debt financing, such as the debt maturity structure of firms and countries (box 3.4).

Although the overall level of lending activity declined during the global financial crisis, the substitution events seem to have mitigated (at least to some extent) the decline in global banks' lending. The drying up of bank credit during financial crises has negative effects on investment, employment, and economic growth (Kroszner, Laeven, and Klingebiel 2007). However, if firms are able

BOX 3.4   Substitution Effects during Crises

In a recent paper, Cortina, Didier, and Schmukler (2016) use issuance data for four different debt markets (domestic and international corporate bonds and syndicated loans) to study (1) how firms use different markets to borrow at different maturities, (2) how corporate- and country-level maturity depend on which markets and which firms are active at each point in time, and (3) whether firms switch across different debt markets during market-specific crises.

The main findings of the authors are as follows. First, debt composition matters because different markets provide financing at different maturities. In particular, bond markets are, on average, of longer maturity than syndicated loans. For high-income countries, domestic and international bonds are significantly longer term than domestic and international syndicated loans. For developing countries, not only the instrument but also the market location is relevant. For example, the unconditional results show that international syndicated loans are the shortest term, followed by domestic bonds, international bonds, and domestic syndicated loans. The maturity of debt issuances consistently varies across markets, even after controlling for time-varying, country-specific factors and firm-level fixed effects, currency of issuance, and use of the proceeds raised. Thus the results indicate that part of the differences in debt maturity across firms and countries lies in differences across types of instrument and market location of the capital raised.

Second, the relative importance of each market for firm financing varies over time, with significant compositional effects, especially during market-specific crises. For example, when the global financial crisis suddenly hit the banking sector of major high-income countries, both domestic and international syndicated loan markets were affected negatively and firms moved toward issuing in domestic and international bond markets. In developing countries, the global financial crisis only affected international syndicated loan markets, and firms reacted by moving toward domestic markets, issuing both syndicated loans and bonds. An analogous pattern of switches occurs during domestic banking crises. Firms mitigate the funding shock in the local banking system by moving away from domestic syndicated loans and toward bond and international markets (table B3.4.1).

Third, the time-varying activity in each market and the ensuing changes in debt composition are reflected in firm- and country-level maturities. During the global financial crisis, the maturity of debt at issuance declined in individual markets. However, because the hardest-hit markets supplied relatively shorter-term maturities, firms' movements toward less affected markets had a positive impact on the maturity of debt issuances. Consequently, the overall maturity at issuance remained stable both at the aggregate country level as well as for those firms able to move across markets. Firms issuing the same type of debt before and in the aftermath of the global financial crisis experienced declining borrowing maturities in both high-income and developing countries. Similar patterns take place during domestic banking crises, when the overall debt maturity increases, despite declines in the maturity of domestic syndicated loans. Thus these switches across markets provide evidence of supply side shocks with significant effects on debt maturity.

Fourth, because larger firms have access to a wider set of debt markets than smaller ones, the composition of firms also changes when shocks hit particular markets. For example, as the largest firms issued bonds and tapped into international markets, they were the ones capable of moving away from syndicated loan markets during the global financial crisis and from local markets during domestic banking crises. Furthermore, in developing countries, as larger firms returned home during the global financial crisis, they might have crowded out funding for smaller firms that rely solely on domestic markets. In both cases, large firms gain relative to small ones, prompting a compositional shift at the firm level with aggregate-level consequences. Overall, access to several markets allows larger firms to use them as complements during good times, obtaining different types of financing in each, and as substitutes when conditions deteriorate, cushioning the decline in volume in certain markets and in maturity across all individual markets. The financing conditions of smaller firms are constrained by the specific market they access.

In summary, the results from this report show that although the demand side can be important for maturity as firms choose their optimal financing, the supply side (or type of market) is also relevant.

(box continued next page)

BOX 3.4   **Substitution Effects during Crises** *(continued)*

TABLE B3.4.1   **Market Choice and Domestic Banking Crises**

	Corporate bonds versus syndicated loans		Domestic versus international loans	
	Dependent variable: dummy (d_{it}) = 1 if the firm issued a bond in quarter t; dummy (d_{it}) = 0 if the firm issued a loan in quarter t		Dependent variable: dummy (d_{it}) = 1 if the firm issued a domestic loan in quarter t; dummy (d_{it}) = 0 if the firm issued an international loan in quarter t	
Mean (d_{it}):	0.41		0.51	
Fixed effects:	Country and year dummies	Firm fixed effects and year dummies	Country and year dummies	Firm fixed effects and year dummies
Domestic banking crises	0.12*** [0.01]	0.14*** [0.01]	−0.15*** [0.01]	−0.12*** [0.02]
No. of observations	110,436	47,354	63,571	19,012
No. of clusters	40,471	6,237	29,303	3,776

Source: Cortina, Didier, and Schmukler (2016).
Note: Robust standard errors in brackets.
*** $p < 0.01$, ** $p < 0.05$, * $p < 0.1$

In other words, the market of issuance matters for the maturity structure of firms and countries, even after controlling for factors that the literature highlights as key determinants of the maturity choice. To the extent that markets specialize in particular types of financing, firms might decide to issue in specific markets to obtain financing at different maturities. When firms cannot choose markets, they will be constrained by the financing available where they can issue. By using issuance data across markets, the authors provide evidence that firms constrained to one market face a different maturity structure than firms that obtain financing in a different market or firms that tap multiple markets. Therefore, by analyzing a wider set of debt markets, the authors reveal a broader perspective on how firm and country financing as well as maturity behave.

to substitute bond financing for bank financing, the negative effects on investments and growth would be reduced (Greenspan 1999a, 1999b). Recent theoretical models show that flexibility in the financial system through access to alternative debt markets helps to cushion the negative real effects (on investment and output) of adverse shocks to the banking system (Crouzet 2016; De Fiore and Uhlig 2015)—not completely, however, because bond markets and bank credit are not perfect substitutes (Crouzet 2016). In the context of the global financial crisis, the access to alternative sources of external finance by firms would have mitigated to some extent the adverse effects of the crisis on the performance of firms and countries. Although empirical assessments of this type of argument are scarce, Levine, Lin, and Xie (2016) show that countries in which firms have easier access to stock markets experience smaller deteriorations in corporate investment following banking crises. Nevertheless, it is also important to consider the compositional change in the types of issuers that are tapping each market over time. For example, during domestic crises, only relatively larger firms will have access to alternative markets (bonds and international loans). During foreign shocks, large international firms switching to domestic markets can potentially crowd small domestic issuers out of the market (Cortina, Didier, and Schmukler 2016).

The shift in the pattern of global financial intermediation that began during the global financial crisis continued during the postcrisis years. Regulatory reforms aimed at avoiding systemic risks (higher capital and liquidity requirements), combined with the higher compliance costs to combat money laundering and the financing of terrorism and to increase transparency, led to a de-risking of global banks from their relatively riskier cross-border activities and a withdrawal from correspondent banking relationships (box 3.5). As such, cross-border lending as a share of

---

BOX 3.5   De-risking in Correspondent Banking

Correspondent banking, in the context of global finance, refers to the services provided by a bank (the correspondent) to another financial institution (the respondent) and its clients by extension. Large international banks typically serve as correspondents to settle payments and clear foreign currency transactions for local and regional banks that in turn support money transfer operators and other businesses. Correspondent banking connects local economies which would otherwise have limited access to the international financial system, and underpins trade finance, remittances, and humanitarian flows.

Global banks' recent retrenchment from correspondent relationships has garnered attention from multiple international institutions for its potential downside impact on financial stability and economic development. A joint World Bank-FSB-CPMI survey found that about half of national banking regulators, three-fifths of local and regional banks, and three-quarters of large international banks indicated declines in correspondent banking (World Bank 2015a). The retrenchment originated in banks in Canada, Switzerland, the United States, the United Kingdom, and other EU economies. It has affected institutions in the Latin America and the Caribbean, Middle East and North Africa, Sub-Saharan Africa, and Europe and Central Asia regions, particularly those located in offshore centers and jurisdictions at a high risk of illicit financing.[a] As pointed out by a new IFC survey, the pervasiveness of withdrawal has challenged the ability of respondent banks to serve clients and further develop banking business needed for economic diversification (Starnes and others 2017).

Although profitability and risk appetite are critical factors in banks' commercial decisions, the retrenchment from correspondent relationships has occurred against a backdrop of more stringent enforcement of the anti–money laundering and combating financing of terrorism (AML-CFT) rules (World Bank 2015a). Because of the ambiguity in regulatory expectations and the unquantifiable potential for reputational impact, many correspondents have chosen to de-risk by restricting or exiting relationships with institutions that are deemed excessively risky (see panel a, figure B3.5.1). Wholesale de-risking at the jurisdiction or sector level, independent of the type of customer, reflects a shift away from case-by-case risk management to risk avoidance (FATF 2014). Humanitarian aid beneficiaries (World Bank 2016b), small exporters (Starnes, Alexander, and Kurdyla 2016), and nonbank international remittance companies (Ramachandran 2016; World Bank 2015b) served by local and regional banks are among the most vulnerable to general de-risking (see panel b, figure B3.5.1 for example).

Early evidence points to the need for further research to determine developmental impacts. For example, analyzing SWIFT bank payment information, the CPMI (2016) found that the number of correspondent relationships had fallen during 2011–15, whereas the volume and value of transactions indicated that those relationships had increased (panel a, figure B3.5.1). This finding reveals the growing concentration and complexity in correspondent banking, consistent with the World Bank-FSB-CPMI survey finding that local and regional banks have gener-

(box continued next page)

BOX 3.5   De-risking in Correspondent Banking *(continued)*

FIGURE B3.5.1   Correspondent Banking: Recent Developments

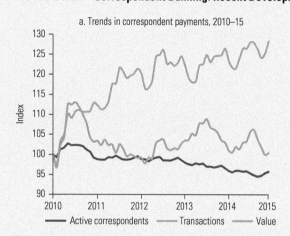

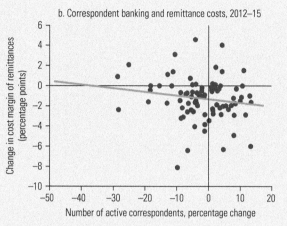

Sources: Deutsche Bank and SWIFT Watch, adapted from CPMI (2016) and World Development Indicators (database).
Note: In panel a, the series are indexed as 100 times the current values divided by those of January 2011.

ally been successful in finding replacement institutions or alternative financing channels. Often, this is achieved through nested correspondent relationships at the cost of excluding part of the respondent customer base, as required by correspondence providers (World Bank 2015a).

Following the large global banks' withdrawal, this condensation through additional layers of financial intermediation carries several risks. In terms of business control, the smaller Tier 2 and 3 correspondent banks are often less well positioned to piece together financial intelligence from complex client relationships and process large-volume transactions in a timely fashion (World Bank 2015a). From a

supervisory perspective, it is becoming increasingly challenging to monitor and enforce the financial integrity of layered arrangements because of their complexity and opacity (Ramachandran 2016). Last but not the least, nested relationships are significantly costlier to establish and service when there is limited coordination in regulatory standards across countries (World Bank 2015b). Hence, a widespread uncontained retrenchment from correspondent banking can threaten progress toward financial stability and inclusive growth, and these trends need to be followed closely. For a rigorous analysis to support the decline in correspondent banking, however, better data going beyond anecdotal evidence are needed.

---

a. The withdrawal of correspondent banking can affect local financial systems significantly. For example, the nonofficial financial sector in Angola lost access to U.S. dollar clearing in December 2015. Access to U.S. dollar payments was merely sustained through the Banco Nacional de Angola. Monetary authorities have also experienced terminations of correspondent relationships, such as in Belize (IMF 2016).

total banking assets declined, driven largely by the retrenchment of European banks (IMF 2015c). Moreover, the higher propensity of developing countries to issue domestic loans continued during 2010–14. The share of domestic loans in the total volume of loans

issued was 18 percent on average during the precrisis years and 50 percent during the postcrisis ones. Bond finance also continued to gain importance during the years following the crisis. The share of bonds of total debt rose from 33 percent to 42 percent in high-income countries and from 42 percent to 57 percent in developing countries when comparing pre- and postcrisis years.

The change in debt market composition during and after the global financial crisis reduced the exposure of borrowing firms and countries to global banking conditions, but it increased their exposure to international bond markets. The expansion of corporate borrowing in bond markets (and away from banks) since the crisis has been labeled the "second phase of global liquidity" (Shin 2013). Unlike in the first phase, in which global banks monopolized global liquidity, international bond markets are taking the lead during the second phase. Thus, international bond markets have taken on a larger role in the transmission of financial conditions across borders since the crisis. Because a large part of the bond issuances has been denominated in U.S. dollars, developing countries have become more exposed to movements in U.S. interest rates and exchange rates (McCauley, McGuire, and Sushko 2015; Shin 2013). Holding large liabilities in foreign currency while having assets in local currency can be risky, as demonstrated during the crises in Mexico and Asia in the 1990s.[19] But this time, the provision of longer-term issuances by bond markets (relative to bank credit) may be mitigating to some extent the risk of capital flow reversals and foreign currency financing (Cortina, Didier, and Schmukler 2016). This new trend can also affect domestic credit through the so-called carry trade (Bruno and Shin 2017). In this sense, low interest rates in high-income countries would fuel nonfinancial corporations in developing countries to issue foreign currency bonds and use the proceeds not solely to support real investment but also to serve as savings in the form of cash holdings or other liquid assets, thereby increasing the domestic credit capacity (Acharya and others 2015; Acharya and Vij 2016; IMF 2015b). For example, Powell (2014) documents a positive correlation between bond issuances by Latin American corporations, corporate deposits in LAC financial institutions, and domestic credit. In this way, nonfinancial institutions become important conduits of international

financial conditions for domestic liquidity and credit growth. As the reliance on international bond markets continues to rise with respect to cross-border banking, the locus of risks shifts from banks to nonbank institutions, which may complicate surveillance of the global financial system (IMF 2015c). Moreover, although the increasing use of domestic loan markets in developing countries reduces their exposure to global financial shocks, it may increase their vulnerability to domestic and regional banking crises.

The patterns highlighted in this section imply that policy discussions would benefit from considering other key components of the global financial system, beyond the single focus on cross-border banking. Because there are different markets where corporates obtain new debt financing, it is important to jointly analyze the dynamics across those markets. For example, firms can better withstand market-specific adverse shocks through their access to alternative sources of external finance. Although this section focuses on the role of capital markets as complements of bank financing during crisis periods, this argument can also be generalized to "good" times and can be a topic for future research. In this way, access to more complete markets may allow firms and countries to diversify their financing sources and reduce the risks associated with financial contagion. However, global financial markets are not perfectly integrated, and several frictions result in different markets providing different types of financing, even for the same firm (such as in terms of maturity or currency denomination). As a result, changes in debt market composition over time also expose firms and countries to new types of risks. Moreover, despite the fact that debt is the main source of external financing for investment projects, most of the theoretical models of debt market frictions are constrained to a single type of debt, typically bank debt. Although this finding might be true for small firms, it does not hold for relatively large corporations, which typically have a broader access to alternative sources of external finance. In this sense, policy initiatives, such as the Capital Markets Union in Europe (European

Commission 2015), the development of capital markets for SMEs, as well as those initiatives aimed at developing innovative instruments, such as minibonds, and securitization may be important tools to broaden external funding choices for a wider set of firms (Borensztein and others 2008; Giovannini and others 2015).

FINTECH AND THE FUTURE OF GLOBAL BANKING

This section provides an overview of some of the latest fintech developments and how they are related to global banking. In particular, it describes how fintech might provide alternative sources of external financing, increase competition, push innovation, and introduce new technologies that can potentially disintermediate many financial processes such as cross-border payments. Consumers and small and medium-sized enterprises (SMEs) are the segments most affected by innovative fintech solutions.

Although there is no consensus on what "fintech" means, and it is typically used to describe disruptive technologies in the financial system, this section uses the term in conjunction with the set of tech-driven new companies providing financial services outside the traditional financial sector. The retrenchment and intensified regulation of the traditional banking system after the global financial crisis, combined with the greater access to information technology and the wider use of mobile devices, have given a new generation of firms outside the traditional banking sector an opportunity to innovate and deliver financial services. These new players, which are still very young (most emerged after the crisis), are bringing new business models and innovations to multiple segments of the financial world, including lending, payments and transfers, and wealth management. This section covers only the first two segments because they are the areas that most significantly affect the traditional banking industry.

Global investment in fintech companies has expanded very rapidly worldwide. Although available data on fintech are very scant, according to some estimates at least 4,000 fintech firms were active in 2015, and over a dozen of them were valued at over $1 billion (*The Economist* 2015). Meanwhile, this trend is growing very quickly. The global investment in fintech was about $22.3 billion in 2015, or more than 12 times the investment amount in 2010 (Accenture 2016). The United States and the United Kingdom appear to be the world leaders in fintech investments, although these firms operate globally, providing services to developing economies as well. Fintech firms in the United States attracted most of the investments between 2010 and 2015—about 63 percent of the total. The United Kingdom is the second-largest attractor of investments, absorbing 11 percent of the total, but Nordic economies such as Sweden are also becoming leading fintech centers globally.[20] In terms of growth, Asia has experienced the fastest expansion of fintech in recent years. Investment in Asian fintech companies accounted for 19 percent of the world's total fintech investment in 2015, up from 6 percent in 2010. China captured most of that growth by absorbing about 45 percent of the total investment in that region by 2015 (box 3.6). The role of India was important as well; it accounted for 38 percent of total Asian investment for the same year (Accenture 2016). Most of fintech funding has been directed at the personal and SME space (lending, payments, and transfers), which has absorbed over 70 percent of the total fintech investments to date (Citigroup 2016). Other fintech areas such as wealth management and insurance, although smaller in size, have recently been attracting a large share of the global investments (Accenture 2016).

In lending, the emerging online platforms are alternative forms of intermediating credit beyond the traditional credit system. Most of the alternative lending platforms emerged using the so-called peer-to-peer (or P2P) model in the aftermath of the global financial crisis, when the availability of traditional bank credit was quite limited.[21] This type of lending model allows direct lending from savers to borrowers, avoiding the traditional system of financial intermediation. However,

BOX 3.6   Fintech in China: An Overview

The fintech sector has seen extraordinary growth in China in recent years. Despite the general scarcity of official statistics on fintech development, China appears to be one of the global leaders in fintech innovation and adoption. Fintech in China attracted $8.8 billion during 2015:Q3–16:Q2 in terms of volume of investment, representing 352 percent of the volume in 2010 (Mittal and Lloyd 2016). In 2016, 30 percent of the fintech firms valued at more than $1 billion were located in China (panel a, figure B3.6.1). In terms of adoption and usage, credit provided by the peer-to-peer (P2P) subsector increased from $4.3 billion in 2013 to $71.4 billion in 2015 (PIIE 2016), and the volume of mobile payments reached $4.4 trillion in 2015, accounting for 40 percent of China's gross domestic product (GDP)—see PBOC (2016).

Payment platforms—which largely derive their user base from thriving e-commerce and social media platforms—by far dominate the fintech space in China (panel b, figure B3.6.1). Service providers have been able to leverage the large economies of scale thanks to the high level of smartphone penetration. For example, Ant Financial (formerly Alipay), the largest payment service provider, supported 451 million active users in 2015 and processed on average 153 million transactions a day (Alibaba Group 2016).[a] Notably, 54 percent of the payment volume

in China as of 2016:Q2 was processed by nonbank institutions, as opposed to traditional payment service providers (Saal, Starnes, and Rehermann 2017). Thanks to their cost-efficiency, reliability, and ease of use, digital payments have enabled large parts of the cash-based Chinese economy to leapfrog over credit card systems, absorbing fees paid to traditional payment intermediaries in the process.

Flourishing within a similar environment, the fintech lending sector exploited the financial needs of households and small and medium-sized enterprises (SMEs) that were not met by traditional service providers.[b] P2P platforms have rapidly seized opportunities not taken by traditional intermediaries, designing competitive products in search of customers and profits under broadly accommodative regulatory conditions.

Although P2P lending can improve efficiency and promote access to underserved segments of SMEs and retail customers, the many platforms operating in China have not been a riskless solution to mitigating the banking industry's primary focus on state-owned enterprises and well-known borrowers. As consolidation among more than 2,000 platforms accelerated in 2015, a more pronounced regulatory approach to credit limits was adopted to improve sectoral soundness. By August 2016, several prominent

FIGURE B3.6.1   **Fintech "Unicorns": Fintech Firms with a Valuation of over $1 Billion, 2016**

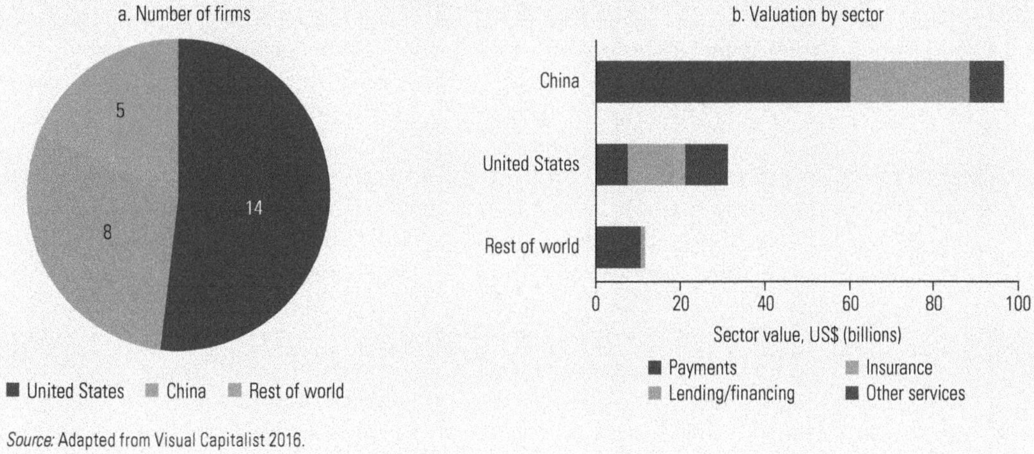

a. Number of firms

b. Valuation by sector

Source: Adapted from Visual Capitalist 2016.

(box continued next page)

BOX 3.6   **Fintech in China: An Overview** *(continued)*

exits had triggered further regulation of loan size and custodian requirements for investor funds (CBRC 2016b), aiming to address concerns about potential systemic risk.

Under an innovative approach to promoting SME capital access and facilitating financial sector reforms, Chinese regulatory authorities are allowing several large technology companies to venture into lending services directly. Precluded from brick-and-mortar operations under special banking licenses, this class of online intermediaries collects deposits, assesses creditworthiness via cloud-based and data-driven analytics (using, for example, the borrowers' marketplace and social network records), and lends using streamlined processes. Being one step closer to the technology sector's vision of integrated financial services, these intermediaries are able to draw on the accumulated expertise of finance as an ecology, possibly leading to further innovations.

Building on domestic experience, large Chinese technology companies are venturing into developing countries such as India, Thailand, the Russian Federation, and Brazil through brownfield investments and collaborative efforts (Mittal and Lloyd 2016). However, the fintech sector is facing challenges as markets, regulations, and perceptions continue to evolve. Incumbent intermediaries are innovating to bridge gaps in financial access, while retail investors are becoming more informed about the risks and returns of fintech products. Because cyber security, AML-CFT (anti–money laundering and combating financing of terrorism), and prudential compliance all remain valid concerns within the current regulatory approach to the fintech sandbox, it helps when both the industry and the regulator are vigilant and proactive about risks in order to maintain an environment conducive to healthy developments in this promising sector.

---

a. The comparable value for Visa is 260 million transactions a day globally; and for MasterCard, 180 million.
b. Total assets in the Chinese banking system constituted 290 percent of GDP by the end of 2015, according to calculations based on the China Banking Regulatory Commission's annual report (CBRC 2016a). Credit to households as of 2015 was 39 percent of GDP (BIS Credit to the Non-financial Sector database, 2016). Furthermore, despite contributing to about four-fifths of urban employment and three-fifths of national GDP, SMEs as a sector receive less than a quarter of bank loans, in part because of their lack of collateral and financial track records (Mittal and Lloyd 2016).

the industry has evolved, and the term *peer-to-peer* has become somewhat inaccurate. Most of the loans include funding from a wide range of investors (including financial institutions and institutional investors). Thus P2P lending can be considered a form of online *crowdfunding*, a term that includes other types of platforms where multiple individuals pool their contributions in a larger fund (Atz and Bholat 2016). Online lending platforms have no retail branches and typically provide faster loan applications and smaller shorter-term loans than traditional credit institutions. These new platforms also involve alternative credit models that help lenders to assess the credit risk of a broader set of borrowers. They replace traditional credit scoring with machine learning and algorithms based on big

data mining to assess credit risk, accelerate lending processes, and lower operating costs. The new digital lending sector is attracting a massive number of entrants. According to Autonomous (2016), in 2006 only two economies were home to digital lenders. By 2016, 67 economies had digital lenders, and over 2,000 players were thought to be operating worldwide (over 200 in the United States).

In payments and transfers, innovative solutions are rapidly changing the way consumers engage in financial transactions. Indeed, the payment industry had largely evolved before the latest fintech expansion. For example, with the adoption of credit cards in the 1950s and the rise of e-commerce during the 1990s, cash and checks were no longer the main means of transaction in many high-income economies (World Economic Forum 2016b).[22] Another likely consequence of the expansion in e-commerce is that the consumer and retail payments segment has been the fastest-growing area in terms of innovative solutions and fintech new entrants (BNY Mellon 2015). In payments, the most recent innovations have focused on the user experience, leveraging mobile devices, and connectivity (front-end processes), but the existing payment infrastructure remains mostly the same. An example is the use of mobile phones to make payments at a physical location (for example, Apple Pay, Samsung Pay). As for transfers, the current system is built on several intermediaries, such as automated clearinghouses and intermediary banks (corresponding banks), which make the process of value transfer sometimes costly and slow. Innovations in this area make transactions between individuals (and sometimes across economies) easier, faster, and cheaper than in the past. For example, mobile money solutions such as M-Pesa make possible peer-to-peer transactions through the use of mobile devices without the need for a bank account. And new business models such as TransferWise and Azimo allow customers to send money across borders by matching transactions with other users trying to send flows in the opposite direction, thereby avoiding the high fees associated with international transfers because the money never really leaves the economy of origin. Perhaps the most important and disruptive types of innovations are those based on new technologies, most prominently the blockchain.

Blockchain is a decentralized payment scheme that does not require a single trusted third party to validate transactions. As the technology behind the bitcoin, the best-known cryptocurrency, blockchain has the potential to disintermediate any type of financial transaction.[23] The total market value of all bitcoins in circulation by September 2017 was over $60 billion.[24] Blockchain is a system of online exchange that uses powerful encryption to allow peer-to-peer transactions of digital assets without the need for a trusted third party, such as a bank, to clear and settle payments. It consists of a log of transactions recorded on a distributed platform—that is, the database is not stored in a single location but distributed among millions of computers, which replace the traditional trusted intermediaries by keeping track of old transactions and verifying new ones (figure 3.11). Blockchain technology records the transaction history better than any other electronic money or means of payment (Schuh and Shy 2016). Thus this technology upends one of the most important tasks of the traditional financial industry, which is to act as a trusted intermediary for transactions between separated (sometimes unknown) entities. In the same way the Internet has revolutionized the diffusion of information, blockchain technology is revolutionizing the way in which parties send funds (see, for example, *Forbes* 2016).

The potential of blockchain technology goes beyond its uses as a digital form of cash because it can be applied to many other transfer processes, including global bank payments. Blockchain technology provides a new payment infrastructure, so it can disintermediate many financial (and nonfinancial) processes ("blockchain 2.0"), thereby increasing speed and efficiency and lowering transaction costs. Several global banks and financial institutions are already collaborating with technology companies to further experiment with blockchain. For example, Ripple and R3 are trying to create their own blockchain network for global banks, avoiding clearinghouses and correspondent banks. The Tokyo Stock Exchange, in the collaboration with IBM, is testing systems to record trades for low-transaction markets using blockchain (Adriano and Monroe 2016). The U.S. Nasdaq stock exchange was the first one to incorporate blockchain services (CoinDesk 2016). Other applications of blockchain are to registries and transactions of other digital assets (such as blockchain-based property registries) and smart contracts, which are self-executing contracts without the third-party interference and without input by lawyers or recourse to the courts (for example, Ethereum). More efficient arrangement and management of syndicated loan contracts could result from the application of smart contracts, and that is one

FIGURE 3.11   **How Blockchain Works**

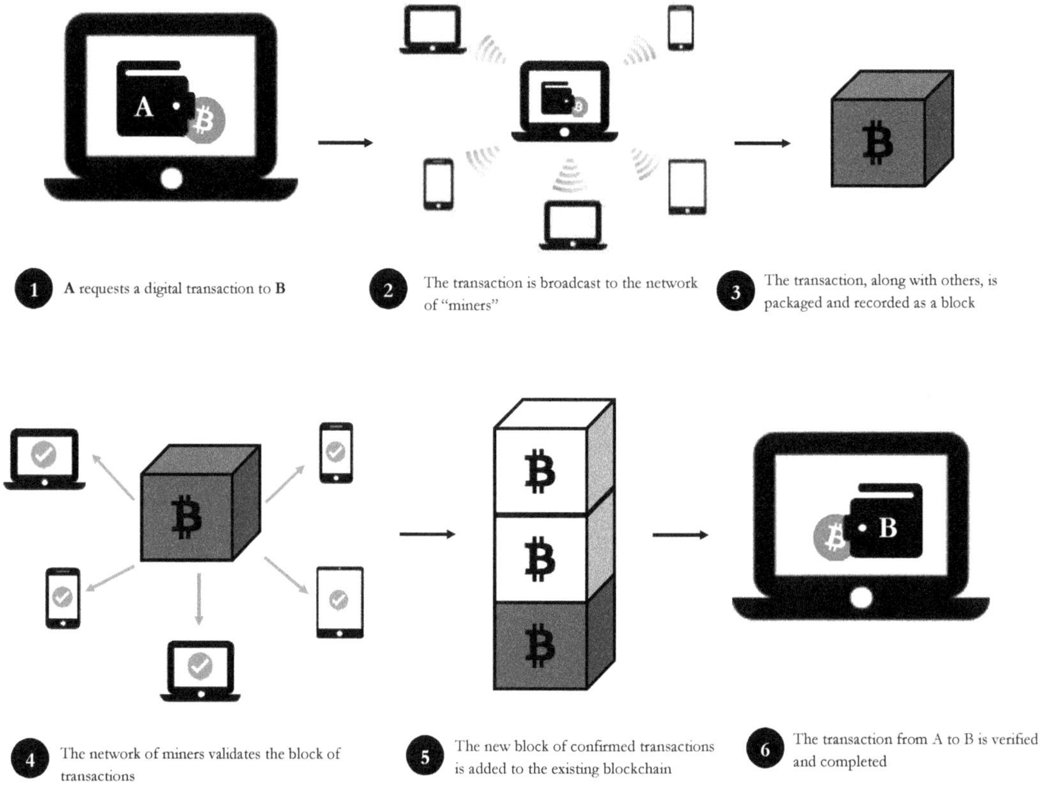

① A requests a digital transaction to **B**

② The transaction is broadcast to the network of "miners"

③ The transaction, along with others, is packaged and recorded as a block

④ The network of miners validates the block of transactions

⑤ The new block of confirmed transactions is added to the existing blockchain

⑥ The transaction from A to B is verified and completed

Sources: Illustration by the GFDR team.

application that directly affects global banking activities (World Economic Forum 2016b).

All recent innovations and business models arising from the latest fintech developments could also affect remittances. Remittances constitute one of the biggest flows of funds from the developed to the developing world (excluding China)—larger than official development aid, FDI flows, and corporate investment (private debt and portfolio equity flows). According to the World Bank (2016a), the global flow of remittances was estimated to exceed $601 billion in 2015. Of that amount, developing economies received an estimated $441 billion. The following developing economies were among the top recipients of global remittances as a percentage of GDP in 2015: Tajikistan (42 percent), Nepal (29 percent), Moldova (26 percent), Haiti (23 percent), and Honduras (17 percent).

Therefore, in many economies, remittances are a pathway to economic development and financial inclusion. However, the existing cross-border payment banking system is slow (it takes days to settle), and the average cost of transactions is high. New digital innovations and the broader use of smartphones and mobile wallets are key to reducing costs and speeding up international transactions. Again, blockchain technology could be especially useful. An example is Rebbit in the Philippines, which builds on blockchain technology to allow users to send remittances to the Philippines with almost no fees. Other companies such as Abra also use blockchain technology for money transfers worldwide.

In fact, innovative digital providers seem to be putting effective pressure on cross-border transfer costs, which have been declining since 2011. The cost of sending remittances fell by 1.7 percentage points between 2011 and 2015, from 9.1 percent in 2011 to 7.4 percent in 2015 (panel a, figure 3.12). This pattern is explained in part by the fact that banks, which charge very high fees to channel remittances, have significantly reduced their market share in the remittances market over the years. The share of remittance transactions handled by banks relative to those handled by money transfer operators (MTOs) declined from 33

percent in 2011 to 22 percent in 2015 (panel a, figure 3.12). Although bank prices have also declined over time, they were still significantly higher than the ones being charged by MTOs by 2015. During that year, the cost of sending remittances through the banking system was 3.2 percentage points higher than the cost of sending them through the traditional MTOs (Western Union, MoneyGram, and Ria) and 5.9 percentage points higher than through

FIGURE 3.12   **The Remittances Market, 2011–16**

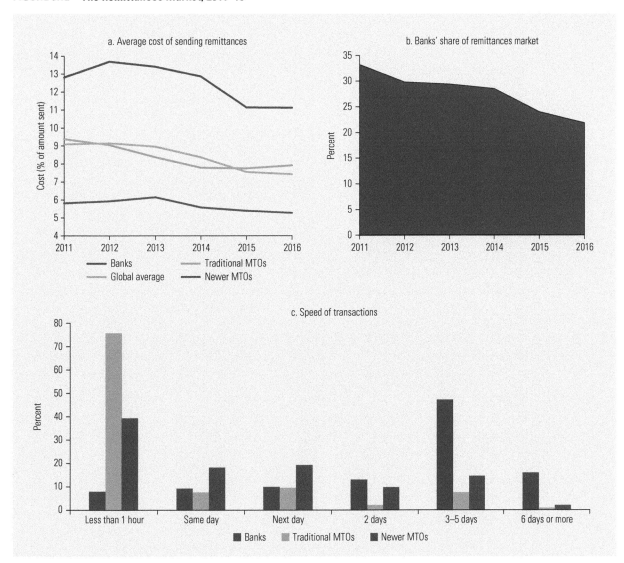

Source: Remittance Prices World Wide (database), World Bank. See http://remittanceprices.worldbank.org.
Note: Panel a shows the average total cost (as a percentage of the remittance) of sending $200 internationally; panel b shows the banks' market share of the remittances market; and panel c shows the average speed of transaction by different methods of sending remittances for the period 2011–16. MTO = money transfer operator.

the newer MTOs such as Transfer Wise and Azimo. Because MTOs provide faster transaction services than banks, they have also allowed faster international transactions worldwide (panel c, figure 3.12).

Increased competition and efficiency are among the main contributions that digital innovators could make to the traditional global financial sector, especially if a significant component of financial sector growth over the last 40 years has been rent seeking (Zingales 2015). For example, according to Philippon (2015), the unit cost of financial intermediation in the United States has remained at about 2 percent for the last 130 years, despite several financial innovations.[25] In other words, the improvements in technology have not been yet transmitted to the end users of financial services. However, such a scenario might change with the entry of new competitors, thereby broadening the competitive landscape in terms of number of players, alternative products, and business models. The current fintech trend is therefore an opportunity to alleviate the tension between private and social returns as well as increase the overall efficiency of the system (Philippon 2016). Lower costs are achievable not only through increased competition but also through the streamlined processes made possible by the new electronic platforms, which allow the innovating businesses to offer prices lower than those of the traditional banking services.

The development of fintech also promotes financial inclusion. Access to financial services allows consumers in developing economies to make longer-term consumption and investment decisions.[26] Historically, there has been a wide gap between the financial needs of households and businesses in developing economies and the set of financial products available to them. Among the traditional barriers of the banking sector faced by this segment have been the high costs relative to the small transaction values involved and the difficulties in identifying and assessing risk. Because mobile phone penetration in developing economies is usually higher than banking penetration (which is often highly underdeveloped), and the share of cash transactions

is large, the rapid spread of digital technologies to access financial services holds special potential to overcome the traditional barriers and financially include the traditionally excluded segments (Demirgüç-Kunt, Kane, and Laeven 2014).[27] For example, mobile money platforms allow unbanked consumers, through the use of basic mobile phones, to make and receive payments much faster (in a matter of seconds) and at a lower cost than in the recent past.[28] They also provide the infrastructure and generate the digitalized data that can be used to create and tailor new financial offerings for the financially excluded. One example is M-Shwari in Kenya, which leverages the mobile money infrastructure and digital information of M-Pesa to make credit-scoring decisions (CGAP 2015). One of the benefits of blockchain technology (see figure 3.11) for financial inclusion is its potential to reform and improve property ownership through blockchain registries such as Bitfury, which would generate proof of collateral (an important problem in developing nations) and thus access to credit. Furthermore, because the digital currencies supported by blockchain technology are also a global means of payment by design, their impact goes beyond the financial arena, as they also facilitate inclusion in global trade. For example, producers in Africa can meet demand in Europe through the use of online platforms and e-payments. In fact, the economic gains from widespread use of digital finance in developing economies would be significant. According to the McKinsey Global Institute (2016), the increased productivity and investment that the widespread use of digital finance generates could boost the annual GDP of all developing economies by 6 percent by 2025 versus a business-as-usual scenario.

Despite the potential benefits, fintech services also pose new types of risks. The lack of safety nets in the business models, misuse of personal data, difficulties in identifying customers, and electronic fraud are among the main vulnerabilities of the new digital financial practices. For example, P2P lending platforms, whose business model is based on loan matching between borrowers and investors (charging fees for that service), do not hold the loans originated in their balance sheets. Therefore, although these fintech companies do not bear the default risk, the profitability of their businesses is highly dependent on the number of loans they intermediate, and thus it might evaporate during economic recessions, whereas banks covered by explicit and implicit deposit insurance schemes are better equipped to cope with economic downturns (Demirgüç-Kunt, Kane, and Laeven 2014). Finally, the new credit assessment techniques that the P2P models incorporate into their processes might involve discriminatory systems against borrowers in poorer areas and other vulnerable segments (U.S. Department of the Treasury 2016). As for payments, the anonymity, speed, and global reach of some digital currencies facilitates the funding of illegal activities. For example, the "Silkroad" was an anonymous e-commerce platform that allowed for the trading of any type of product (including illegal ones) through the use of Tor (an anonymous browser) and bitcoin (an anonymous form of payment). These are some of the risks that have been identified so far, but there still exist several unknown risks related to the new digital financial providers.

At the center of the policy debate is how this new area of finance should be regulated and supervised. For example, lending discrimination against some customers, disclosure requirements for SMEs, and the sharing of customer data, are some of the areas of concern for U.S. regulators brought by the new online platforms (*Politico* 2016). Recent irregularities in the P2P intermediation process have also led to calls for stricter regulation.[29] Moreover, consumer protection and education measures are much needed because many fintechs serve segments of more vulnerable customers (some of them are accessing financial services for the first time). Another area of concern is the cross-border activity of the new digital financial services. Although many fintech companies operate globally or offer digital products involving multiple economies, financial regulation remains region-specific and highly fragmented. Therefore, it is not clear which economy's laws should

prevail. However, excessive regulation might not be desirable, as it may be deadly for fintech start-ups. Understating this, regulators in some economies are developing regulatory sandboxes to manage the transition to a new financial landscape. The aim of this approach is twofold. On the one hand, it allows fintech companies to live test their services with real customers while facing a low level of regulation during a predefined period of time. On the other hand, it helps financial authorities to better understand the functioning of these new services as well as their advantages and risks, ensuring that appropriate consumer protection safeguards are built into the new products and services before they reach the mass market (Financial Conduct Authority 2015). The United Kingdom has launched its sandbox, and other economies, such as Australia, Singapore, and Hong Kong SAR, China, are pursuing similar initiatives (*Financial Times* 2016a). The sandbox strategy has also been contemplated by U.S. regulators (*Wall Street Journal* 2016). The new digitally enabled methods could also be used to address compliance requirements and to monitor digital financial services ("regtech")—see Arner, Barberis, and Buckley (forthcoming) and *Financial Times* (2016b).

Despite the rapid expansion of fintech companies, so far the level of disruption seems to be low. To date, about 1 percent of the consumer banking revenue in North America has been disrupted by fintech players (Citigroup 2016).[30] Moreover, total household and SME lending intermediated by online platforms remains small. According to Citigroup (2016), household lending intermediated through P2P platforms remains at less than 1 percent of total retail loans outstanding in the United States and the United Kingdom. Although online credit to SMEs has grown continually since 2008, it represented less than $10 billion in outstanding loans in the United States by 2013, compared with a total of $700 billion in bank credit outstanding for small businesses (Mills and McCarthy 2014).[31] Moreover, as noted earlier, nonbank MTOs have gained a considerable share of the remittance business. However, the MTO dominating the nonbank market is Western Union, a traditional player, and yet it is holding about 15 percent of the total market share. This traditional MTO provides more expensive services than the new initiatives, but it allows the transfer of cash in real time and without the need for bank accounts (a useful feature in developing economies). Meanwhile, the volume of cryptocurrency transactions is rather limited compared with other electronic means (Schuh and Shy 2016), and the potential uses of blockchain for other applications are still in their infancy.

The low level of disruption to date is driven in part by the complementarity of the services provided by many fintech providers and traditional banks. In many instances, the new fintech companies complement (rather than substitute for) traditional banking, bringing alternative sources of external finance to households and SMEs. For example, a large fraction of the market value in fintech has been created within the relatively new e-commerce ecosystem, which includes firms such as Alipay in China and Paypal in the United States. So, in that case, it seems like an opportunity lost rather than a loss of existing earnings. Moreover, online lending is an alternative for the types of borrowers usually underserved by traditional banks: SMEs and higher-risk households. This alternative lending method expanded worldwide during the banking crunch that followed the global financial crisis, which hit small firms relatively hard. Since then, SMEs have been less able to secure traditional bank credit, and the new online lenders have opened up new pools of capital for them (Mills and Mc-Carthy 2014). This is of special relevance for households and firms in the developing world, where the banking system is often underdeveloped, but also for underserved borrowers in high-income economies. For example, Roure, Pelizzon, and Tasca (2016) find that P2P loans in Germany serve riskier customers than traditional bank loans. Blaseg and Koetter (2016) show that young firms in Germany are more likely to use online equity crowdfunding platforms when their banks are affected by credit crunches.

Finally, because a bank account is needed to perform many of the new fintech services, it would be hard to imagine fintech companies overtaking banks completely and becoming involved in the current accounts niche. There will always be a need for that highly regulated service, which allows households and firms to keep their money safe and accessible, and banks seem to be the players best suited to do that.

Despite their small scale, fintech firms and the newly developed digital technologies in the global financial sector are expected to continue gaining importance over the years, and incumbents are responding with collaborative strategies. Meanwhile, the trend toward digitalization and technological innovation will likely reshape the global financial sector and the ways in which financial companies interact with their customers. For example, some global banks appear to be already shifting their distribution channels from brick-and-mortar operations to nonphysical channels, which will probably be the main channel of interaction between banks and consumers in the future. The proliferation of mobile devices and new demographics are two of the driving forces in this development, as well as the new solutions and products that are better addressing customer needs by increasing accessibility, speed, and convenience. These developments are likely increasing customer expectations for financial services, and banks will find it difficult to control all parts of the value chain using traditional business models (Forrester Consulting 2015; PwC 2011). Recognizing this, banks seem to be shifting toward viewing fintech companies as partners and enablers rather than disruptors and competitors (Economist Intelligence Unit 2015). Incumbent banks are realizing that they need to take advantage of fintech capabilities to grow business, retain existing customers, and attract new ones (some of them previously unbanked) in the medium to long runs. Meanwhile, without access to a client base, client trust, capital, licenses, and a robust global infrastructure, the new fintech companies will discover that there are limits to their growth. Collaboration between incumbents and new players is already taking place, and incumbent financial institutions seem to be pouring increasing amount of investments into the fintech sector through fintech acquisitions, fintech investment funds, and fintech incubators and accelerators (KPMG 2016).

NOTES

1. In the context of this chapter, the "North" comprises Austria, Belgium, Canada, Denmark, Finland, France, Germany, Greece, Iceland, Ireland, Italy, Japan, Luxembourg, the Netherlands, Norway, Portugal, San Marino, Spain, Sweden, Switzerland, the United Kingdom, and the United States. The "South" includes all other economies not in the North. Throughout this chapter, offshore financial centers are excluded from the analysis.

2. Data on international bank claims consider the asset side and use the liability side to augment incomplete reporting. Countries in the North have reported consistently since the 1980s, implying good coverage of North–North and North–South transactions and reasonable coverage of South–North transactions (through the liabilities reported by countries in the North). Reporting of South–South transactions remains relatively sparse, arguably leading to an underestimation of the value of these connections.

   Locational banking statistics categorize banks according to the residency principle. For example, the claims that Spanish bank branches and subsidiaries operating in Chile might have in Brazil would be counted as Chilean claims on Brazil, not as Spanish claims on Brazil, as the BIS Consolidated Banking Statistics would report.

3. Because flows are more volatile than stocks, syndicated loans are averaged across years, and different time periods are used to describe the trends in cross-border bank claims (2001 versus 2014) and syndicated loans (1996–2001 versus 2002–14).

   The value of each syndicated loan is divided equally among the number of lenders, splitting each transaction into several loans with a common borrower and different lenders. Data are then aggregated at the bilateral country level by summing the value of all transactions from a given source economy to a given recipient economy for every year in the sample.

4. The ACIA, which came into effect in March 2012, aims to boost cross-border investments across ASEAN economies by establishing a free, open, transparent, and integrated investment regime. The ACMF is a forum comprising capital market regulators from Brunei Darussalam, Cambodia, Indonesia, the Lao People's Democratic Republic, Malaysia, Myanmar, the Philippines, Singapore, Thailand, and Vietnam. It seeks to achieve greater integration of the region's capital markets through the harmonization of capital market regulations.

5. Several reports have already highlighted the rising presence of the South in international finance, which has accounted for most of the growth in world capital flows since the 1990s (Aykut and Goldstein 2006; Aykut and Ratha 2004; Broner and others 2017; de la Torre and others 2015; World Bank 2006, 2011, 2013).

6. With the exception of South–North bank claims, which have expanded at a slower pace than North–North claims.

7. The largest 20 economies in the South are classified according to their GDP in 2014.

8. Interregional lending refers to cross-border transactions with economies outside the region, whereas intraregional lending refers to cross-border transactions with economies inside the region.

9. The Gulf Cooperation Council economies are Bahrain, Kuwait, Oman, Qatar, Saudi Arabia, and the United Arab Emirates.

10. For cross-border bank claims, old connections are those country-pair links that were established in 2001, and the new connections are those that were established later. For cross-border syndicated loans, old connections are those country-pair links that were established in the period 1996–2001, and new connections are those that were established later.

11. Total EAP lending to the South (EAP-South) also includes cross-border intraregional lending (EAP-EAP).

12. For example, the three largest Icelandic banks increased their assets from 100 percent of GDP in 2000 to more than 800 percent by 2007 (Wade and Sigurgeirsdottir 2011).

13. However, increasing regionalization could also constrain the global diffusion of banking technology and practices across economies as well as the efficient allocation of capital around the world.

14. One indication of the increased size and sophistication of developing economies' financial systems is the growing presence of their banks in syndicated lending—syndicated loans typically include banks that are relatively reliable and well known.

15. This section is based on transaction-level data on corporate bonds and syndicated loans issued domestically and internationally, considering issuances by both listed and nonlisted firms with an original maturity of one year or longer. Classification of corporate bonds as domestic or international was undertaken by comparing the market location of the bond issuance with the issuing firm's nationality. For syndicated loans, the nationality of the banks that participate in the deal is used to distinguish between domestic and cross-border lending. Following the criterion used in the previous section, syndicated loans are divided into tranches according to the number of lenders. Domestic loans are defined as those loans in which the nationality of the lender bank is the same as the one of the issuing firm. Data on firms' capital-raising activity come from the SDC Platinum database.

   Financial sector issuances are excluded throughout this section.

16. This approach is similar to the one pioneered by Khwaja and Mian (2008) for firms borrowing from different banks within a country and addresses the concern about compositional changes in the set of firms raising debt.

17. See Cortina, Didier, and Schmukler (2016) for details about calculation of the logit regressions.

18. Switching issuers not only changed the composition between bond and loan issuances after 2008, but also compensated for the decline in syndicated loan financing—that is, for those issuers, the increase in the amount raised through corporate bonds during the crisis years compensated for the decline in their syndicated loan issuances.

19. See Pesenti and Tille (2000) for a review of this topic.

20. See http://www.businessinsider.com/william -garrity-associates-global-fintech-heat-map -2015-9?r=UK&IR=T.

21. However, the first P2P lending platform was launched in 2005 by Zopa in the United Kingdom.

22. Electronic payments accounted for 68 percent of U.S. transactions in 2012 (World Economic Forum 2016b).

23. The bitcoin system emerged in 2008 in a paper published by Nakamoto (2008), the alias used by the author, whose actual identity is still unknown.

24. See https://blockchain.info.

25. Bazot (2013) finds similar results in other major countries such as France, Germany, and the United Kingdom.

26. See World Bank (2014) and Cull, Ehrbeck, and Holle (2014) for a summary of the research on the economic benefits of financial inclusion.

27. According to the Global Findex Database (http://www.worldbank.org/en/programs/globalfindex), over 2 billion people are financially excluded, but 90 percent of them have access to mobile phones.

28. Mobile payment options are growing more slowly in some high-income markets such as the United States, where the share of cash transactions is much lower (about 14 percent of all transactions) and the established electronic payment system (credit and debit cards) is well developed and efficient (Crowe, Rysman, and Stavins 2010).

29. For example, Lending Club, the largest P2P platform in the United States, which became public in 2014, encountered irregularities in its loan origination and trading processes that caused its shares to plummet and its CEO to resign (Reuters 2016). The failure of several P2P platforms in Asia also led to calls for more regulation (Ecns.cn 2016).

30. According to Citigroup (2016), consumer banking revenue in North America disrupted by fintech companies is projected to grow to about 17 percent by 2023.

31. In a recent survey, only about 2 percent of SMEs in the United States reported using nonbank loans (NSBA 2016).

Statistical Appendixes

This section consists of two appendixes.

Appendix A presents basic economy-by-economy data on financial system characteristics around the world. It also presents averages of the same indicators for peer groups of countries, together with summary maps. It is an update on information from the 2015/2016 *Global Financial Development Report*.

Appendix B provides additional economy-by-economy information on key aspects of international banking around the world. It is specific to the 2017/2018 *Global Financial Development Report*.

These appendixes present only a small part of the Global Financial Development Database (GFDD), available at http://www.worldbank .org/financialdevelopment. The 2017/2018 *Global Financial Development Report* is also accompanied by *Financial Development Data Tables,* which is a concise online edition of the GFDD for convenient reference, available at http://data .worldbank.org/ldbfd. It presents country-by-country and also regional data for a larger set of variables than what are shown here.

APPENDIX A

BASIC DATA ON FINANCIAL SYSTEM CHARACTERISTICS, 2013–15

TABLE A.1   **Economies and Their Financial System Characteristics, 2013–15**

Economy	Financial institutions				Financial markets			
	Private credit by deposit money banks to GDP (%)	Account at a formal financial institution (%, age 15+)	Bank lending-deposit spread (%)	Bank Z-score	Stock market capitalization to GDP (%)	Market capitalization excluding top 10 companies to total market capitalization (%)	Stock market turnover ratio (%)	Stock price volatility
Afghanistan	3.8	9.6		10.8				
Albania	37.2	34.7	6.6	15.3				
Algeria	17.6	44.7	6.3	21.1				
Andorra				22.4				
Angola	20.4	32.6	13.0	11.3				
Antigua and Barbuda	61.9		7.2	32.2				
Argentina	11.7	44.5	3.2	7.3	7.9	30.1	7.3	34.0
Armenia	41.9	17.3	5.1	9.6	1.2		0.8	
Aruba	61.5		6.5	24.5				
Australia	125.8	98.9	3.1	7.6	87.7	52.8	58.8	12.2
Austria	89.1	96.8	3.4	20.3	24.8	40.7	28.7	18.7
Azerbaijan	28.3	24.4	8.5	2.8	0.1			
Bahamas, The	75.5		3.2	16.6				
Bahrain	67.5	76.1	4.6	15.5	62.2	27.7	2.2	7.1
Bangladesh	40.1	30.0	2.8	7.8	14.5		65.1	15.2
Barbados	77.5		6.3	13.1	107.3		0.4	
Belarus	21.2	67.5	0.2	4.4				
Belgium	57.1	97.5	5.2	14.7	72.3		30.2	15.7
Belize	55.4	48.2	7.9	8.1				
Benin	21.9	14.1	2.0	10.9				
Bermuda				13.7			3.0	15.3
Bhutan	43.0	33.7	9.3	32.7	9.6			
Bolivia	42.1	36.5	7.6	9.7	15.9		0.4	
Bosnia and Herzegovina	52.5	53.9	3.9	7.8	13.5			9.2
Botswana	30.9	42.9	6.3	10.1	28.5		2.7	3.6
Brazil	66.4	64.0	24.3	10.5	37.2	48.9	72.4	22.7
Brunei Darussalam	34.2		5.2	9.0				
Bulgaria	61.8	59.6	6.7	8.9	13.6		5.0	14.3
Burkina Faso	25.8	13.4	3.2	7.4				
Burundi	16.5	7.0	8.0	11.6				
Cabo Verde	61.8		7.1	23.7				
Cambodia	48.3	9.6		10.7				
Cameroon	14.6	12.5	10.8	11.2				
Canada	126.6	98.0	2.5	14.0	106.0	72.3	64.4	11.1

(appendix continued next page)

TABLE A.1   **Economies and Their Financial System Characteristics, 2013–15** *(continued)*

Economy	Financial institutions				Financial markets			
	Private credit by deposit money banks to GDP (%)	Account at a formal financial institution (%, age 15+)	Bank lending-deposit spread (%)	Bank Z-score	Stock market capitalization to GDP (%)	Market capitalization excluding top 10 companies to total market capitalization (%)	Stock market turnover ratio (%)	Stock price volatility
Cayman Islands				17.1			1.0	
Central African Republic	13.8	3.3	10.8	7.4				
Chad	7.9	8.1	10.8	11.9				
Channel Islands							0.1	
Chile	75.5	56.2	3.4	7.1	91.8	54.4	12.0	12.6
China	132.4	73.9	2.9	22.7	50.7	81.1	331.6	20.7
Colombia	40.5	35.7	6.8	7.8	46.1	25.8	10.3	14.9
Comoros	23.2	21.7	8.8					
Congo, Dem. Rep.	5.4	8.5	15.0	4.6				
Congo, Rep.	14.5	14.5	10.8	5.0				
Costa Rica	51.0	59.8	11.6	18.2	3.8		1.9	37.9
Côte d'Ivoire	18.7	15.1	1.0	6.6	35.8		3.7	
Denmark	178.7	99.9	4.7	13.6	61.2		53.5	16.2
Croatia	68.8	86.8	7.7	4.7	37.0		2.4	9.2
Cuba				14.0				
Curaçao				7.8				
Cyprus	255.3	88.5	3.3	6.0	12.5	10.7	2.7	45.6
Czech Republic	49.6	81.7	3.9	4.5	17.6		28.1	15.2
Djibouti	29.4	12.3	10.6	16.4				
Dominica	54.9		6.1	10.0				
Dominican Republic	23.3	48.7	7.7	22.3	0.7			
Ecuador	26.3	43.1	9.7	5.1	6.7		2.3	5.9
Egypt, Arab Rep.	25.2	12.3	4.7	18.6	20.3	52.8	28.8	23.7
El Salvador	41.0	27.7	4.6	24.9	34.1		0.6	
Equatorial Guinea	9.8		10.8	17.5				
Eritrea	12.7			6.3				
Estonia	69.3	97.4	4.4	9.3	8.5		9.4	10.7
Ethiopia	17.2	21.8	3.3	7.5				
Fiji	58.3		3.7	25.3	10.7		1.6	
Finland	92.9	99.9	2.7	10.2	57.2		86.1	16.9
France	94.9	96.7	4.4	19.7	76.9		53.2	18.2
Gabon	14.1	26.4	10.8	10.9				
Gambia, The	13.6		12.8	6.3				
Georgia	41.0	37.4	3.6	6.2	5.5		0.2	
Germany	79.7	98.6	7.0	22.6	46.9	54.5	78.6	17.1
Ghana	16.0	32.9	9.1	7.2	7.5		1.7	8.1

TABLE A.1   **Economies and Their Financial System Characteristics, 2013–15** *(continued)*

Economy	Financial institutions				Financial markets			
	Private credit by deposit money banks to GDP (%)	Account at a formal financial institution (%, age 15+)	Bank lending-deposit spread (%)	Bank Z-score	Stock market capitalization to GDP (%)	Market capitalization excluding top 10 companies to total market capitalization (%)	Stock market turnover ratio (%)	Stock price volatility
Gibraltar				31.1				
Greece	117.8	84.3	4.3	7.6	26.2	19.9	42.1	37.0
Grenada	67.5		6.9	11.9				
Guatemala	31.3	34.6	8.1	21.9	0.8		6.6	
Guinea	10.3	5.3	11.9	5.2				
Guinea-Bissau	11.9		4.2	4.8				
Guyana	35.0		11.9	22.2	18.4		0.3	
Haiti	17.4	19.0	8.3	19.2				
Honduras	53.0	26.9	9.7	31.8	684.5			
Hong Kong SAR, China	211.5	93.7	5.0	17.6	1062.4	66.0	51.3	16.5
Hungary	43.6	72.4	3.0	3.2	13.2	3.4	48.2	18.1
Iceland	102.7		7.2	3.1	16.6		29.1	11.2
India	49.7	46.9		8.9	66.3	71.7	50.9	15.6
Indonesia	30.7	30.5	4.5	4.1	40.9	54.2	24.3	17.1
Iran, Islamic Rep.	48.3	86.0	0.1		41.9	50.7	15.9	
Iraq	7.4	10.8		27.6				
Ireland	95.3	94.4	2.6	10.0	60.8	8.8	12.6	15.8
Israel	64.7	90.1	3.0	24.7	67.1	42.3	26.4	11.4
Italy	90.5	81.9	4.9	9.9	27.4	38.1	273.5	24.2
Jamaica	28.4	75.9	12.7	8.0	45.2		3.1	11.9
Japan	103.9	96.6	0.8	14.0	86.7	83.1	135.0	20.3
Jordan	69.0	24.9	4.5	33.2	72.7	35.1	13.0	7.9
Kazakhstan	34.1	50.0		2.1	11.7	17.0	5.6	23.6
Kenya	31.0	50.9	7.9	16.5	25.4		7.9	10.7
Korea, Rep.	127.7	93.9	1.7	9.9	89.6	67.0	122.1	12.9
Kosovo	33.0	46.6		9.7				
Kuwait	72.5	77.5	2.3	14.7	56.7		23.3	10.2
Kyrgyz Republic	17.3	13.6	20.2	18.6	2.4		3.4	
Lao PDR	18.9	26.8	19.6	7.2				17.5
Latvia	54.7	90.0	5.8	4.3	3.7		3.0	14.0
Lebanon	92.8	43.6	1.3	20.8	23.8		4.0	7.1
Lesotho	19.2	18.5	7.6	8.4				
Liberia	16.7	18.8	9.5	10.0				
Libya	14.5		3.5	30.3				
Lithuania	42.0	76.5	4.3	5.6	9.2		4.4	9.0
Luxembourg	90.6	95.6	2.0	34.8	106.5	4.7	0.2	15.7

(appendix continued next page)

TABLE A.1 **Economies and Their Financial System Characteristics, 2013–15** *(continued)*

Economy	Financial institutions				Financial markets			
	Private credit by deposit money banks to GDP (%)	Account at a formal financial institution (%, age 15+)	Bank lending-deposit spread (%)	Bank Z-score	Stock market capitalization to GDP (%)	Market capitalization excluding top 10 companies to total market capitalization (%)	Stock market turnover ratio (%)	Stock price volatility
Macao SAR, China	74.5		5.2	17.8				
Macedonia, FYR	47.3	72.4	3.9	5.3	5.7		5.6	15.4
Madagascar	11.8	5.7	47.3	6.3				
Malawi	11.2	16.3	30.5	10.6	13.7		2.0	
Malaysia	116.4	75.8	1.5	16.0	138.8	64.0	29.7	8.6
Maldives	31.8		7.2	9.5				
Mali	22.3	11.6	3.3	7.6				
Malta	102.3	96.0	2.6	13.8	37.8	10.8	1.9	8.4
Mauritania	27.5	19.5	11.2	19.9				
Mauritius	102.0	81.5	1.9	14.8	67.0	40.2	5.1	4.4
Mexico	21.7	34.9	2.8	18.8	38.4	44.3	27.5	14.0
Micronesia, Fed. Sts.	20.8		15.0	23.7				
Moldova	34.5	17.9	4.2	6.7	2.7		111.8	
Monaco				17.9				
Mongolia	53.3	87.1	6.6	21.4	11.7		2.9	17.2
Montenegro	51.3	56.7		7.2	86.6		1.2	13.4
Morocco	66.4	39.1	8.0	39.9	48.1	28.4	6.0	9.0
Mozambique	28.2	39.9	6.4	4.0				
Myanmar	13.3	22.6	5.0	2.5				
Namibia	47.4	58.1	4.5	7.9	8.9		1.8	17.6
Nepal	55.6	31.0	4.4	25.4	20.1		1.3	
Netherlands	115.3	99.1	0.2	8.9	90.5		60.4	15.0
New Zealand	139.2	99.5	1.8	24.0	52.4	56.2	13.4	8.1
Nicaragua	29.0	17.3	12.5	12.2				
Niger	13.8	2.8	3.5	11.0				
Nigeria	12.8	39.3	7.9	9.4	12.2	28.2	8.1	14.8
Norway	109.1	100.0	2.0	8.6	47.6	26.0	44.7	15.7
Oman	48.6	73.6	3.0	15.5	48.2	66.2	13.9	10.4
Pakistan	15.4	9.2	4.8	10.8	16.9		31.5	13.0
Panama	69.2	37.2	4.8	25.6	30.8		1.0	6.3
Papua New Guinea	25.0		9.1	6.4	68.0		0.6	
Paraguay	46.7	21.7	16.0	12.7	3.8		5.6	
Peru	31.7	26.1	14.4	14.8	39.3	37.9	3.3	15.5
Philippines	36.2	27.6	4.1	15.7	83.1	60.1	17.8	17.2
Poland	51.3	75.3	3.3	8.0	33.6	45.4	35.3	17.1

TABLE A.1　**Economies and Their Financial System Characteristics, 2013–15** *(continued)*

Economy	Financial institutions				Financial markets			
	Private credit by deposit money banks to GDP (%)	Account at a formal financial institution (%, age 15+)	Bank lending-deposit spread (%)	Bank Z-score	Stock market capitalization to GDP (%)	Market capitalization excluding top 10 companies to total market capitalization (%)	Stock market turnover ratio (%)	Stock price volatility
Portugal	134.7	85.3	2.8	12.9	29.7		63.5	18.7
Puerto Rico		69.7						
Qatar	47.9	65.9	3.4	24.5	86.2	27.6	20.1	12.8
Romania	32.3	55.4	5.4	4.7	10.2		12.3	13.3
Russian Federation	52.2	61.0	5.2	5.2	28.4	38.7	32.3	20.7
Rwanda	18.6	36.4	9.2	6.4				
Samoa	41.5		7.1	12.0				
San Marino	123.5			9.2				
São Tomé and Príncipe	27.6		13.0	2.9				
Saudi Arabia	44.8	61.7		14.6	63.2	47.0	100.7	15.8
Senegal	31.4	9.9	1.0	5.4				
Serbia	43.9	76.1	8.4	11.4	17.7		4.0	11.0
Seychelles	21.5		9.1	8.7				
Sierra Leone	4.7	14.5	12.9	4.9				
Singapore	124.4	97.0	5.2	19.8	240.5	72.9	31.2	10.3
Slovak Republic	48.8	78.0	2.0	14.4	4.9		2.3	17.4
Slovenia	61.6	97.2	4.5	2.1	14.6	62.7	7.3	16.4
Solomon Islands	20.4		10.4					
Somalia		15.6						
South Africa	65.9	63.7	3.3	13.4	245.2	77.2	28.2	13.8
South Sudan	1.4		12.2	8.3				
Spain	134.5	96.1	1.8	18.7	73.8	32.2	100.5	21.4
Sri Lanka	26.2	78.0	0.6	11.4	25.7	59.6	9.7	10.3
St. Kitts and Nevis	59.8		5.9	13.6	81.1		0.9	
St. Lucia	103.2		6.3	4.8				
St. Vincent and the Grenadines	52.3		6.8	15.3				
Sudan	8.0	12.5		23.8				
Suriname	28.1		5.0	14.9				
Swaziland	19.3	28.6	6.6	14.8	6.3		1.7	
Sweden	127.9	99.5	2.5	11.9	92.8		74.5	15.8
Switzerland	169.3	98.0	2.7	13.9	213.7	29.2	54.3	14.2
Syrian Arab Republic	20.4	23.3	3.7	10.7				
Taiwan, China		90.0		13.3		69.7		
Tajikistan	17.0	8.5	19.5	12.0				
Tanzania	12.8	18.4	6.2	11.9	4.3		1.6	14.5

(appendix continued next page)

TABLE A.1 **Economies and Their Financial System Characteristics, 2013–15** *(continued)*

	Financial institutions				Financial markets			
Economy	Private credit by deposit money banks to GDP (%)	Account at a formal financial institution (%, age 15+)	Bank lending-deposit spread (%)	Bank Z-score	Stock market capitalization to GDP (%)	Market capitalization excluding top 10 companies to total market capitalization (%)	Stock market turnover ratio (%)	Stock price volatility
Thailand	111.6	76.3	4.7	3.2	93.5	62.9	81.8	16.4
Timor-Leste	13.2		12.1					
Togo	32.5	15.1	2.9	3.1				
Tonga	30.0		6.1	4.9				
Trinidad and Tobago	32.2	75.9	6.2	25.3	65.2		0.8	
Tunisia	71.2	28.9	2.5	23.2	19.4		14.3	7.0
Turkey	60.4	56.9		7.7	26.9	52.4	175.6	23.9
Turkmenistan		1.3		2.6				
Tuvalu				10.9				
Uganda	12.4	25.3	10.7	10.6	30.7		0.2	
Ukraine	55.2	48.9	6.8	5.2	13.1		5.2	30.6
United Arab Emirates	65.2	75.4	4.4	27.2	45.9	23.3	39.7	15.2
United Kingdom	145.9	98.4	2.7	13.6	112.1	69.0	84.9	12.6
United States	49.5	91.7		27.9	139.5	74.6	156.0	12.6
Uruguay	27.9	38.1	9.6	5.5	0.3		0.8	
Uzbekistan		34.6		6.7			5.9	
Vanuatu	69.5		3.2	9.7				
Venezuela, RB	27.9	52.6	2.8	6.8	3.7		0.3	32.5
Vietnam	96.4	27.7	2.8	5.9	23.6		38.7	17.9
West Bank and Gaza	29.0	22.6		17.6	25.1		9.6	10.6
Yemen, Rep.	5.6	5.5	6.8	19.1				
Zambia	12.5	28.0	3.7	2.9	13.8		5.7	
Zimbabwe	8.0	24.7		3.4	136.5		0.0	

Source: Data from and calculations based on the Global Financial Development Database. For more information, see Čihák and others 2013.
Note: Empty cells indicate a lack of data.

NOTES

Economy: A territorial entity for which statistical data are maintained and provided internationally on a separate and independent basis (not necessarily a state as understood by international law and practice). The term, used interchangeably with *country,* does not imply political independence or official recognition by the World Bank.

Table layout: The layout of the table follows the 4x2 matrix of financial system characteristics introduced in the 2013 *Global Financial Development Report*, with four variables approximating depth, access, efficiency, and stability of financial institutions and financial markets, respectively.

Additional data: The table above presents a small fraction of observations in the Global Financial Development Database, accompanying this report. For additional variables, historical data, and detailed metadata, see

the full data set at http://www.worldbank
.org/financialdevelopment.

Period covered: The table shows averages of
values for 2013–15, where available.

Averaging: Each observation is an arithmetic
average of the corresponding variable over
2013–15. When a variable is not reported
or not available for a part of this period, the
average is calculated using the forwarded
value from the most recent observation
available.

Visualization: To illustrate where an economy's observation is in relation to the global
distribution of the variable, the table includes
four bars on the left of each observation. The
four-bar scale is based on the location of
the economy in the statistical distribution of
the variable in the Global Financial Development Database: values below the 25th percentile show only one full bar, values equal
to or greater than the 25th and less than the
50th percentile show two full bars, values
equal to or greater than the 50th and less
than the 75th percentile show three full bars,
and values greater than the 75th percentile
show four full bars. At the economy level,
bars are calculated using winsorized and rescaled values, as described in the 2013 *Global
Financial Development Report*. To prepare
for this, the 95th and 5th percentile for each
variable for the entire pooled economy-year
data set are calculated, and the top and
bottom 5 percent of observations are trun-
cated. Specifically, all observations from the
5th percentile to the minimum are replaced
by the value corresponding to the 5th percentile, and all observations from the 95th
percentile to the maximum are replaced by
the value corresponding to the 95th percentile. To convert all the variables to a 0–100
scale, each score is rescaled by the maximum
and the minimum for each indicator. The
rescaled indicator can be interpreted as the
percent distance between the worst (0) and
the best (100) financial development out-
come, defined by the 5th and 95th percen-
tiles of the original distribution. The four
bars on the left of the economy name show

the unweighted arithmetic average of the
rescaled variables (dimensions) for each
economy. This average is reported only for
those economies for which data for 2013–
15 are available for at least four variables
(dimensions).

**Private credit by deposit money banks to
GDP (%)** measures the domestic private
credit to the real sector by deposit money
banks as a percentage of local currency GDP.
Data on domestic private credit to the real
sector by deposit money banks are from the
International Financial Statistics (IFS), line
FOSAOP/22D, published by the Interna-
tional Monetary Fund (IMF). Local currency
GDP is also from IFS.

**Account at a formal financial institution (%,
age 15+)** measures the percentage of adults
with an account (self or together with some-
one else) at a bank, credit union, another
financial institution (e.g., cooperative,
microfinance institution), or the post office
(if applicable), including adults who report
having a debit card. The data are from the
Global Financial Inclusion (Global Findex)
Database (Demirgüç-Kunt, Klapper, and
others 2014).

**Bank lending-deposit spread (percentage
points)** is lending rate minus deposit rate.
Lending rate is the rate charged by banks
on loans to the private sector, and deposit
interest rate is the rate paid by commercial
or similar banks for demand, time, or savings deposits. The lending and deposit rates
are from IFS lines FILR/60P and FIDR/60L,
respectively.

Bank Z-score is calculated as [ROA + (equity /
assets)] / (standard deviation of ROA). To
approximate the probability that a an economy's banking system defaults, the indicator compares the system's buffers (returns
and capitalization) with the system's riskiness (volatility of returns). Return on Assets
(ROA), equity, and assets are economy-level
aggregate figures (calculated from underlying bank-by-bank unconsolidated data from
Bankscope and Orbis Bank Focus).

Stock market capitalization to GDP (%) measures the capitalization of all equity markets as percentage of GDP. Market capitalization (also known as market value) is the share price times the number of shares outstanding. Listed domestic companies are the domestically incorporated companies listed on the economy's stock exchanges at the end of the year. Listed companies do not include investment companies, mutual funds, or other collective investment vehicles. Data are from World Federation of Exchanges (WFE), Standard & Poor's Global Stock Markets Factbook, and supplemental Standard & Poor's data, and are compiled and reported by the World Development Indicators.

Market capitalization excluding top 10 companies to total market capitalization (%) measures the ratio of market capitalization outside of the top 10 largest companies to total market capitalization. The WFE provides data on the exchange level. This variable is aggregated up to the economy level by taking a simple average over exchanges.

Stock market turnover ratio (%) is the total value of shares traded during the period divided by the average market capitalization for the period. Average market capitalization is calculated as the average of the end-of-period values for the current period and the previous period. Data are from the WFE, Standard & Poor's Global Stock Markets Factbook, and supplemental Standard & Poor's data, and are compiled and reported by the World Development Indicators.

Stock price volatility is the 360-day standard deviation of the return on the primary national stock market index. The data are from Bloomberg.

MAP A.1   DEPTH—FINANCIAL INSTITUTIONS

To approximate financial institutions' depth, this map uses domestic private credit to the real sector by deposit money banks as a percentage of local currency GDP. Data on domestic private credit to the real sector by deposit money banks are from the International Financial Statistics (IFS), line

FOSAOP/22D, published by the International Monetary Fund (IMF). Local currency GDP is also from IFS. The four shades of blue in the map are based on the average value of the variable in 2013–15: the darker the blue, the higher the quartile of the statistical distribution of the variable.

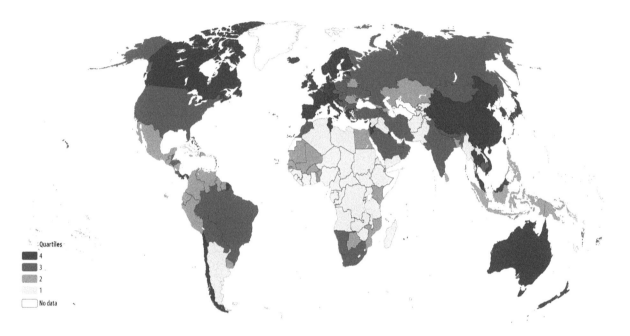

Quartiles
- 4
- 3
- 2
- 1
- No data

TABLE A.1.1   **Depth—Financial Institutions**

Private credit by deposit money banks to GDP (%)	Number of countries	Average	Median	Standard deviation	Minimum	Maximum	Weighted average
World	185	51.4	41.5	41.3	1.4	255.3	83.1
By developed/developing economies							
Developed economies	56	89.6	76.5	46.1	21.5	255.3	85.9
Developing economies	129	34.9	28.4	24.9	1.4	132.4	78.3
By income level							
High income	56	89.6	76.5	46.1	21.5	255.3	85.9
Upper-middle income	50	47.9	45.3	28.7	7.4	132.4	90.1
Lower-middle income	50	32.4	29	18.8	5.6	96.4	38.1
Low income	29	16.6	13.8	10.9	1.4	55.6	17.1
By region							
High income: OECD	33	97.5	94.9	36.5	43.6	178.7	86
High income: non-OECD	23	78.3	65.2	56.1	21.5	255.3	83
East Asia and Pacific	18	52	38.9	38	13.2	132.4	120.4
Europe and Central Asia	19	40.1	41	13.6	17	61.8	50.6
Latin America and the Caribbean	25	42.2	40.5	20.4	11.7	103.2	42.5
Middle East and North Africa	13	38.2	29	28.2	5.6	92.8	35
South Asia	8	33.2	36	17.5	3.8	55.6	44.7
Sub-Saharan Africa	46	21.3	16.2	17.8	1.4	102	26.6

Source: Global Financial Development Database, 2013–15 data.
Note: OECD = Organization for Economic Co-operation and Development. Weighted average by current GDP.

MAP A.2   ACCESS—FINANCIAL INSTITUTIONS

To approximate access to financial institutions, this map uses the percentage of adults (age 15+) who reported having an account at a formal financial institution. The data are taken from the Global Financial Inclusion (Global Findex) Database. The four shades of blue in the map are based on the value of the variable in 2014: the darker the blue, the higher the quartile of the statistical distribution of the variable.

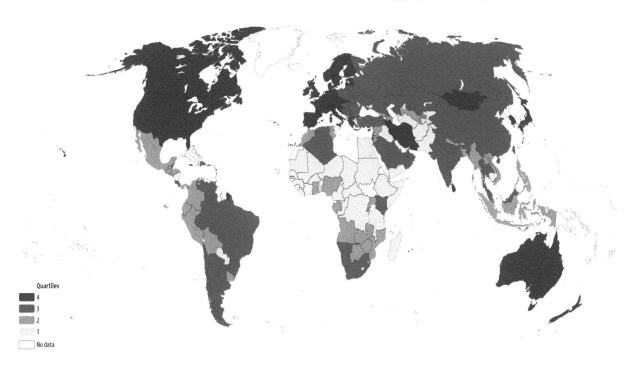

Quartiles
- 4
- 3
- 2
- 1
- No data

TABLE A.1.2   Access—Financial Institutions

Account at a formal financial institution (%, age 15+)	Number of countries	Average	Median	Standard deviation	Minimum	Maximum	Weighted average
World	157	49.8	43.6	31.5	1.3	100	53.7
By developed/developing economies							
Developed economies	48	87.1	92.7	13.6	38.1	100	91.1
Developing economies	109	33.4	28	21.5	1.3	87.1	46.5
By income level							
High income	48	87.1	92.7	13.6	38.1	100	91.1
Upper-middle income	41	49.8	50	19.9	1.3	86	64.8
Lower-middle income	42	28	27.2	17	5.5	87.1	36.2
Low income	26	16.1	14.8	9.6	2.8	39.9	17.1
By region							
High income: OECD	32	91.8	96.6	10.2	56.2	100	92.5
High income: non-OECD	16	77.7	76.3	15	38.1	97	72.2
East Asia and Pacific	10	45.8	29.1	28.7	9.6	87.1	62
Europe and Central Asia	21	42.6	48.9	21.8	1.3	76.1	52
Latin America and the Caribbean	19	39.7	36.5	15.8	17.3	75.9	46.5
Middle East and North Africa	12	29.5	24.1	22	5.5	86	36.3
South Asia	7	34.1	31	23.6	9.2	78	40.7
Sub-Saharan Africa	40	23.4	18.5	17.3	2.8	81.5	26.2

Source: Global Financial Development Database, 2014 data.
Note: OECD = Organization for Economic Co-operation and Development. Weighted average by total adult population in 2014.

MAP A.3   EFFICIENCY—FINANCIAL INSTITUTIONS

To approximate efficiency of financial institutions, this map uses the spread (difference) between lending rate and deposit interest rate. Lending rate is the rate charged by banks on loans to the private sector, and deposit interest rate is the rate paid by commercial or similar banks for demand, time, or savings deposits. The lending and deposit rates are from IFS, lines FILR/60P and FIDR/60L, respectively. The four shades of blue in the map are based on the average value of the variable in 2013–15: the darker the blue, the higher the quartile of the statistical distribution of the variable.

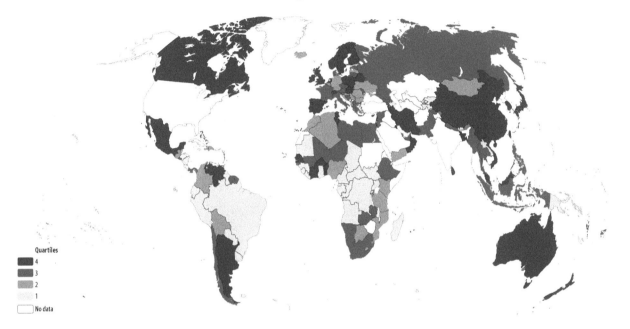

Quartiles
4
3
2
1
No data

TABLE A.1.3   Efficiency—Financial Institutions

Bank lending-deposit spread (%)	Number of countries	Average	Median	Standard deviation	Minimum	Maximum	Weighted average
World	170	6.7	5.2	5.5	0.1	47.3	5.1
By developed/developing economies							
Developed economies	53	4.1	3.4	2	0.2	9.6	3.8
Developing economies	117	7.9	6.8	6.1	0.1	47.3	6.5
By income level							
High income	53	4.1	3.4	2	0.2	9.6	3.8
Upper-middle income	46	6.7	6.2	4.6	0.1	24.3	6.1
Lower-middle income	45	7.9	7.1	4.6	0.6	20.2	6.8
Low income	26	10	8.5	9.7	1	47.3	7.9
By region							
High income: OECD	32	3.3	3	1.6	0.2	7.2	3.2
High income: non-OECD	21	5.3	5.2	2	2.3	9.6	4.8
East Asia and Pacific	17	7	5	4.9	1.5	19.6	4.8
Europe and Central Asia	15	7.2	5.4	5.5	0.2	20.2	6.1
Latin America and the Caribbean	25	8.7	7.7	4.8	2.8	24.3	9.3
Middle East & North Africa	11	4.7	4.5	3.1	0.1	10.6	4
South Asia	6	4.9	4.6	3.1	0.6	9.3	4.9
Sub-Saharan Africa	43	9.1	8	7.9	1	47.3	7.2

Source: Global Financial Development Database, 2013–15 data.
Note: OECD = Organization for Economic Co-operation and Development. Weighted average by total banking assets.

MAP A.4 STABILITY—FINANCIAL INSTITUTIONS

To approximate stability of financial institutions, this map uses the Z-score for commercial banks. The indicator is estimated as follows: [ROA + (equity / assets)] / (standard deviation of ROA). Return on assets (ROA), equity, and assets are economy-level aggregate figures (calculated from underlying bank-by-bank unconsolidated data from Bankscope). The indicator compares the banking system's buffers (returns and capital) with its riskiness (volatility of returns). The four shades of blue in the map are based on the average value of the variable in 2013–15: the darker the blue, the higher the quartile of the statistical distribution of the variable.

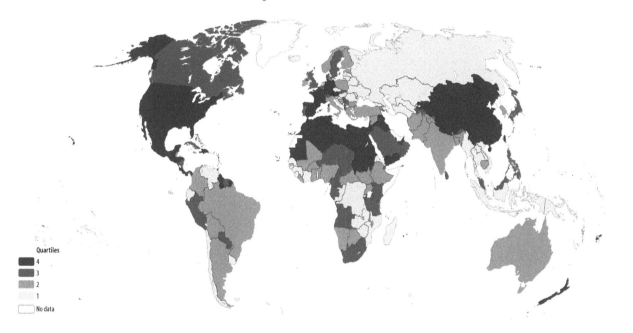

Quartiles
- 4
- 3
- 2
- 1
- No data

TABLE A.1.4 **Stability—Financial Institutions**

Bank Z-score	Number of countries	Average	Median	Standard deviation	Minimum	Maximum	Weighted average
World	192	12.9	10.9	7.7	2.1	39.9	13.7
By developed/developing economies							
Developed economies	63	14.4	13.7	7.6	2.1	34.8	14
Developing economies	129	12.1	10.5	7.6	2.1	39.9	13.4
By income level							
High income	63	14.4	13.7	7.6	2.1	34.8	14
Upper-middle income	52	12.6	10.9	7.6	2.1	33.2	13.4
Lower-middle income	49	13.5	10.8	8.4	2.5	39.9	14.8
Low income	28	8.7	7.5	4.8	3.1	25.4	9.2
By region							
High income: OECD	33	13	11.9	7.6	2.1	34.8	13.3
High income: non-OECD	30	16	15.1	7.5	4.7	32.2	15.3
East Asia and Pacific	17	11.9	10.7	7.6	2.5	25.3	12.7
Europe and Central Asia	21	7.6	6.7	4.1	2.1	18.6	7.7
Latin America and the Caribbean	26	14.6	13.3	7.1	4.8	31.8	14.2
Middle East and North Africa	12	23.2	21	8.1	10.7	39.9	24.5
South Asia	8	14.7	10.8	9.2	7.8	32.7	15.4
Sub-Saharan Africa	45	9.5	8.3	5.1	2.9	23.8	10.4

Source: Global Financial Development Database, 2013–15 data.
Note: OECD = Organization for Economic Co-operation and Development. Weighted average by total banking assets.

MAP A.5   DEPTH—FINANCIAL MARKETS

To approximate depth of financial markets, this map uses stock market capitalization as percentage of GDP. Market capitalization (also known as market value) is the share price times the number of shares outstanding. Listed domestic companies are the domestically incorporated companies listed on the economy's stock exchanges at the end of the year. Listed companies do not include investment companies, mutual funds, or other collective investment vehicles. Data are from WFE, Standard & Poor's Global Stock Markets Factbook, and supplemental S&P data, and are compiled and reported by the *World Development Indicators*. The four shades of blue in the map are based on the average value of the variable in 2013–15: the darker the blue, the higher the quartile of the statistical distribution of the variable.

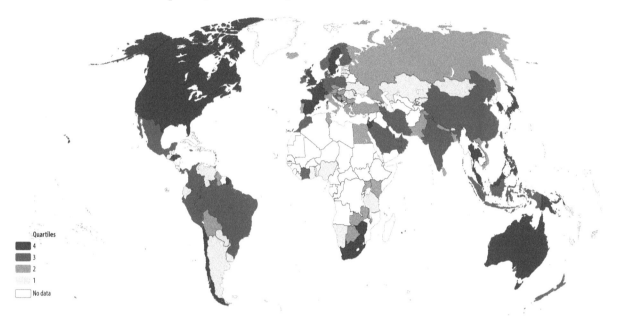

TABLE A.1.5   **Depth—Financial Markets**

Stock market capitalization to GDP (%)	Number of countries	Average	Median	Standard deviation	Minimum	Maximum	Weighted average
World	117	72.4	38.4	125.3	0.1	1077.7	130.8
By developed/developing economies							
Developed economies	49	110.8	79.3	154.4	0.3	1077.7	164.3
Developing economies	68	44.8	19.7	90.8	0.1	684.5	68.6
By income level							
High income	49	110.8	79.3	154.4	0.3	1077.7	164.3
Upper-middle income	35	42.9	24.6	56.1	0.1	262.7	74.1
Lower-middle income	28	47.7	18.1	126.6	0.8	684.5	48.3
Low income	5	41.1	20.1	54.2	4.3	136.5	30.3
By region							
High income: OECD	33	102.3	99.2	63	3.7	231.4	162.1
High income: non-OECD	16	128.5	59.5	259.4	0.3	1077.7	207
East Asia and Pacific	9	73.2	68	60.5	10.7	190.8	90.1
Europe and Central Asia	15	16.6	11.7	21.8	0.1	86.6	28.4
Latin America and the Caribbean	17	63.1	18.4	161.6	0.7	684.5	50
Middle East and North Africa	7	36	25.1	19.6	19.4	72.7	35
South Asia	6	26.3	18.5	22.6	9.6	71.2	60.1
Sub-Saharan Africa	14	46.7	19.6	71.3	4.3	262.7	90

Source: Global Financial Development Database, 2013–15 data.
Note: OECD = Organization for Economic Co-operation and Development. Weighted average by current GDP.

MAP A.6   ACCESS—FINANCIAL MARKETS

To approximate access to financial markets, this map uses the ratio of market capitalization excluding the top 10 largest companies to total market capitalization. The WFE provides data on the exchange level. This variable is aggregated up to the economy level by taking a simple average over exchanges. The four shades of blue in the map are based on the average value of the variable in 2013–15: the darker the blue, the higher the quartile of the statistical distribution of the variable.

Quartiles
- 4
- 3
- 2
- 1
- No data

TABLE A.1.6   **Access—Financial Markets**

Market capitalization excluding top 10 companies to total market capitalization (%)	Number of countries	Average	Median	Standard deviation	Minimum	Maximum	Weighted average
World	53	45.7	47	21.1	3.4	83.1	55
By developed/developing economies							
Developed economies	31	43.8	45.4	23.5	3.4	83.1	54.2
Developing economies	22	48.2	49.8	17.4	17	81.1	56.8
By income level							
High income	31	43.8	45.4	23.5	3.4	83.1	54.2
Upper-middle income	15	47.1	44.3	18.2	17	81.1	57.4
Lower-middle income	7	50.7	54.2	16.5	28.2	71.7	54.9
Low income	0						
By region							
High income: OECD	21	44.6	45.4	23.4	3.4	83.1	47.9
High income: non-OECD	10	42.2	37.3	25	10.7	72.9	60
East Asia and Pacific	5	64.5	62.9	10	54.2	81.1	64.1
Europe and Central Asia	3	36	38.7	17.9	17	52.4	40.4
Latin America and the Caribbean	5	37.4	37.9	9.6	25.8	48.9	38.1
Middle East and North Africa	4	41.8	42.9	11.9	28.4	52.8	38.9
South Asia	2	65.7	65.7	8.6	59.6	71.7	68.4
Sub-Saharan Africa	3	48.5	40.2	25.5	28.2	77.2	67.7

Source: Global Financial Development Database, 2013–15 data.
Note: OECD = Organization for Economic Co-operation and Development. Weighted average by stock market capitalization.

MAP A.7 EFFICIENCY—FINANCIAL MARKETS

To approximate efficiency of financial markets, this map uses the total value of shares traded during the period divided by the average market capitalization for the period. Average market capitalization is calculated as the average of the end-of-period values for the current period and the previous period. Data are from WFE, Standard & Poor's Global Stock Markets Factbook, and supplemental S&P data, and is compiled and reported by the *World Development Indicators*. The four shades of blue in the map are based on the average value of the variable in 2013–15: the darker the blue, the higher the quartile of the statistical distribution of the variable.

Quartiles
- 4
- 3
- 2
- 1
- No data

TABLE A.1.7 Efficiency—Financial Markets

Stock market turnover ratio (%)	Number of countries	Average	Median	Standard deviation	Minimum	Maximum	Weighted average
World	116	30.6	9.5	50.5	0	331.6	43.7
By developed/developing economies							
Developed economies	52	42.2	28.9	50.2	0.1	273.5	51.7
Developing economies	64	21.3	5.6	49.2	0	331.6	28.1
By income level							
High income	52	42.2	28.9	50.2	0.1	273.5	51.7
Upper-middle income	32	27.9	5.3	65.3	0.2	331.6	38.1
Lower-middle income	27	17.2	6.6	25.1	0.4	111.8	17.2
Low income	5	1	1.3	0.9	0	2	0.3
By region							
High income: OECD	33	57.3	48.2	54.8	0.2	273.5	66.3
High income: non-OECD	19	15.8	2.7	25.6	0.1	100.7	36.9
East Asia and Pacific	9	58.8	24.3	105.4	0.6	331.6	61.6
Europe and Central Asia	14	26.4	5.4	51.9	0.2	175.6	28.7
Latin America and the Caribbean	15	9.5	3.1	18.7	0.3	72.4	14
Middle East and North Africa	7	13.1	13	8.2	4	28.8	12.3
South Asia	5	31.7	31.5	26.9	1.3	65.1	35.7
Sub-Saharan Africa	14	5	2.4	7.2	0	28.2	12.5

Source: Global Financial Development Database, 2013–15 data.
Note: OECD = Organization for Economic Co-operation and Development. Weighted average by stock market capitalization.

MAP A.8 STABILITY—FINANCIAL MARKETS

To approximate stability of financial markets, this map uses the 360-day standard deviation of the return on the primary national stock market index. Data are from Bloomberg. The four shades of blue in the map are based on the average value of the variable in 2013–15: the darker the blue, the higher the quartile of the statistical distribution of the variable.

Quartiles
4
3
2
1
No data

TABLE A.1.8   **Stability—Financial Markets**

Stock price volatility	Number of countries	Average	Median	Standard deviation	Minimum	Maximum	Weighted average
World	92	15.5	15.1	7.2	3.6	45.6	15.9
By developed/developing economies							
Developed economies	46	15.6	15.2	6.7	7.1	45.6	15.5
Developing economies	46	15.4	14.7	7.7	3.6	37.9	17.2
By income level							
High income	46	15.6	15.2	6.7	7.1	45.6	15.5
Upper-middle income	28	15.7	14.1	8.8	3.6	37.9	17.4
Lower-middle income	17	15	15.2	5.9	7	30.6	16
Low income	1	14.5	14.5		14.5	14.5	14.5
By region							
High income: OECD	33	16.1	15.7	5	8.1	37	15.6
High income: non-OECD	13	14.3	10.4	9.9	7.1	45.6	15.4
East Asia and Pacific	8	16.6	17.2	3.5	8.6	20.7	17.4
Europe and Central Asia	10	17.5	14.8	6.9	9.2	30.6	22.6
Latin America and the Caribbean	10	19.6	15.2	11.6	5.9	37.9	19.2
Middle East and North Africa	6	10.9	8.4	6.4	7	23.7	12.3
South Asia	4	13.5	14.1	2.4	10.3	15.6	15.1
Sub-Saharan Africa	8	10.9	12.2	5.1	3.6	17.6	13.2

Source: Global Financial Development Database, 2013–15 data.
Note: OECD = Organization for Economic Co-operation and Development. Weighted average by total value of stocks traded.

APPENDIX B
KEY ASPECTS OF INTERNATIONAL BANKING

TABLE B.1 Foreign Penetration and Internationalization of Financial Systems, 2014

Economy	Foreign bank penetration					Internationalization		
	Foreign bank claims to GDP (%)	Foreign bank local claim share (%)	Foreign bank asset share (%)	Foreign bank share (%)	Foreign developing economy bank share (%)	Foreign liability ratio (%)	Foreign developing economy liability ratio (%)	Foreign host countries
Albania	46.6	78.1	89	85	15			
Algeria	5.2	91.6	15	60	27	1.7	0	
Andorra	36.5	56.6				3.2	0	1
Angola	12.9	67.0	54	46	8			1
Antigua and Barbuda				29	29			
Argentina	6.4	85.2	25	32	8			6
Armenia	8.5	56.8	85	80	33	0.6	0	
Australia	29.2	53.4	2	35	13	9.3	0.3	7
Austria	52.4	40.5	26	11	5	2.5	1.5	18
Azerbaijan	4.5	0.01	4	14	14	6.3	0	
Bahamas, The	320.6	23.4				55.0	55.0	1
Bahrain	37.8	44.2	52	71	21	27.4	17.3	6
Bangladesh	6.1	66.7	3	3	0	0.9	0.9	1
Barbados	128.4	63.1	100	100	25	3.7	3.7	1
Belarus	3.5	11.0	31	65	45			1
Belgium	81.6	60.2	47	46	4	11.8	0.1	10
Benin	4.7	83.5	98	89	88			
Bolivia	1.1	3.0	16	30	30			
Bosnia and Herzegovina	42.8	79.8	87	64	18			
Botswana	14.7	77.5	78	60	40	7.1	7.1	3
Brazil	18.0	59.9	15	40	3	0.9	0	9
Bulgaria	56.2	83.0	62	65	4			2
Burkina Faso	6.8	79.9	100	100	71			1
Burundi	1.6	0	73	50	25			
Cambodia	10.2	68.8	60	61	33			
Cameroon	9.0	43.6	76	73	36			
Canada	22.5	41.5	3	37	8	21.7	1.2	22
Chile	42.5	74.0	33	41	10			3
China	7.8	37.0	2	20	2	1.3	0.1	12
Colombia	11.7	66.3	15	42	0	0.7	0.6	9
Congo, Dem. Rep.	0.7	25.3	70	83	58			
Costa Rica	11.6	60.9	26	21	14	2.9	2.9	1
Croatia	103.8	62.6	90	52	6			1

(appendix continued next page)

TABLE B.1   **Foreign Penetration and Internationalization of Financial Systems, 2014** *(continued)*

Economy	Foreign bank penetration					Internationalization		
	Foreign bank claims to GDP (%)	Foreign bank local claim share (%)	Foreign bank asset share (%)	Foreign bank share (%)	Foreign developing economy bank share (%)	Foreign liability ratio (%)	Foreign developing economy liability ratio (%)	Foreign host countries
Cuba	1.0	8.7	0	0	0			1
Cyprus	108.0	33.9	12	63	38	0.3	0	5
Czech Republic	83.2	86.3	85	62	10			2
Côte d'Ivoire	11.9	58.9	100	71	36	8.0	8.0	
Denmark	79.8	50.5	18	8	0	3.6	0	8
Dominican Republic	6.6	35.3	8	8	3			1
Ecuador	2.7	23.8	12	22	6	7.2	6.2	3
Egypt, Arab Rep.	8.7	84.3	21	54	13	1.7	0.8	4
El Salvador	18.7	82.4	100	91	64			2
Estonia	79.6	92.9	97	75	13			1
Ethiopia	0.7	0	0	0	0			
Finland	69.9	53.0	84	22	0			3
France	38.2	13.5	5	4	0	10.0	0.7	46
Gabon	6.9	11.9						1
Gambia, The	12.4	82.8						1
Georgia	6.7	59.5	64	77	38			2
Germany	33.1	38.4	13	14	0	6.7	0.3	32
Ghana	16.0	31.4	69	63	44	6.2	0	
Greece	19.9	6.8	0	0	0	14.9	11.7	13
Guatemala	5.5	34.2	30	53	31	14.3	10.1	3
Haiti	4.0	61.8	0	0	0			
Honduras	5.2	14.7	53	53	35			2
Hong Kong SAR, China	236.8	78.8	92	73	27	1.8	1.6	1
Hungary	50.0	67.3	56	80	8	10.6	8.9	7
Iceland	33.2	0.1	0	0	0	6.3	0	1
India	12.9	38.9	3	12	0	0.2	0.1	11
Indonesia	12.7	45.6	27	48	9	1.6	1.5	1
Iran, Islamic Rep.	0.2	0.8	0	0	0	0.5	0	5
Iraq	0.3	17.1						1
Ireland	143.1	22.6	36	85	0	20.0	0	2
Israel	4.7	23.0	0	0	0	10.8	0.2	6
Italy	32.2	47.7	6	12	1	16.1	1.1	26
Jamaica	33.5	67.6	91	75	0	2.0	0	1
Japan	15.8	63.3	1	2	0	3.0	0.5	18
Jordan	9.2	19.8	25	40	20	1.0	0	5

TABLE B.1   **Foreign Penetration and Internationalization of Financial Systems, 2014** *(continued)*

Economy	Foreign bank penetration					Internationalization		
	Foreign bank claims to GDP (%)	Foreign bank local claim share (%)	Foreign bank asset share (%)	Foreign bank share (%)	Foreign developing economy bank share (%)	Foreign liability ratio (%)	Foreign developing economy liability ratio (%)	Foreign host countries
Kazakhstan	3.1	30.7	13	33	21	0.2	0.2	5
Kenya	10.1	49.0	36	32	18	0.9	0.9	4
Korea, Rep.	20.3	53.8	7	13	0	1.1	0.7	11
Kuwait	8.8	9.5	7	11	0	10.4	7.7	8
Kyrgyz Republic	0.6	0	79	83	80			
Latvia	52.8	89.4	58	55	25	3.2	0	2
Lebanon	10.1	24.6	29	36	18	0.9	0.1	10
Libya	0.3	1.4	0	0	0	4.5	1.8	17
Liechtenstein	72.9	0.3				11.1	0	6
Lithuania	53.7	79.1	91	75	0	14.0	0	1
Luxembourg	743.3	12.4	92	95	3	2.0	0	3
Macedonia, FYR	30.1	80.1	68	67	17			
Madagascar	11.9	33.0	100	100	50			
Malawi	0.9	0	34	25	25			3
Malaysia	50.4	70.3	17	42	9			6
Mali	1.6	37.4	61	67	63			11
Malta	167.3	36.5				1.1	0	1
Mauritania	6.3	0	4	38	25			
Mauritius	60.9	34.2	55	60	33	0.9	0.9	6
Mexico	27.7	78.7	70	37	0	0.5	0	4
Moldova	8.6	64.5	27	50	0			
Monaco						2.4	0	
Mongolia	6.1	0	7	13	13			
Montenegro	25.5	37.9	89	88	25			
Morocco	28.5	72.3	19	36	0			7
Mozambique	41.0	83.7	94	85	38			
Namibia	2.2	0	52	43	43	5.3	5.3	
Nepal	1.4	35.9	11	10	7			
Netherlands	67.3	16.9	4	47	17	10.9	0.6	24
New Zealand	157.1	94.9	94	78	0	0.2	0	
Nicaragua	4.4	48.9	39	60	40			6
Niger	1.2	0	69	71	67			
Nigeria	2.7	19.1	19	28	12	3.4	0.6	12
Norway	42.5	56.4	14	2	0	1.6	0	8
Oman	12.8	53.2	11	17	0			2

(appendix continued next page)

TABLE B.1   Foreign Penetration and Internationalization of Financial Systems, 2014 *(continued)*

Economy	Foreign bank penetration					Internationalization		
	Foreign bank claims to GDP (%)	Foreign bank local claim share (%)	Foreign bank asset share (%)	Foreign bank share (%)	Foreign developing economy bank share (%)	Foreign liability ratio (%)	Foreign developing economy liability ratio (%)	Foreign host countries
Pakistan	3.5	76.9	52	43	5	1.3	0	5
Panama	83.5	10.2	67	69	54	49.9	49.9	3
Paraguay	9.4	77.2	51	64	36			1
Peru	25.7	75.1	51	69	13			2
Philippines	13.0	38.4	1	12	2	3.2	3.0	2
Poland	51.0	79.8	76	76	0	0.1	0.1	2
Portugal	54.6	63.2	23	36	5	0.9	0.7	11
Qatar	16.6	16.7	0	0	0	1.1	0	5
Romania	44.0	66.9	79	82	4	0.6	0	1
Russian Federation	7.5	38.8	8	17	3	8.0	3.5	24
Rwanda	0.6	0	13	50	50			
San Marino	41.7	16.2						1
Saudi Arabia	8.5	7.3	0	0	0	0.04	0.04	3
Senegal	18.8	59.1	94	83	56			
Serbia	48.7	77.8	75	66	6			3
Seychelles	106.9	14.5	65	40	20			
Singapore	125.1	67.5	6	55	5			8
Slovak Republic	69.5	68.4	75	67	7	17.0	0	1
Slovenia	39.2	65.8	25	35	6	3.1	3.1	4
South Africa	29.3	71.5	23	24	4	2.4	1.9	18
Spain	33.6	27.3	2	13	2	33.4	11.4	21
Sri Lanka	9.4	66.4	0	0	0			
Sudan	0.2	0	9	21	21			
Swaziland	1.9	2.4	100	60	60			
Sweden	23.7	11.4	0	1	0	36.6	0.03	11
Switzerland	47.4	31.4	2	20	5	7.9	1.4	22
Syrian Arab Republic	0.8	2.8				2.6	2.6	1
Tanzania	5.7	68.6	47	67	52			1
Thailand	30.4	78.9	7	25	10	0.4	0.4	4
Togo	12.2	1.8	0	17	17	28.2	28.2	15
Trinidad and Tobago	32.5	82.3	57	75	13			1
Tunisia	15.7	64.5	28	47	29			
Turkey	27.6	54.3	14	38	11	4.4	0.1	15
Uganda	6.5	41.1	85	83	67			
Ukraine	11.3	69.2	28	39	14	7.4	1.0	4
United Arab Emirates	29.1	51.6	1	22	11	0.4	0.4	7

TABLE B.1   **Foreign Penetration and Internationalization of Financial Systems, 2014** *(continued)*

Economy	Foreign bank penetration					Internationalization		
	Foreign bank claims to GDP (%)	Foreign bank local claim share (%)	Foreign bank asset share (%)	Foreign bank share (%)	Foreign developing economy bank share (%)	Foreign liability ratio (%)	Foreign developing economy liability ratio (%)	Foreign host countries
United Kingdom	82.2	64.3	14	58	18	13.8	1.8	55
United States	31.8	61.8	11	31	0	5.1	0.4	62
Uruguay	22.9	82.8	92	78	26			2
Uzbekistan	1.3	0	6	20	13			1
Venezuela, RB	9.9	86.3	18	27	12			3
Vietnam	17.4	48.6	5	23	10	0.1	0.0	1
Yemen, Rep.	2.3	0	0	0	0			
Zambia	8.8	62.7	99	94	56			1
Zimbabwe	4.9	27.8	36	38	23			

NOTES

Additional data: The table above presents information from various databases and research papers, including the Bank for International Settlements (BIS) Consolidated Banking Statistics (CBS), World Bank Global Financial Development Database (GFDD), Claessens and van Horen (2015), and Bertay, Demirgüç-Kunt, and Huizinga (2017).

Period covered: The table shows the most recently available data, up to 2014.

Economy: A territorial entity for which statistical data are maintained and provided internationally on a separate and independent basis (not necessarily a state as understood by international law and practice). The term, used interchangeably with *country,* does not imply political independence or official recognition by the World Bank.

Foreign bank claims to GDP (%): Consolidated foreign bank claims on a counterparty economy. A bank is foreign if it is headquartered outside an economy's jurisdiction. Consolidated claims capture worldwide positions by bank offices, including foreign subsidiaries and branches and excluding inter-office activity. Bank claims include loans and deposits,

holdings of debt securities, equity securities, participations, derivatives instruments with positive market value, and any other residual on-balance-sheet financial claims. This indicator provides an aggregate measure of the size of foreign bank funding for an economy. The data are based on BIS CBS table B4 and World Development Indicators.

Foreign bank local claims share (%): Share of local claims among consolidated foreign bank claims on a counterparty country. Local claims are booked by foreign bank offices inside counterparty economy and can be in either local or foreign currency. This indicator provides a measure of the importance of brick and mortar business by foreign banks for an economy, as opposed to its reliance on cross-border foreign funding. The data are based on BIS CBS table B4 and World Development Indicators.

Foreign bank asset share (%): Percentage of the total banking assets that are held by foreign banks. A foreign bank is a bank where a majority its shares are owned by foreigners. This indicator provides a measure of the importance of foreign bank assets within an economy's banking system. The data are from the GFDD, using input from Claessens and van Horen (2015). The values represent 2013.

Foreign bank share (%): Percentage of the number of foreign-owned banks to the number of the total banks in an economy. A foreign bank is a bank where a majority of its shares are owned by foreigners. This indicator provides a measure of the presence of foreign bank offices within an economy's banking system. The data are from the GFDD, using input from Claessens and van Horen (2015). The values represent 2013.

Foreign developing economy bank share (%): Percentage of the number of foreign developing economy–owned banks to the number of the total banks in an economy. A foreign bank is a bank where a majority of its shares are owned by foreigners. This indicator provides a measure of the presence of developing economy banks within a economy's banking system. The data are from the GFDD, using input from Claessens and van Horen (2015). The values represent 2013.

Foreign liability ratio (%): Percentage of liabilities located in a foreign economy by an economy's banking system, calculated by aggregating liabilities of majority-owned subsidiaries in foreign countries and dividing by the total liabilities of the banking system. This indicator provides a proxy measure for the extent of internationalization of an economy's banking system. The data are computed by the *Global Financial Development Report* team as part of Bertay, Demirgüç-Kunt, and Huizinga (2017).

Foreign developing economy liability ratio (%): Percentage of liabilities located in a foreign developing economy by economy's banking system, calculated by aggregating liabilities of majority-owned subsidiaries in foreign developing countries and dividing by the total liabilities of the banking system. This indicator provides a proxy measure for the extent of internationalization into developing countries of economy's banking system. The data are computed by the *Global Financial Development Report* team as part of Bertay, Demirgüç-Kunt, and Huizinga (2017).

Foreign host countries: Number of foreign host countries for subsidiaries and branches controlled through direct majority ownership by an economy's banking system. This indicator provides a measure for the immediate geographic outreach of an economy's banking system. The data are from the GFDD, using input from Claessens and van Horen (2015). The values represent 2013.

Bibliography

Accenture. 2016. *Fintech and the Evolving Landscape: Landing Points for the Industry.* Dublin: Accenture.

Acharya, V. V. 2003. "Is the International Convergence of Capital Adequacy Regulation Desirable?" *Journal of Finance* 58 (6): 2745–82.

Acharya, V. V., S. G. Cecchetti, J. De Gregorio, S. Kalemli-Ozcan, P. R. Lane, and U. Panizza. 2015. *Corporate Debt in Emerging Economies: A Threat to Financial Stability?* Washington, DC: Brookings Institution.

Acharya, V. V., and S. Vij. 2016. "Foreign Currency Borrowing of Corporations as Carry Trades: Evidence from India." NSE-NYU Conference on Indian Financial Markets 2016, New York, December 21–22.

Adrian, T., P. Colla, and H. S. Shin. 2013. "Which Financial Frictions? Parsing Evidence from the Financial Crisis of 2007–09." *NBER Macroeconomics Annual* 2012 (27): 159–214.

Adriano, A., and H. Monroe. 2016. "The Internet of Trust." *Finance and Development* 53 (2).

Agenor, P. R. 2003. "Benefits and Costs of International Financial Integration: Theory and Facts." *World Economy* 26 (8): 1089–118.

Ahmed, U., T. Beck, C. McDaniel, and S. Schropp. 2015. "Filling the Gap: How Technology Enables Access to Finance for Small-and Medium-Sized Enterprises." *Innovations* 103 (4): 35–48.

Aiyar, S. 2012. "From Financial Crisis to Great Recession: The Role of Globalized Banks." *American Economic Review* 102 (3): 225–30.

Aiyar, S., C. W. Calomiris, and T. Wieladek. 2014. "Does Macro Prudential Regulation Leak? Evidence from a UK Policy Experiment." *Journal of Money, Credit and Banking* 46 (s1): 181–214.

Albertazzi, U., and M. Bottero. 2014. "Foreign Bank Lending: Evidence from the Global Financial Crisis." *Journal of International Economics* 92: S22–35.

Alfaro, L., T. Beck, and C. W. Calomiris. 2015. "Foreign Bank Entry and Entrepreneurship." Working Paper, Columbia University, New York.

Alibaba Group. 2016. *Ant Financial.* Investor Day Document: June 2016. San Mateo, CA.

Allen, F., T. Beck, E. Carletti, P. R. Lane, D. Schoenmaker, and W. Wagner. 2011. "Cross-Border Banking in Europe: Implications for Financial Stability and Macroeconomic Policies." London: Centre for Economic Policy Research.

Allen, F., A. Demirgüç-Kunt, L. F. Klapper, and M. S. Martínez Pería. 2012. "The Foundations of Financial Inclusion: Understanding Ownership and Use of Formal Accounts." Policy Research Working Paper 6290, World Bank, Washington, DC.

Álvarez, J. M., J. P. García, and O. Gouveia. 2016. "The Globalization of Banking: How Is Regulation Affecting Global Banks?" BBVA Research.

Anginer, D., E. Cerutti, and M. S. Martínez Pería. 2017. "Foreign Bank Subsidiaries' Default Risk during the Global Crisis: What Factors Help Insulate Affiliates from Their Parents ?" *Journal of Financial Intermediation* 29: 19–31.

Arena, M., C. Reinhart, and F. Vazquez. 2007. "The Lending Channel in Emerging Economics: Are Foreign Banks Different?" IMF Working Paper 07/48, International Monetary Fund, Washington, DC.

Arner, D. W., J. Barberis, and R. P. Buckley. 2016. "The Evolution of Fintech: A New Paradigm?" *Georgetown Journal of International Law* 47: 1271–319.

———. Forthcoming. "FinTech, RegTech and the Reconceptualization of Financial Regulation." *Northwestern Journal of International Law and Business.* SSRN: https://ssrn.com/abstract=2847806.

Atz, U., and D. Bhola. 2016. "Peer-to-Peer Lending and Financial Innovation in the United Kingdom." Staff Working Paper 598, Bank of England, London.

Autonomous. 2016. "Digital Lending: The 100 Billion Dollar Question." http://www.autonomous.com/fintech/af8fe529-c188-46ba-bf25-d25e9596a09d.

Avdjiev, S., Z. Kuti, and E. Takats. 2012. "The Euro Area Crisis and Cross-Border Bank Lending to Emerging Markets." *BIS Quarterly Review* (December): 37–47.

Avdjiev, S., R. N. McCauley, and H. S. Shin. 2015. "Breaking Free of the Triple Coincidence in International Finance." BIS Working Paper 524, Bank for International Settlements, Basel.

Aviat, A., and N. Coeurdacier. 2007. "The Geography of Trade in Goods and Asset Holdings." *Journal of International Economics* 71 (1): 22–51.

Aykut, D., and A. Goldstein. 2006. "Developing Country Multinationals: South-South Investment Comes of Age." OECD Development Centre Working Paper 257, OECD Publishing, Paris.

Aykut, D., and D. Ratha. 2004. "South-South FDI Flows: How Big Are They?" *Transnational Corporations Journal* 13 (1).

Baker, M., and M. Collins. 1999. "Financial Crises and Structural Change in English Commercial Bank Assets, 1860–1913 ." *Explorations in Economic History* 36 (4): 428–44.

Barajas, A., R. Steiner, and N. Salazar. 2000. "The Impact of Liberalization and Foreign Investment in Colombia's Financial Sector." *Journal of Development Economics* 63 (1): 157–96.

Barth, J. R., G. Caprio, and R. Levine. 2004. "Bank Regulation and Supervision: What Works Best?" *Journal of Financial Intermediation* 13 (2): 205–48.

———. 2013. "Bank Regulation and Supervision in 180 Countries from 1999 to 2011." *Journal of Financial Economic Policy* 5 (2): 111–219.

Basel Committee on Banking Supervision (BCBS). 2016. "Global Systemically Important Banks: Assessment Methodology and the Additional Loss Absorbency Requirement." November 21. https://www.bis.org/bcbs/gsib/index.htm.

Battilossi, S. 2006. "The Determinants of Banking during the First Globalisation, 1880–1914." *European Review of Economic History* 10 (3): 361–88.

Bayraktar, N., and Y. Wang. 2008. "Banking Sector Openness and Economic Growth." *Margin: The Journal of Applied Economic Research* 2: 145.

Bazot, G. 2013. "Financial Consumption and the Cost of Finance: Measuring Financial Efficiency in Europe (1950–2007)." Working paper, Paris School of Economics.

Beck, R., P. Jakubik, and A. Piloiu. 2013. "Non-performing loans: What Matters in Addition to the Economic Cycle?" ECB Working Paper 1515, European Central Bank, Frankfurt.

Beck, T. 2002. "Financial Development and International Trade: Is There a Link?" *Journal of International Economics* 57 (1): 107–31.

Beck, T., and M. Brown. 2013. "Foreign Bank Ownership and Household Credit." *Journal of Financial Intermediation* 24 (4): 466–86.

Beck, T., and R. Cull. 2013. "Banking in Africa." Policy Research Working Paper 6684, World Bank, Washington, DC. http://elibrary.worldbank.org/doi/pdf/10.1596/1813-9450-6684.

Beck, T., H. Degryse, R. De Haas, and N. van Horen. 2014. "When Arm's Length Is Too Far: Relationship Banking over the Business Cycle." Discussion Paper 2014-042, Center for Economic Research, Tilburg University, The Netherlands. http://www.ebrd.com/downloads /research/economics/workingpapers/wp0169 .pdf.

Beck, T., M. Fuchs, D. Singer, and M. Witte. 2014. *Making Cross-Border Banking Work for Africa.* Washington, DC: World Bank.

Beck, T., V. Ioannidou, and L. Schäfer. 2012. "Foreigners vs. Natives: Bank Lending Technologies and Loan Pricing." Discussion Paper 2012-014, European Banking Center, Tilburg University, The Netherlands. http://papers.ssrn.com/sol3 /papers.cfm?abstract_id=2101037.

Beck, R., P. Jakubik, and A. Piloiu. 2013. "Non-performing loans: What matters in addition to the economic cycle?" ECB Working Paper 1515.

Beck, T., R. Levine, and A. Levkov. 2010. "Big Bad Banks? The Winners and Losers from Bank Deregulation in the United States." *Journal of Finance* 65 (5): 1637–67.

Beck, T., and M. S. Martínez Pería. 2010. "Foreign Bank Participation and Outreach: Evidence from Mexico." *Journal of Financial Intermediation* 19 (1): 52–73.

Beck, T., C. Silva-Buston, and W. Wagner. 2015. "Cross-Border Banking Cooperation: From Actual to Optimal Arrangements." Unpublished paper.

Beck, T., R. Todorov, and W. Wagner. 2013. "Supervising Cross-Border Banks: Theory, Evidence and Policy." *Economic Policy* 28 (73): 5–44.

Beck, T., and W. Wagner. 2016. "Supranational Supervision: How Much and for Whom?" *International Journal of Central Banking* 12 (2): 221–68.

Becker, B., and V. Ivashina. 2014. "Cyclicality of Credit Supply: Firm-Level Evidence." *Journal of Monetary Economics* 62: 76–93.

Behn, M., R. Haselmann, A. Seru, and V. Vig. 2014. "Does Financial Structure Shape Industry Structure? Evidence from Timing of Bank Liberalization." Unpublished paper, London Business School.

Berger, A. N., G. R. Clarke, R. Cull, L. Klapper, and G. F. Udell. 2005. "Corporate Governance and Bank Performance: A Joint Analysis of the Static, Selection, and Dynamic Effects of Domestic, Foreign, and State Ownership." *Journal of Banking & Finance* 29 (8): 2179–221.

Berger, A. N., R. DeYoung, H. Genay, and G. F. Udell. 2000. "The Globalization of Financial Institutions: The Evidence from Cross-Border Banking Performance." *Brookings-Wharton Papers on Financial Services* 3: 23–158.

Berger, A. N., S. El Ghoul, O. Guedhami, and R. A. Roman. 2016. "Internationalization and bank risk." *Management Science 2017* 63 (7): 2283–2301.

Berger, A. N., I. Hasan, and M. Zhou. 2009. "Bank Ownership and Efficiency in China: What Will Happen in the World's Largest Nation?" *Journal of Banking & Finance* 33 (1): 113–30.

Berger, A. N., L. F. Klapper, M. S. M. Peria, and R. Zaidi. 2008. "Bank Ownership Type and Banking Relationships." *Journal of Financial Intermediation* 17 (1): 37–62.

Berger, A. N., L. F. Klapper, and G. F. Udell. 2001. "The Ability of Banks to Lend to Informationally Opaque Small Businesses." *Journal of Banking and Finance* 25 (12): 2127–67.

Berger, A. N., and G. F. Udell. 2006. "A More Complete Conceptual Framework for SME Finance." *Journal of Banking and Finance*, 30 (11), 2945–66.

Berlin, Mitchell. 2015. "New Rules for Foreign Banks: What's at Stake?" *Business Review Q* 1: 1–10.

Bertay, A. C. 2014. "The Transmission of Real Estate Shocks through Multinational Banks." Discussion Paper 2014-001, European Banking Center, Tilburg University, The Netherlands.

Bertay, A. C., A. Demirgüç-Kunt, and H. Huizinga. 2013. "Do We Need Big Banks? Evidence on Performance, Strategy and Market Discipline." *Journal of Financial Intermediation* 22 (4): 532–558.

———. 2015. "Bank Ownership and Credit over the Business Cycle: Is Lending by State Banks Less Procyclical?" *Journal of Banking and Finance* 50: 326–39.

———. 2016. "Should Cross-Border Banking Benefit from the Financial Safety Net?" *Journal of Financial Intermediation* 27: 51–67.

————. 2017. "Are Internationally Active Banks Different? Evidence on Bank Performance and Strategy." Unpublished paper, World Bank.

Bhattacharya, A., C. K. Lovell, and P. Sahay. 1997. "The Impact of Liberalization on the Productive Efficiency of Indian Commercial Banks." *European Journal of Operational Research* 98 (2): 332–45.

Bircan, C., and R. De Haas. 2015. "The Limits of Lending: Banks and Technology Adoption across Russia." Discussion paper 2015-011, Center for Economic Research, Tilburg University, The Netherlands.

BIS (Bank for International Settlements). 2013. "Global Systemically Important Banks: Updated Assessment Methodology and the Higher Loss Absorbency Requirement." Basel. http://www.bis.org/publ/bcbs255.pdf.

————. 2015. "Guidelines for Reporting BIS International Banking Statistics." Basel. http://www.bis.org/statistics/bankstatsguide.htm.

Blanchard, O. J., M. Griffiths, and B. Gruss. 2013. "Boom, Bust, Recovery: Forensics of the Latvia Crisis." In *Brookings Papers on Economic Activity: Fall 2013,* edited by D. H. Romer and J. Wolfers, 325–388. Washington, DC: Brookings Institute.

Blaseg, D., and M. Koetter. 2016. "Friend or Foe? Crowdfunding versus Credit When Banks Are Stressed." IWH Discussion Paper, Halle Institute for Economic Research, Halle, Germany.

BNY Mellon. 2015. "Innovation in Payments: The Future Is Fintech." London. https://www.bnymellon.com/global-assets/pdf/our-thinking/innovation-in-payments-the-future-is-fintech.pdf.

Bolton, Patrick, and Martin Oehmke. 2015. "Bank Resolution and the Structure of Global Banks." Working paper, Columbia University, New York.

Bonaccorsi di Patti, E., and D. C. Hardy. 2005. "Financial Sector Liberalization, Bank Privatization, and Efficiency: Evidence from Pakistan." *Journal of Banking and Finance* 29 (8): 2381–406.

Bonin, J. P., and D. Louie. Forthcoming. "Did Foreign Banks Stay Committed to Emerging Europe during Recent Financial Crises?" *Journal of Comparative Economics.*

Bonin, J., and P. Wachtel. 2003. "Financial Sector Development in Transition Economies: Lessons from the First Decade." *Financial Markets, Institutions and Instruments* 12 (1): 1–66.

Borensztein, E., K. Cowan, B. Eichengreen, and U. Panizza. 2008. "Building Bond Markets in Latin America." In *Bond Markets in Latin America: On the Verge of a Big Bang?* 1–28. Cambridge, MA: MIT Press.

Borio, C., R. McCauley, and P. McGuire. 2012. "Global Credit and Domestic Credit Booms." *BIS Quarterly Review* (September): 43–57.

Bremus, F., and C. M. Buch. 2014. "Granularity in Banking and Growth: Does Financial Openness matter?" DIW Berlin Discussion Paper 1346. http://papers.ssrn.com/sol3/papers.cfm?abstract_id=2387571.

Broner, F., T. Didier, S. L. Schmukler, and G. Von Peter. 2017. "Global Capital Flows: The Big Sur?" World Bank Working Paper, World Bank.

Brüggemann, B., J. Kleinert, and E. Prieto. 2011. "A Gravity Equation of Bank Loans." Paper presented at Deutsche Bundesbank Workshop, The Costs and Benefits of International Banking, Eltville am Rhein, Germany.

Bruno, V., and R. Hauswald. 2013. "The Real Effect of Foreign Banks." *Review of Finance* 18 (5): 1683–716.

Bruno, V., and H. S. Shin. 2015a. "Cross-Border Banking and Global Liquidity." *The Review of Economic Studies* 82: 535–64.

————. 2015b. "Capital Flows and the Risk-Taking Channel of Monetary Policy." *Journal of Monetary Economics* 71: 119–32.

————. 2017. "Global Dollar Credit and Carry Trades: A Firm-Level Analysis." *Review of Financial Studies* 30 (3): 703–49.

Buch, C. M. 2003. "Information or Regulation: What Drives the International Activities of Commercial Banks?" *Journal of Money, Credit and Banking* 35 (6): 851–69.

Buch, C. M., K. Carstensen, and A. Schertler. 2009. "Macroeconomic Shocks and Banks' Foreign Assets." *Journal of Money, Credit and Banking* 42 (1): 171–88.

Buch, C. M., J. C. Driscoll, and C. Ostergaard. 2010. "Cross-Border Diversification in Bank Asset Portfolios." *International Finance* 13 (1): 79–108.

Buch, C. M., and L. S. Goldberg. 2014. "International Banking and Liquidity Risk Transmission: Lessons from Across Countries." NBER Working Paper 20286, National Bureau of Economic Research, Cambridge, MA.

———. 2015. "International Banking and Liquidity Risk Transmission: Lessons from across Countries." *IMF Economic Review* 63 (3): 377–410.

Buch, C. M., C. T. Koch, and M. Koetter. 2011. "Size, Productivity, and International Banking." *Journal of International Economics* 85 (2): 329–34.

———. 2012. "Do Banks Benefit from Internationalization? Revisiting the Market Power–Risk Nexus." *Review of Finance* 17 (4): 1401–35.

———. 2014. "Should I Stay or Should I Go? Bank Productivity and Internationalization Decisions." *Journal of Banking and Finance* 42: 266–82.

Buiter, W., and A. Sibert. 2011. "The Icelandic Banking Crisis and What to Do About It: The Lender of Last Resort Theory of Optimal Currency Areas." In *Preludes to the Icelandic Financial Crisis*, edited by R. Aliber and G. Zoega, 241–75. London: Palgrave Macmillan.

Calvo, G. A., L. Leiderman, and C. Reinhart. 1993. "Capital Inflows and Real Exchange Rate Appreciation in Latin America: The Role of External Factors." *IMF Staff Papers* 40 (1): 108–51.

———. 1996. "Capital Flows to Developing Countries in the 1990s: Causes and Effects." *Journal of Economic Perspectives* 10: 123–39.

Calzolari, Giacomo, and Gyongyi Loranth. 2011. "Regulation of Multinational Banks: A Theoretical Inquiry." *Journal of Financial Intermediation* 20 (2): 178–98.

Carbo-Valverde, S., E. J. Kane, and F. Rodriguez-Fernandez. 2012. "Regulatory Arbitrage in Cross-Border Banking Mergers within the EU." *Journal of Money, Credit and Banking* 44 (8): 1609–29.

Carmassi, J., and R. J. Herring. 2015. "The Corporate Complexity of Global Systematically Important Banks." IBEFA 2016 ASSA Session on Banking Risk and Complexity, International Banking, Economics and Finance Association, Atlanta.

Cassis, Y. 2013. "Baring Brothers: A London Merchant Bank in Historical and Comparative Perspective." Baring Archive Symposium. http://www.baringarchive.org.uk/materials/yousseff_cassis.pdf.

CBRC (China Banking Regulatory Commission). 2016a. "China Banking Regulatory Commission Annual Report 2015." http://www.cbrc.gov.cn/chinese/home/docView/C41C682055714362AF1C86FEA7486BB5.html (Chinese).

———. 2016b. "Interim Measures for the Business Activities of Online Lending Information Intermediary Institutions." CBRC Order 1, Beijing.

Cerutti, E., S. Claessens, and L. Laeven. 2015. "The Use and Effectiveness of Macroprudential Policies: New Evidence." Unpublished paper, International Monetary Fund, Washington, DC.

Cerutti, E., S. Claessens, and P. McGuire. 2012. "Systemic Risk in Global Banking: What Can Available Data Tell Us and What More Data Are Needed?" Working Paper 376, Bank for International Settlements, Basel. http://www.bis.org/publ/work376.pdf.

Cerutti, E., S. Claessens, and L. Ratnovski. 2016. "Global Liquidity and Cross-Border Bank Flows." *Economic Policy* 32: 81–125.

Cerutti, E., G. Dell'Ariccia, and M. S. M. Pería. 2007. "How Banks Go Abroad: Branches or Subsidiaries?" *Journal of Banking and Finance* 31 (6): 1669–92.

Cerutti, E., G. Hale, and C. Minoiu. 2015. "Financial Crises and the Composition of Cross-border Lending." *Journal of International Money and Finance* 52: 60–81.

Cerutti, E., A. Ilyina, Y. Makarova, and C. Schmieder. 2010. "Bankers without Borders? Implications of Ring-Fencing for European Cross-Border Banks." International Monetary Fund, Washington, DC.

Cerutti, E., and C. Schmieder. 2014. "Ring Fencing and Consolidated Banks' Stress Tests." *Journal of Financial Stability* 11: 1–12.

Cetorelli, N., and L. S. Goldberg. 2011. "Global Banks and International Shock Transmission: Evidence from the Crisis." *IMF Economic Review* 59 (1): 41–76.

———. 2012a. "Liquidity Management of US Global Banks: Internal Capital Markets in the

Great Recession." *Journal of International Economics* 88 (2): 299–311.

———. 2012b. "Banking Globalization and Monetary Transmission." *Journal of Finance* 67 (5): 1811–43.

———. 2012c. "Follow the Money: Quantifying Domestic Effects of Foreign Bank Shocks in the Great Recession." *American Economic Review* 102 (3): 213–18.

———. 2014. "Measures of Global Bank Complexity." *Federal Reserve Bank of New York Economic Policy Review* (December): 107–26.

CGAP (Consultative Group to Assist the Poor). 2015. "How M-Shwari Works: The Story So Far." Washington, DC.

CGFS (Committee on the Global Financial System), 2014. "Trade Finance: Developments and Issues." CGFS Paper 50, Bank for International Settlements, Basel.

Chang, C., I. Hasan, and W. C. Hunter. 1998. "Efficiency of Multinational Banks: An Empirical Investigation." *Applied Financial Economics* 8 (6): 689–96.

Chava, S., and A. Purnanandam. 2011. "The Effect of Banking Crisis on Bank-Dependent Borrowers." *Journal of Financial Economics* 99 (1): 116–35.

Chinn, M., and H. Ito. 2006. "What Matters for Financial Development? Capital Controls, Institutions and Interactions." *Journal of Development Economics* 81 (1): 163–92.

———. 2008. "A New Measure of Financial Openness." *Journal of Comparative Policy Analysis* 10 (3): 309–22.

Choi, M. J., E. Gutierrez, and M. S. Martínez Pería. 2014. "Dissecting Foreign Bank Lending Behavior during the 2008–2009 Crisis." Working Paper 2014-7, Bank of Korea, Seoul.

Chui, M. K., D. Domanski, P. Kugler, and J. Shek. 2010. "The Collapse of International Bank Finance during the Crisis: Evidence from Syndicated Loan Markets." *BIS Quarterly Review* (September).

Čihák, M., D. S. Mare, and M. Melecky. 2016. "The Nexus of Financial Inclusion and Financial Stability: A Study of Trade-offs and Synergies." Policy Research Working Paper 7722, World Bank, Washington, DC. http://documents.worldbank.org/curated /en/138991467994676130/The-Nexus-of

-financial-inclusion-and-financial-stability-a -study-of-trade-offs-and-synergies.

Citigroup, 2016. "Digital Disruption: How FinTech Is Forcing Banking to a Tipping Point." New York.

Claessens, S. 2016. "Global Banking: Recent Developments and Insights from Research." *Review of Finance* 21 (4): 1513–55.

Claessens, S., A. Demirgüç-Kunt, and H. Huizinga. 2001. "How Does Foreign Bank Entry Affect Domestic Banking Markets?" *Journal of Banking and Finance* 25: 891–911.

Claessens, S., O. Hassib, and N. van Horen. 2014. "How Foreign Banks Facilitate Trade in Tranquil and Crisis Times: Finance or Information." International Monetary Fund, Washington, DC.

Claessens, S., and L. Laeven. 2004. "What Drives Bank Competition? Some International Evidence." *Journal of Money, Credit, and Banking* 36 (3): 563–83.

Claessens, S., and N. van Horen. 2007. "Location Decisions of Foreign Banks and Competitive Advantage." Policy Research Working Paper 4113, World Bank, Washington, DC.

———. 2012. "Being a Foreigner among Domestic Banks: Asset or Liability?" *Journal of Banking and Finance* 36: 1276–90.

———. 2014a. "Location Decisions of Foreign Banks and Competitor Remoteness." *Journal of Money, Credit and Banking* 46 (1): 145–70.

———. 2014b. "Foreign Banks: Trends and Impact." *Journal of Money, Credit and Banking* 46 (s1): 295–326.

———. 2015. "The Impact of the Global Financial Crisis on Banking Globalization." *IMF Economic Review* 63 (4): 868–918.

———. 2016. "The Role of Foreign Banks in Local Credit Booms." *The Future of Large, Internationally Active Banks* 55: 273.

Claeys, S., and C. Hainz. 2006. "Foreign Banks in Eastern Europe: Mode of Entry and Effects on Bank Interest Rates." Discussion Paper 95, Governance and the Efficiency of Economic Systems (GESY), Mannheim, Germany. http:// www.sfbtr15.de/uploads/media/95.pdf.

———. 2014. "Modes of Foreign Bank Entry and Effects on Lending Rates: Theory and Evidence." *Journal of Comparative Economics* 421, 160–77.

Clarke, G., R. Cull, and M. S. Martínez Pería. 2006. "Foreign Bank Participation and Access to Credit across Firms in Developing Countries." *Journal of Comparative Economics* 34 (4): 774–95.

Clarke, G., R. Cull, M. S. Martínez Pería, and S. M. Sánchez. 2005. "Bank Lending to Small Businesses in Latin America: Does Bank Origin Matter? *Journal of Money, Credit and Banking* 83–118.

CoinDesk. 2016. "Nasqad Opens Blockchain Services to Global Exchange Partners." May 26. http://www.coindesk.com/nasdaqs-blockchain-services-global-exchange/.

Cordero, J. A., 2009. "The IMF's Stand-by Arrangements and the Economic Downturn in Eastern Europe: The Cases of Hungary, Latvia, and Ukraine." Center for Economic and Policy Research Report, London.

Cortina, J. J., T. Didier, and S. L. Schmukler. 2016. "How Long Is the Maturity of Corporate Borrowing? Evidence from Bond and Loan Issuances across Markets." Policy Research Working Paper 7815, World Bank, Washington, DC.

Cortina, J. J., S. Ismail, and S. L. Schmukler. 2016. "Firm Financing and Growth in the Arab Region." Policy Research Working Paper 7756, World Bank, Washington, DC.

CPMI (Committee on Payments and Market Infrastructures). 2016. "Correspondent Banking." Bank for International Settlements, Basel.

Crouzet, N. 2016. "Aggregate Implications of Corporate Debt Choices." Working paper, Northwestern University, Evanston, IL. https://www.scholars.northwestern.edu/en/publications/aggregate-implications-of-corporate-debt-choices.

Crowe, M., M. Rysman, and J. Stavins. 2010. "Mobile Payments in the United States at Retail Point of Sale: Current Market and Future Prospects." Public Policy Discussion Paper 10-2, Federal Reserve Bank of Boston.

Crystal, J. S., G. Dages, and L. Goldberg. 2001. "Does Foreign Ownership Contribute to Sounder Banks? The Latin American Experience." In *Open Doors: Foreign Participation in Emerging Financial Systems*, edited by R. E. Litan, P. Masson, and M. Pomerleano. Washington, DC: Brookings Institution Press.

———. 2002. "Has Foreign Bank Entry Led to Sounder Banks in Latin America?" *Current Issues in Economics and Finance* 8 (1): 1–6.

Cull, R., T. Ehrbeck, and N. Holle. 2014. "Financial Inclusion and Development: Recent Impact Evidence." Focus Note 92, World Bank, Washington, DC. http://documents.worldbank.org/curated/en/269601468153288448/Financial-inclusion-and-development-recent-impact-evidence.

Cull, R., S. Harten, I. Nishida, A. B. Rusu, and G. Bull. 2015. "Benchmarking the Financial Performance, Growth, and Outreach of Greenfield MFIs in Africa." *Emerging Markets Review* 25 (c): 92–124.

Cull, R., and M. S. Martínez Pería. 2010. "Foreign Bank Participation in Developing Countries: What Do We Know about the Drivers and Consequences of This Phenomenon?" Policy Research Working Paper 5398, World Bank, Washington, DC.

———. 2013. "Bank Ownership and Lending Patterns during the 2008–2009 Financial Crisis: Evidence from Latin America and Eastern Europe." *Journal of Banking & Finance* 37(12): 4861–78.

Cull, R., M. S. Martínez Pería, and J. Verrier. 2017. *Bank Ownership: Trends and Implications.* Washington, DC: International Monetary Fund.

Dailami, M., S. Kurlat, and J. Lim. 2012. "Bilateral M&A Activity from the Global South." Policy Research Working Paper 5953, World Bank, Washington, DC.

Danisewicz, P., D. Reinhardt, and R. Sowerbutts. 2015. "On a Tight Leash: Does Bank Organisational Structure Matter for Macroprudential Spillovers?" Working Paper 524, Bank of England, London.

Daude, C., and M. Fratzscher. 2008. "The Pecking Order of Cross-Border Investment." *Journal of International Economics* 74 (1): 94–119

De Fiore, F., and H. Uhlig. 2015. "Corporate Debt Structure and the Financial Crisis." *Journal of Money, Credit and Banking* 47 (8): 1572–98.

De Haas, R., D. Ferreira, and A. Taci. 2010. "What Determines the Composition of Banks' Loan Portfolios? Evidence from Transition Countries." *Journal of Banking and Finance* 34 (2): 388–98.

De Haas, R., Y. Korniyenko, A. Pivovarsky, and T. Tsankova. 2015. "Taming the Herd? Foreign Banks, the Vienna Initiative and Crisis Transmission." *Journal of Financial Intermediation* 24 (3): 325–55.

De Haas, R., and N. van Horen. 2013. "Running for the Exit? International Bank Lending during a Financial Crisis." *Review of Financial Studies* 26 (1): 244–85.

De Haas, R., and I. van Lelyveld. 2004. "Foreign Bank Penetration and Private Sector Credit in Central and Eastern Europe." *Journal of Emerging Market Finance* 3 (2): 125–51.

———. 2006. "Foreign Banks and Credit Stability in Central and Eastern Europe: A Panel Data Analysis." *Journal of Banking and Finance* 30 (7): 1927–52.

———. 2010. "Internal Capital Markets and Lending by Multinational Bank Subsidiaries." *Journal of Financial Intermediation* 19 (1): 1–25.

———. 2014. "Multinational Banks and the Global Financial Crisis: Weathering the Perfect Storm?" *Journal of Money, Credit and Banking* 46 (s1): 333–64.

de la Torre, A., M. S. Martínez Pería, and S. L. Schmukler. 2010. "Bank Involvement with SMEs: Beyond Relationship Lending." *Journal of Banking and Finance* 34 (9): 2280–93.

de la Torre, A., T. Didier, A. Ize, D. Lederman, and S. Schmukler, 2015. "Latin America and the Rising South: Changing World, Changing Priorities." World Bank, Washington, DC.

De Roover, R. 1963. "The Rise and Decline of the Medici Bank, 1397–1494." *Harvard Studies in Business History* 21.

De Santis, R., and B. Gerard. 2009. "International Portfolio Reallocation: Diversification Benefits and European Monetary Union." *European Economic Review* 53 (8): 1010–27.

Delis, M. D., I. Hasan, and N. Mylonidis. 2016. "Foreign Bank Ownership and Income Inequality: Empirical Evidence." Unpublished paper, Fordham University, Bronx, NY, April.

Delis, M. D., S. Kokas, and S. Ongena. 2014. "Foreign Ownership and Market Power in Banking: Evidence from a World Sample." https://mpra.ub.uni-muenchen.de/55805/.

Dell'Ariccia, G., and R. Marquez. 2004. "Information and Bank Credit Allocation." *Journal of Financial Economics* 72 (1): 185–214.

———. 2006a. "Lending Booms and Lending Standards." *Journal of Finance* 61 5: 2511–46.

———. 2006b. "Competition among Regulators and Credit Market Integration." *Journal of Financial Economics* 79 (2): 401–30.

Demirgüç-Kunt, A., T. Beck, and P. Honohan. 2008. "Finance for All? Policies and Pitfalls in Expanding Access." World Bank, Washington, DC.

Demirgüç-Kunt, A., and E. Detragiache. 2002. "Does Deposit Insurance Increase Banking System Stability? An Empirical Investigation." *Journal of Monetary Economics* 49 (7): 1373–1406.

Demirgüç-Kunt, A., D. D. Evanoff, and G. G., eds. Kaufmann G. G. (Eds.). 2016. *The Future of Large, Internationally Active Banks.* Vol. 55. World Scientific.

Demirgüç-Kunt, A., B. L. Horváth, and H. Huizinga. 2017. "Foreign Banks and International Transmission of Monetary Policy: Evidence from the Syndicated Loan Market." Policy Research Working Paper 7937, World Bank, Washington, DC.

Demirgüç-Kunt, A., and H. Huizinga. 1999. "Determinants of Commercial Bank Interest Margins and Profitability: Some International Evidence." *World Bank Economic Review* 13 (2): 379–408.

———. 2013. "Are Banks Too Big to Fail or Too Big to Save? International Evidence from Equity Prices and CDS Spreads." *Journal of Banking and Finance* 37 (3): 875–94.

Demirgüç-Kunt, A., E. Kane, and L. Laeven. 2014. "Deposit Insurance Database." Policy Research Working Paper 6934, World Bank, Washington, DC.

Demirgüç-Kunt, A., and L. Klapper. 2012. "Measuring Financial Inclusion: The Global Findex Database." World Bank, Washington, DC.

Demirgüç-Kunt, A., L. Klapper, D. Singer, and P. V. Oudheusden. 2014. "The Global Findex Database 2014: Measuring Financial Inclusion around the World." Policy Research Working Paper 7255, World Bank, Washington, DC.

Demirgüç-Kunt, A., R. Levine, and H. Min. 1998. "Opening to Foreign Banks: Issues of Stability, Efficiency, and Growth. In *Proceedings of the Bank of Korea Conference on the Implications of Globalisation of World Financial Markets.* Seoul: Bank of Korea.

Demirgüç-Kunt, A., M. S. Martínez Pería, and T. Tressel. 2017. "The Global Financial Crisis and the Capital Structure of Firms: Was the Impact More Severe among SMEs and Non-Listed Firms?" Unpublished paper, World Bank.

Detragiache, E., and P. Gupta. 2006. "Foreign Banks in Emerging Market Crises: Evidence from Malaysia." *Journal of Financial Stability* 2 (3): 217–42.

Detragiache, E., Tressel, T., and Gupta, P. 2008. "Foreign Banks in Poor Countries: Theory and Evidence." *Journal of Finance* 635: 2123–60.

DeYoung, R., and D. E. Nolle. 1996. "Foreign-Owned Banks in the United States: Earning Market Share or Buying It?" *Journal of Money, Credit and Banking* 28 (4): 622–36.

D'Hulster, K. 2014. "Ring-Fencing Cross Border Banks: How Is It Done and How Important Is It?" Unpublished paper, World Bank, Washington, DC.

D'Hulster, K., and I., Ötker-Robe. 2015. "Ring-fencing cross-border banks: An effective supervisory response?" *Journal of Banking Regulation* 16 (3): 169–187.

Diamond, D. W. 1984. "Financial Intermediation and Delegated Monitoring." *Review of Economic Studies* 51 (3): 393–414.

Diamond, D. W., and P. Dybvig. 1983. "Bank Runs, Deposit Insurance, and Liquidity." *Journal of Political Economy* 91 (3): 401–19.

Diamond, D. W., and R. G. Rajan. 2001. "Liquidity Risk, Liquidity Creation, and Financial Fragility: A Theory of Banking." *Journal of Political Economy* 109 (2): 287–327.

Didier, T., R. Levine, and S. L. Schmukler. 2015. "Capital Market Financing, Firm Growth, and Firm Size Distribution." Policy Research Working Paper 7353, World Bank, Washington, DC.

Didier, T., R. Llovet, and S. L. Schmukler. 2017. "International Financial Integration of East Asia and Pacific." *Journal of the Japanese and International Economies* 44: 52–66.

Dinc, I. S. 2005. "Politicians and Banks: Political Influences on Government-Owned Banks in Emerging Markets." *Journal of Financial Economics* 77 (2): 453–79.

Dong, H., F. M. Song, and L. Tao. 2011. "Regulatory Arbitrage: Evidence from Bank Cross-border M&As." Unpublished working paper, University of Hong Kong.

Duenwald, C. K., N. Gueorguiev, and A. Schaechter. 2005. "Too Much of a Good Thing? Credit Booms in Transition Economies: The Cases of Bulgaria, Romania, and Ukraine." IMF Working Paper WP/05/128, International Monetary Fund, Washington, DC. https://www.imf.org /external/pubs/ft/wp/2005/wp05128.pdf.

Düwel, C., R. Frey, and A. Lipponer. 2011. "Cross-Border Bank Lending, Risk Aversion and the Financial Crisis." Discussion Paper Series 1: Economic Studies, Deutsche Bundesbank, Frankfurt.

Earne, J., T. Jansson, A. Koning, and M. Flaming. 2014. *Greenfield MFIs in Sub-Saharan Africa: A Business Model for Advancing Access to Finance.* Washington, DC: CGAP and International Finance Corporation. http://documents.worldbank.org/curated /en/244571468191940035/pdf/679970NWP0 CGAP00Box385295B00PUBLIC0.pdf.

Ecns.cn. 2016. "Tougher Times for P2P Sector." February.

Ecobank. 2017. "Performance/Reports." https:// www.ecobank.com/group/investor-relations/ key-figures/performance.

The Economist. 2013a. "Too Much of a Good Thing." Special Report on the World Economy, October.

———. 2013b. "In the Cooler: A Court Ruling over an Icelandic Bank Is a Blow to Global Banking." February 2.

———. 2015. "Why Fintech Won't Kill Banks." June.

Economist Intelligence Unit. 2015. "The Disruption of Banking." October 20.

Eichengreen, B., K. Walsh, and G. Weir. 2014. "Internationalization of the Renminbi: Pathways, Implications, and Opportunities." CIFR Research Report, Centre for International Finance and Regulation, Sydney, Australia. http://www.cifr.edu.au/assets/document /CIFR%20Internationalisation%20of%20the %20RMB%20Report%20Final%20web.pdf.

Enoch, C. 2007. "Credit Growth in Central and Eastern Europe." In *Rapid Credit Growth in Central and Eastern Europe*, edited by Charles Enoch and Inci Ökter-Robe, 3–12. London: Palgrave Macmillan UK.

European Commission. 2015. "Building a Capital Markets Union." Green Paper, Brussels.

Faia, E., and B. Weder di Mauro. 2015. "Cross-border Resolution of Global Banks." Discussion Paper 11, European Commission, Brussels. http://ec.europa.eu/info/publications/cross-border-resolution-global-banks_en.

Fama, E. F. 1985. "What's Different about Banks?" *Journal of Monetary Economics* 15 (1): 29–39.

FATF (Financial Action Task Force). 2014. "FATF Clarifies Risk-Based Approach: Case-by-Case, Not Wholesale De-Risking." Paris.

Fernández, A., M. W. Klein, A. Rebucci, M. Schindler, and M. Uribe. 2016. "Capital Control Measures: A New Dataset." *IMF Economic Review* 64 (3): 548–74.

Feyen, E., R. Letelier, I. Love, S. Maimbo, and R. Rocha. 2014. "The Impact of Funding Models and Foreign Bank Ownership on Bank Credit Growth: Is Central and Eastern Europe Different?" *World Bank Policy Research Working Paper* 6783.

Fiechter, J., M. I. Ötker, A. Ilyina, M. Hsu, M. A. Santos, and J. Surti. 2011. *Subsidiaries or Branches: Does One Size Fit All?* Washington, DC: International Monetary Fund.

Financial Conduct Authority. 2015. "Regulatory Sandbox." London, November.

Financial Times. 2016a. "Banks in Charge at Hong Kong's Sandbox." September 6. https://www.ft.com/content/38a662ee-740f-11e6-bf48-b372cdb1043a.

———. 2016b. "Market Grows for 'Regtech,' or AI for Regulation." October 14. https://www.ft.com/content/fd80ac50-7383-11e6-bf48-b372cdb1043a

Fischer, M., C. Hainz, J. Rocholl, and S. Steffen. 2014. "Government Guarantees and Bank Risk Taking Incentives." Research Working Paper, European School of Management and Technology, Berlin.

Fischer, S. 2014. "The Federal Reserve and the Global Economy." Speech by Vice Chairman of the Board of Governors of the Federal Reserve System delivered as the Per Jacobson Foundation Lecture at the 2014 Annual Meetings of the International Monetary Fund and World Bank Group, Washington, DC.

Focarelli, D., and A. Pozzolo. 2000. "The Determinants of Cross-Border Shareholding: An Analysis with Bank-Level Data from OECD Countries." In *Federal Reserve Bank of Chicago Bank Structure Conference*, 226–30, Federal Reserve Bank of Chicago, May 3–5. Chicago.

Forbes. 2016. "How the Blockchain Will Transform Everything from Banking to Government to Our Identities." May 26.

Forbes, K. 2010. "Why Do Foreigners Invest in the United States?" *Journal of International Economics* 80 (1): 3–21.

Forbes, K. J., and Warnock, F. E. 2012. "Capital Flow Waves: Surges, Stops, Flight, and Retrenchment." *Journal of International Economics* 88(2): 235–51.

Forrester Consulting. 2015. "Digital Transformation in the Age of the Consumer." Accenture, Dublin. https://www.accenture.com/ca-en/insight-digital-transformation-age-customer.

Fratzscher, M. 2012. "Capital Flows, Push versus Pull Factors and the Global Financial Crisis." *Journal of International Economics* 88 (1): 341–56.

FSB (Financial Stability Board). 2011. *Financial Stability Issues in Emerging Market and Developing Economies.* Report to the G20 Finance Ministers and Central Bank Governors, November 2, 2011.

———. 2013. *Monitoring the Effects of Agreed Regulatory Reforms on Emerging Market and Developing Economies,* November 12, 2014.

———. 2015. *Thematic Review on Supervisory Frameworks and Approaches for SIBs: Peer Review Report,* May 26, 2015.

Fungáčová, Z., R. Herrala, and L. Weill. 2013. "The Influence of Bank Ownership on Credit Supply: Evidence from the Recent Financial Crisis." *Emerging Markets Review* 15: 136–47.

Galema, R., M. Koetter, and C. Liesegang. 2016. "Lend Global, Fund Local? Price and Funding Cost Margins in Multinational Banking." *Review of Finance* 20 (5): 1981–2014.

García-Herrero, A., and M. S. Martínez Pería. 2007. "The Mix of International Banks' Foreign Claims: Determinants and Implications." *Journal of Banking and Finance* 31 (6): 1613–31.

García-Herrero, A., and F. Vázquez. 2013. "International Diversification Gains and Home Bias in Banking." *Journal of Banking and Finance* 37 (7): 2560–71.

Gennaioli, N., A. Martin, and S. Rossi. 2014. "Sovereign Default, Domestic Banks, and Financial Institutions." *Journal of Finance* 69 (2): 819–66.

Giannettia, M., and S. Ongena. 2012. "'Lending by Example': Direct and Indirect Effects of Foreign Banks in Emerging Markets." *Journal of International Economics* 86 (1): 167–80.

Giovannini, A., C. Mayer, S. Micossi, C. Di Noia, M. Onado, M. Pagano, and A. Polo. 2015. "Restarting European Long-Term Investment Finance." Green Paper Discussion Document, Centre for Economic Policy Research, London. http://reltif.cepr.org/sites/default/files/RELTIF_Green%20Paper.pdf.

Goldberg, L., B. G. Dages, and D. Kinney. 2000. "Foreign and Domestic Bank Participation in Emerging Markets: Lessons from Mexico and Argentina." NBER Working Paper 7714, National Bureau of Economic Research, Cambridge, MA.

Goldberg, L. G., and D. Johnson. 1990. "The Determinants of US Banking Activity Abroad." *Journal of International Money and Finance* 9 (2): 123–37.

Goldberg, L. S. 2009. "Understanding Banking Sector Globalization." *IMF Staff Papers* 561, 171–97.

Goodhart, Charles A. E. 2013. "Global Macroeconomic and Financial Supervision: Where Next?" In *Globalization in an Age of Crisis: Multilateral Economic Cooperation in the Twenty-First Century*, edited by Robert C. Feenstra and Alan M. Taylor, 343–63. Chicago: University of Chicago Press.

Gormley, T. A. 2005. "Banking Competition in Developing Countries: Does Foreign Bank Entry Improve Credit Access?" Department of Economics, Massachusetts Institute of Technology, Cambridge, MA.

———. 2010. "The Impact of Foreign Bank Entry in Emerging Markets: Evidence from India." *Journal of Financial Intermediation* 19 (1): 26–51.

———. 2014. "Costly Information, Entry, and Credit Access." *Journal of Economic Theory* 154: 633–67.

Gourinchas, P. O., and O. Jeanne. 2009. "Capital Mobility and Reform." 2009 Meeting Papers 107, Society for Economic Dynamics, Minneapolis.

Gozzi, J. C., R. Levine, M. S. Martínez Pería, and S. L. Schmukler. 2015. "How Firms Use Domestic and International Corporate Bond Markets." *Journal of Banking and Finance* 58: 532–51.

Greenspan, A. 1999a. "Do Efficient Financial Markets Mitigate Financial Crises?" Speech to Financial Markets Conference of the Federal Reserve Bank of Atlanta, Sea Island, GA.

———. 1999b. "Lessons from the Global Crises." Speech to World Bank Group and International Monetary Fund, Program of Seminars.

Gulamhussen, M. A., C. Pinheiro, and A. F. Pozzolo. 2014. "International Diversification and Risk of Multinational Banks: Evidence from the Pre-Crisis Period." *Journal of Financial Stability* 13: 30–43.

Hagendorff, J., I. Hernando, M. J. Nieto, and L. D. Wall. 2012. "What Do Premiums Paid for Bank M&As Reflect? The Case of the European Union." *Journal of Banking and Finance* 36 (3): 749–59.

Hale, G., T. Kapan, and C. Minoiu. 2016. "Crisis Transmission in the Global Banking Network." IMF Working Paper 16/91, International Monetary Fund, Washington, DC.

Hanson, G. 2012. "The Rise of Middle Kingdoms: Emerging Economies in Global Trade." *Journal of Economic Perspectives* 26 (2): 41–64.

Hasan, I., and W. C. Hunter. 1996. "Efficiency of Japanese Multinational Banks in the United States." *Research in Finance* 14: 157–74.

Havrylchyk, O., and P. E. Jurzyk. 2011. "Profitability of Foreign and Domestic Banks in Central and Eastern Europe: Does the Mode of Entry Matter?" *Economics of Transition* 19: 443–72.

Hayden, E., D. Porath, and N. V. Westernhagen. 2007. "Does Diversification Improve the Performance of German Banks? Evidence from Individual Bank Loan Portfolios." *Journal of Financial Services Research* 32 (3): 123–40.

Herrmann, S., and D. Mihaljek. 2013. "The Determinants of Cross-Border Bank Flows to Emerging Markets." *Economics of Transition* 21 (3): 479–508.

Hesse, H., S. Bakhache, and T. Asonuma. 2015. "Is Banks' Home Bias Good or Bad for Public Debt Sustainability?" IMF Working Paper 15/44, International Monetary Fund, Washington, DC.

Heuchemer, S., S. Kleimeier, and H. Sander. 2009. "The Determinants of Cross-Border Lending in the Euro Zone." *Comparative Economic Studies* 51 (4): 467–99.

Hoggarth, G., J. Hooley, and Y. Korniyenko. 2013. "Which Way Do Foreign Branches Sway? Evidence from the Recent UK Domestic Credit Cycle." Financial Stability Paper 22, Bank of England, London.

Hoggarth, G., L. Mahadeva, and J. Martin. 2010. "Understanding International Bank Capital Flows during the Recent Financial Crisis." Financial Stability Paper 8, Bank of England, London.

Honohan, P., and Beck, T. 2007. *Making Finance Work for Africa*. Washington, DC: World Bank.

Horváth, B. L., H. Huizinga, and V. Ioannidou. 2015. "Determinants and Valuation Effects of the Home Bias in European Banks' Sovereign Debt Portfolios." CEPR Discussion Paper DP10661, Centre for Economic Policy Research, London.

Houston, J. F., C. Lin, and Y. Ma. 2012. "Regulatory Arbitrage and International Bank Flows." *Journal of Finance* 67 (5): 1845–95.

Huang, R. R. 2008. "Evaluating the Real Effect of Bank Branching Deregulation: Comparing Contiguous Counties across US State Borders." *Journal of Financial Economics* 87 (3): 678–705.

Hughes, J. P., and L. J. Mester. 2013. "Who Said Large Banks Don't Experience Scale Economies? Evidence from a Risk-Return-Driven Cost Function." *Journal of Financial Intermediation* 22 (4): 559–85.

Iapadre, L., and L. Tajoli. 2014. "Emerging Countries and Trade Regionalization: A Network Analysis." *Journal of Policy Modeling* 36 (1): S89–110.

ICC (International Chamber of Commerce). 2016. "Rethinking Trade and Finance: An ICC Private Sector Development Perspective." ICC Banking Commission, Paris.

Ichiue, H., and F. Lambert. 2016. "International Banking: An Analysis with New Regulatory Survey Data." IMF Working Paper WP/16/88, International Monetary Fund, Washington, DC. https://www.imf.org/external/pubs/ft/wp/2016/wp1688.pdf.

IMF (International Monetary Fund). 2003. "Trade Finance in Financial Crises: Assessment of Key Issues." IMF, Washington, DC.

———. 2010. "Resolution of Cross-Border Banks—A Proposed Framework for Enhanced Coordination." IMF Staff Paper. IMF: Washington, DC.

———. 2014. "Global Liquidity—Issues for Surveillance." IMF Policy Paper, Washington, DC.

———. 2015a. *Global Financial Stability Report—Navigating Monetary Policy Challenges and Managing Risks*. Washington, DC: IMF.

———. 2015b. "Corporate Leverage in Emerging Markets: A Concern?" Chapter 3, in *Global Financial Stability Report*, 55-91. Washington, DC: IMF.

———. 2015c. "International Banking after the Crisis: Increasingly Local and Safer?" Chapter 2 in *Global Financial Stability Report*, 55-91. Washington, DC: IMF.

———. 2016. "The Withdrawal of Correspondent Banking Relationships: A Case for Policy Action." IMF Staff Discussion Note 16/6, Washington, DC.

Independent Evaluation Group (IEG). 2012. *The World Bank's Response to the Global Economic Crisis: Phase II*. Washington, DC: World Bank.

Isik, I., and M. K. Hassan. 2002. "Cost and Profit Efficiency of the Turkish Banking Industry: An Empirical Investigation." *Financial Review* 37 (2): 257–79.

Jeanneau, S., and M. Micu. 2002. "Determinants of International Bank Lending to Emerging Market Countries." BIS Working Paper 112, Bank for International Settlements, Basel, Switzerland.

Jeon, B. N., M. P. Olivero, and J. Wu. 2011. "Do Foreign Banks Increase Competition? Evidence from Emerging Asian and Latin American Banking Markets." *Journal of Banking and Finance* 35 (4): 856–75.

———. 2013. "Multinational Banking and the International Transmission of Financial Shocks: Evidence from Foreign Bank Subsidiaries."

Journal of Banking and Finance 37 (3): 952–72.

Jeon, B. N., J. Wu, M. Chen, and R. Wang. 2016. "Does Foreign Bank Penetration Affect the Risk of Domestic Banks? Evidence from Emerging Economies." Unpublished paper. https://ssrn.com/abstract=2843638.

Kalemli-Ozcan, S., E. Papaioannou, and J. L. Peydró. 2010. "What Lies Beneath the Euro's Effect on Financial Integration? Currency Risk, Legal Harmonization, or Trade?" *Journal of International Economics* 81 (1): 75–88.

Kamil, H., and K. Rai. 2010. "The Global Credit Crunch and Foreign Banks' Lending to Emerging Markets: Why Did Latin America Fare Better?" IMF Working Paper 10/102, International Monetary Fund, Washington, DC.

Kaminsky, G. L., and S. L. SchmuklerL. 2008. "Short-Run Pain, Long-Run Gain: Financial Liberalization and Stock Market Cycles." *Review of Finance* 12 (2): 253–92.

Karolyi, G. A., and A. G. Taboada. 2015. "Regulatory Arbitrage and Cross-Border Bank Acquisitions." *Journal of Finance* 70 (6): 2395–450.

Kashyap, A., J. Stein, and D. Wilcox. 1993. "Monetary Policy and Credit Conditions: Evidence from the Composition of External Finance." *American Economic Review* 83 (1): 78–98.

Khwaja, A., and A. Mian. 2008. "Tracing the Impact of Bank Liquidity Shocks: Evidence from an Emerging Market." *American Economic Review* 98 (4): 1413–42.

Klomp, J., and J. De Haan, 2014. "Bank Regulation, the Quality of Institutions, and Banking Risk in Emerging and Developing Countries: An Empirical Analysis." *Emerging Markets Finance and Trade* 50 (6): 19–40.

Kouretas, G., and C. Tsoumas. 2016. "Foreign Bank Presence and Business Regulations." *Journal of Financial Stability* 24: 104–116.

KPMG. 2016. "The Pulse of Fintech Q2 2016: Global Analysis of Fintech Venture Funding." Montreal.

Kroszner, R. S., L. Laeven, and D. Klingebiel. 2007. "Banking Crises, Financial Dependence, and Growth." *Journal of Financial Economics* 84: 187–228.

Landau, J. P. 2013. "Global Liquidity: Public and Private." Unpublished paper.

Lane, P., and G. M. Milesi-Ferretti. 2008. "International Investment Patterns." *Review of Economics and Statistics* 90 (3): 538–49.

Lehner, M. 2009. "Entry Mode Choice of Multinational Banks." *Journal of Banking and Finance* 33 (10): 1781–92.

Lehner, M., and M. Schnitzer. 2008. "Entry of Foreign Banks and Their Impact on Host Countries." *Journal of Comparative Economics* 36 (3): 430–52.

Levchenko, A. A., and P. Mauro. 2007. "Do Some Form of Financial Flows Help Protect against 'Sudden Stops'?" *World Bank Economic Review* 21 (3): 389–412.

Levine, R. 1997. "Financial Development and Economic Growth: Views and Agenda." *Journal of Economic Literature* 35 (2): 688–726.

Levine, R., C. Lin, and W. Xie. 2016. "Spare Tire? Stock Markets, Banking Crises, and Economic Recoveries." *Journal of Financial Economics* 120 (1): 81–101.

Lothian, J. R. 2002. "The Internationalization of Money and Finance and the Globalization of Financial Markets." *Journal of International Money and Finance* 21 (6): 699–724.

Manova, K. 2013. "Credit Constraints, Heterogeneous Firms, and International Trade." *Review of Economic Studies* 80 (2): 711–44.

Matoušek, R., and A. Taci. 2004. "Efficiency in Banking: Empirical Evidence from the Czech Republic." *Economics of Planning* 37 (3): 225–44.

McGuire, P., and N. A. Tarashev. 2008. "Bank Health and Lending to Emerging Markets." *BIS Quarterly Review* (December): 67–80.

McCauley, R. N., P. McGuire, and G. Von Peter. 2010. "The Architecture of Global Banking: From International to Multinational?" *BIS Quarterly Review* (March): 25–37.

McCauley, R., P. McGuire, and V. Sushko. 2015. "Global Dollar Credit: Links to U.S. Monetary Policy and Leverage." *Economic Policy* 30 (82): 187–229.

McKinsey Global Institute. 2016. *Digital Finance for All: Powering Inclusive Growth in Emerging Economies.* New York: McKinsey Global Institute.

Mehigan, C. 2016. "Foreign Bank Identity: Does It Matter for Credit Growth?" http://dx.doi.org/10.2139/ssrn.2788417.

Mian, A. 2003. "Foreign, Private Domestic, and Government Banks: New Evidence from Emerging Markets." *Journal of Banking and Finance* 27 (7): 1219–410.

———. 2006. "Distance Constraints: The Limits of Foreign Lending in Poor Economies." *Journal of Finance* 61 (3): 1465–505.

Micco, A., U. Panizza, and M. Yañez. 2007. "Bank Ownership and Performance: Does Politics Matter? *Journal of Banking and Finance* 31 (1): 219–41.

Mihaljek, D. 2011. "How Have External Factors Affected Monetary Policy in the EMEs? The Influence of External Factors on Monetary Policy Frameworks and Operations." *BIS Papers* 57: 1–9.

Milesi-Ferretti, G. M., and C. Tille. 2011. "The Great Retrenchment: International Capital Flows during the Global Financial Crisis." *Economic Policy* 26 (66): 289–346.

Miller, S. R., and A. Parkhe. 2002. "Is There a Liability of Foreignness in Global Banking? An Empirical Test of Banks' X Efficiency." *Strategic Management Journal* 23 (1): 55–75.

Mills, K., and B. McCarthy. 2014. "The State of Small Business Lending: Credit Access during the Recovery and How Technology May Change the Game." Working Paper 15-004, Harvard Business School, Cambridge, MA.

Mittal, S., and J. Lloyd. 2016. "The Rise of Fintech in China: Redefining Financial Services." Collaborative Report by DBS (Development Bank of Singapore) and EY (Ernst & Young).

Morais, B., J. L. Peydró, Jessica Roldan and C. Ruiz Ortega. Forthcoming. "The International Bank Lending Channel of Monetary Policy Rates and Quantitative Easing: Credit Supply, Reach-for-Yield, and Real Effects." *Journal of Finance*.

Morgan, D. P., B. Rime, and P. E. Strahan. 2004. "Bank Integration and State Business Cycles." *Quarterly Journal of Economics* 119 (4): 1555–84

Morrison, A. D., and L. White. 2009. "Leveling Playing Fields in International Financial Regulation." *Journal of Finance* 64 (3): 1099–142.

Moyo, J., B. Nandwa, D. E. Council, J. Oduor, and A. Simpasa. 2014. "Financial Sector Reforms, Competition and Banking System Stability in Sub-Saharan Africa." IMF RES-SPR Macroeconomic Challenges Facing Low-Income Countries Conference Paper, International Monetary Fund, Washington, DC. https://www.imf.org /external/np/seminars/eng/2014/lic/pdf/Moyo .pdf.

Müller, O., and A. Uhde. 2013. "Cross-Border Bank Lending: Empirical Evidence on New Determinants from OECD Banking Markets." *Journal of International Financial Markets Institutions and Money* 23: 136–62.

Nakamoto, S. 2008. "Bitcoin: A Peer-to-Peer Electronic Cash System." https://bitcoin.org/en/ bitcoin-paper.

Niepman, F., and T. Schmidt-Eisenlohr. 2013. "International Trade, Risk and the Role of Banks." Staff Report 633, Federal Reserve Bank of New York.

NSBA (National Small Business Association). 2016. *2016 Mid-Year Economic Report.* Washington, DC.

Nyantakyi, E. B., and M. Sy. 2015. "The Banking System in Africa: Main Facts and Challenges." African Economic Brief, African Development Bank, Abidjan, Nigeria. https://www.afdb.org /fileadmin/uploads/afdb/Documents/Knowledge /AEB_Vol_6_Issue_5_2015_The_Banking _System_in_Africa__Main_Facts_and _Challenges-10_2015.pdf.

Oliner, S., and G. C. Rudebusch. 1996. "Monetary Policy and Credit Conditions: Evidence from the Composition of External Finance: Comment." *American Economic Review* 86 (1): 300–09.

Ongena, S., A. Popov, and N. van Horen. 2016. "The Invisible Hand of the Government: 'Moral Suasion' during the European Sovereign Debt Crisis." DNB Working Paper 505, De Nederlandsche Bank, Amsterdam.

Ongena, S., A. Popov, and G. F. Udell. 2013. "'When the Cat's Away the Mice Will Play': Does Regulation at Home Affect Bank Risk-Taking Abroad?" *Journal of Financial Economics* 108 (3): 727–50.

Ongena, S., S. Qi, and F. Qin. 2014. "The Impact of Foreign Bank Presence on Foreign Direct Investment in China." *China and World Economy* 23 (4): 40–59.

Papaioannou, E. 2009. "What Drives International Financial Flows? Politics, Institutions and

Other Determinants." *Journal of Development Economics* 88 (2): 269–81.

PBOC (People's Bank of China). 2016. "China Payment System Development Report." Beijing.

Peek, J., and E. S. Rosengren. 1997. "The International Transmission of Financial Shocks: The Case of Japan." *American Economic Review* 87 (4): 495–505.

———. 2000. "Collateral Damage: Effects of the Japanese Bank Crisis on Real Activity in the United States." *American Economic Review* 90 (1): 30–45.

Peek, J., E. S. Rosengren, and F. Kasirye. 1999. "The Poor Performance of Foreign Bank Subsidiaries: Were the Problems Acquired or Created?" *Journal of Banking and Finance* 23 (2): 579–604.

Pesenti, P., and C. Tille. 2000. "The Economics of Currency Crises and Contagion: An Introduction." *Federal Reserve Bank of New York Economic Policy Review* 6: 3–16.

Philippon, T. 2015. "Has the US Finance Industry Become Less Efficient? On the Theory and Measurement of Financial Intermediation." *American Economic Review* 105 (4): 1408–38.

———. 2016. "The FinTech Opportunity." NBER Working Paper 22476, National Bureau of Economic Research, Cambridge, MA.

PIIE (Peterson Institute for International Economics). 2016. *Peering into China's Growing Peer-to-Peer Lending Market.* China Economic Watch, P2P Series. Washington, DC: PIIE.

Poelhekke, S. 2015. "Do Global Banks Facilitate Foreign Direct Investment?" *European Economic Review* 76: 25–46.

Politico. 2016. "Can Washington Control High-Tech Lending?" September 28, 2016.

Popov, A., and G. F. Udell. 2012. "Cross-Border Banking, Credit Access, and the Financial Crisis." *Journal of International Economics* 87 (1): 147–61.

Portes, R., and H. Rey. 2005. "The Determinants of Cross-Border Equity Flows." *Journal of International Economics* 65 (2): 269–96.

Powell, A. 2014. "Global Recovery and Monetary Normalization: Escaping a Chronicle Foretold?" In *Latin American and Caribbean Macroeconomic Report* (chapter 4). Washington, DC: Inter-American Development Bank.

PwC (PricewaterhouseCoopers). 2011. "The New Digital Tipping Point." https://www.pwc.com/gx/en/banking-capital-markets/publications/assets/pdf/pwc-new-digital-tipping-point.pdf.

———. 2016. "Review and Outlook of China's Banking Industry in 2015." Banking Newsletter, April 30, 2016. http://www.pwccn.com/webmedia/doc/635987551331759799_banking_newsletter_2015.pdf.

Quinn, D. P., and A. M. Toyoda. 2008. "Does Capital Account Liberalization Lead to Growth?" *Review of Financial Studies* 21 (3): 1403–49.

Rabobank. 2015. "Financial Inclusion and Rural Development 2015." Rabo Development Impact Report, Utrecht.

Rajan, R. 2014. "Competitive Monetary Easing: Is It Yesterday Once More?" Speech, Brookings Institution, Washington, DC, April 10.

Ramachandran, V. 2016. "Mitigating the Effects of De-Risking in Emerging Markets in Order to Preserve Remittance Flows." EMCompass Note 22, International Finance Corporation, Washington, DC.

Reinhart, C. M., and K. S. Rogoff. 2008. "This Time Is Different: A Panoramic View of Eight Centuries of Financial Crises." NBER Working Paper w13882, National Bureau of Economic Research, Cambridge, MA. http://www.nber.org/papers/w13882.

Reinhardt, D., and R. Sowerbutts. 2015. "Regulatory Arbitrage in Action: Evidence from Banking Flows and Macroprudential Policy." Staff Working Paper 546, Bank of England, London.

Reuters. 2013. *'Doom Loop' Tying European Banks and Governments Reinforced.* December 16. http://uk.reuters.com/article/uk-eu-banks-idUKBRE9BF13O20131216.

———. 2014. *Global Equity Capital Markets Review: Managing Underwriters.* http://dmi.thomsonreuters.com/Content/Files/4Q2013_Thomson_Reuters_Equity_Capital_Markets_Review.pdf.

———. 2016. *Lending Club CEO Resigns after Internal Probe, Shares Plummet.* May 9, 2016.

Rey, H. 2015. "Dilemma Not Trilemma: The Global Cycle and Monetary Policy Independence." NBER Working Paper No. 21162.

National Bureau of Economic Research, Cambridge, MA.

Roure, C., L. Pelizzon, and P. Tasca. 2016. "How Does P2P Lending Fit into the Consumer Credit Market." Discussion Paper 30/2016, Deutsche Bundesbank, Frankfurt.

Roussakis, E. N. 1997. "Global Banking: Origins and Evolution." *Revista de Administração de Empresas* 37 (4): 45–53.

Saal, M., S. Starnes, and T. Rehermann. 2017. "The Challenges and Opportunities for Emerging Markets Banks from the Digitalization of Financial Services." Unpublished paper.

Schindler, M. 2009. "Measuring Financial Integration: A New Data Set." *IMF Staff Papers* 56 (1): 222–38.

Schnabl, P. 2012. "The International Transmission of Bank Liquidity Shocks: Evidence from an Emerging Market." *Journal of Finance* 67 (3): 897–932.

Schoenmaker, D. 2013. *Governance of International Banking: The Financial Trilemma.* Oxford: Oxford University Press.

Schuh, S., and O. Shy. 2016. "U.S. Consumers' Adoption and Use of Bitcoin and Other Virtual Currencies." Working paper, Federal Reserve Bank of Boston.

Sensarma, R. 2006. "Are Foreign Banks Always the Best? Comparison of State-Owned, Private and Foreign Banks in India." *Economic Modelling* 23 (4): 717–35.

Seth, R., D. E. Nolle, and S. K. Mohanty. 1998. "Do Banks Follow Their Customers Abroad?" *Financial Markets, Institutions, and Instruments* 7 (4): 1–25.

Shin, H. S. 2013. "The Second Phase of Global Liquidity and Its Impact on Emerging Economies." Keynote address at Asia Economic Policy Conference, Federal Reserve Bank of San Francisco, November 7.

Siregar, R., and K. M. Choy. 2010. "Determinants of International Bank Lending from the Developed World to East Asia." *IMF Staff Papers* 57 (2): 484–516.

Škarica, B. 2014. "Determinants of Non-Performing Loans in Central and Eastern European Countries." *Financial Theory and Practice* 38 (1): 38-59.

Smith, R. C., I. Walter, and G. DeLong. 2012. *Global Banking.* Oxford: Oxford University Press.

Starnes, S., A. J. Alexander, and M. Kurdyla. 2016. "De-Risking by Banks in Emerging Markets— Effects and Responses for Trade." EMCompass Note 24, International Finance Corporation, Washington, DC.

Starnes, S., M. Kurdyla, A. Prakash, A. Volk, and S. Wang, 2017. "Impact of De-Risking: Emerging Market Banks' Capacity to Serve Clients and Countries." Unpublished report, IFC.

Temesvary, J. 2015a. "Foreign Activities of US Banks since 1997: The Roles of Regulations and Market Conditions in Crises and Normal Times." *Journal of International Money and Finance* 56: 202–22.

———. 2015b. "The Role of Regulatory Arbitrage in US Banks' International Flows: Bank-Level Evidence." https://ssrn.com/abstract=2585464 or http://dx.doi.org/10.2139/ssrn.2585464.

U.S. Department of the Treasury. 2016. "Opportunities and Challenges in Online Marketplace Lending." Washington, DC.

van Horen, N. 2007. "Foreign Banking in Developing Countries: Origin Matters." *Emerging Markets Review* 8 (2): 81–105.

Viñals, José, Ceyla Pazarbasioglu, Jay Surti, Aditya Narain, Michaela Erbenova, and Julian Chow. 2013. "Creating a Safer Financial System: Will the Volcker, Vickers, and Liikanen Structural Measures Help." IMF Staff Discussion Note SDN/13/4, International Monetary Fund, Washington, DC.

Visual Capitalist. 2016. "27 Fintech Unicorns, and Where They Were Born." September 7.

Wade, R., and S. Sigurgeirsdottir. 2011. "Iceland's Rise, Fall, Stabilization and Beyond." *Cambridge Journal of Economics* 36 (1): 127–44.

Wagner, C. 2012. "From Boom to Bust: How Different Has Microfinance Been from Traditional Banking?" *Development Policy Review* 30 (2): 187–210.

Wall Street Journal. 2016. "U.S. House Bill Aims to Set Up Sandbox for Fintech Innovation." September 22.

Weill, L. 2003. "Banking Efficiency in Transition Economies." *Economics of Transition* 11 (3): 569–92.

Weisbrot, M., and J. Montecino. 2010. "The IMF and Economic Recovery: Is Fund Policy Contributing to Downside Risks?" Center for Economic and Policy Research Report, London.

Wiggins, R. Z., N. Tente, and A. Metrick. 2014. "European Banking Union C: Cross Border Resolution-Fortis Group." Yale Program on Financial Stability Case Study 2014-5C-V1, New Haven, CT, November.

World Bank. 2006. *Global Development Finance: The Development Potential of Surging Capital Flows.* Washington, DC: World Bank.

———. 2011. *Global Development Horizons 2011: Multipolarity—The New Global Economy.* Washington, DC: World Bank.

———. 2013. *Global Development Horizons: Capital for the Future—Saving and Investment in an Interdependent World.* Washington, DC: World Bank.

———. 2014. *Global Financial Development Report: Financial Inclusion.* Washington, DC: World Bank.

———. 2015a. "Report on the G20 Survey on De-Risking Activities in the Remittance Market." Working paper, Washington, DC.

———. 2015b. "Withdrawal from Correspondent Banking: Where, Why, and What to Do About It." Working paper, Washington, DC.

———. 2016a. "Migration and Remittances Factbook, 2016." Washington, DC.

———. 2016b. "Stakeholder Dialogue on De-Risking: Findings and Recommendations." Washington, DC.

World Economic Forum. 2016a. "The Future of Financial Infrastructure. An Ambitious Look at How Blockchain Can Reshape Financial Services." Cologny, Switzerland.

———. 2016b. "The Role of Financial Services in Society: Understanding the Impact of Technology-Enabled Innovation on Financial Stability." Geneva.

Wu, H. L., C. H. Chen, and M. H. Lin. 2007. "The Effect of Foreign Bank Entry on the Operational Performance of Commercial Banks in the Chinese Transitional Economy." *Post-Communist Economies* 19 (3): 343–57.

Wu, J., H. Lim, and B. N. Jeon. 2016. "The Impact of Foreign Banks on Monetary Policy Transmission during the Global Financial Crisis of 2008–2009: Evidence from Korea." *Emerging Markets Finance and Trade* 52 (7): 1574–86.

Wu, J., A. C. Luca, and B. N. Jeon. 2011. "Foreign Bank Penetration and the Lending Channel in Emerging Economies: Evidence from Bank-Level Panel Data." *Journal of International Money and Finance* 30 (6): 1128–56.

Yamori, N. 1998. "A Note on the Location Choice of Multinational Banks: The Case of Japanese Financial Institutions." *Journal of Banking and Finance* 22 (1): 109–20.

Zeissler, A., T. Piontek, and A. Metrick. 2015. "Ireland and Iceland in Crisis C: Iceland's Landsbanki Icesave." No. 57246, Yale School of Management YPFS Cases, Yale School of Management, New Haven, CT

Zhu, M. 2012. "The Impact of Foreign Bank Entry in Emerging Markets: Knowledge Spillovers or Competitive Pressure?" CCP Working Paper 12-4, Centre for Competition Policy, University of East Anglia, Norwich, U.K.

Zingales, L. 2015. "Presidential Address: Does Finance Benefit Society?" *Journal of Finance* 70 (4): 1327–63.

ECO-AUDIT

Environmental Benefits Statement

The World Bank Group is committed to reducing its environmental footprint. In support of this commitment, we leverage electronic publishing options and print-on-demand technology, which is located in regional hubs worldwide. Together, these initiatives enable print runs to be lowered and shipping distances decreased, resulting in reduced paper consumption, chemical use, greenhouse gas emissions, and waste.

We follow the recommended standards for paper use set by the Green Press Initiative. The majority of our books are printed on Forest Stewardship Council (FSC)–certified paper, with nearly all containing 50–100 percent recycled content. The recycled fiber in our book paper is either unbleached or bleached using totally chlorine-free (TCF), processed chlorine–free (PCF), or enhanced elemental chlorine–free (EECF) processes.

More information about the Bank's environmental philosophy can be found at http://www.worldbank.org/corporateresponsibility.